The Seventh Daughter

CECILIA CHIANG

with Lisa Weiss

The Seventh Daughter

My Culinary Journey from Beijing to San Francisco

foreword by

Alice Waters

photography by

Leigh Beisch

TEN SPEED PRESS

Berkeley | Toronto

To the memory of my parents, Sun Long Guang and Sun Shueh Yun Hui

10

Ten Speed Press
PO Box 7123
Berkeley, California 94707
www.tenspeed.com

Distributed in Australia by Simon and Schuster Australia, in
Canada by Ten Speed Press Canada, in New Zealand by
Southern Publishers Group, in South Africa by Real Books, and
in the United Kingdom and Europe by Publishers Group UK.

Design: **Catherine Jacobes**
Food Styling: **Karen Shinto**
Prop Styling: **Sara Slavin**
Food Stylist Assistant: **Jeffrey Larsen**
Photography Assistant: **Lauren Grant**

Library of Congress Cataloging-in-Publication Data
Chiang, Cecilia.
The seventh daughter : my culinary journey from Beijing to
San Francisco / by Cecilia Chiang with Lisa Weiss ; photography
by Leigh Beisch and Ed Anderson.
p.   cm.
Includes index.
ISBN-13: 978-1-58008-822-0
ISBN-10: 1-58008-822-8
1. Cookery, Chinese. 2. Mandarin (Restaurant : San Francisco,
Calif.) 3. Chiang, Cecilia. 4. China--Social life and customs.
I. Weiss, Lisa, 1951– II. Title.
TX724.5.C5C55385 2007
641.5951--dc22

                    2007012884

Printed in China
First printing, 2007

1 2 3 4 5 6 7 8 9 10 — 11 10 09 08 07

Contents

ACKNOWLEDGMENTS

I'VE LIVED A VERY LONG LIFE so it would be impossible to truly thank all the people who have loved me, befriended me, supported me, comforted me, aided me, and advised me on my long journey from last century's China to this century's America. Sadly many of those people are gone now, and while it probably would take another entire book to mention everyone, I hope that by telling my story I will have honored them all in some small measure. At the very least, all I can say is thank you, thank you, (xie xie) to the following people who helped make this book a reality.

Jane Dystel, my agent, who believed in this project at a time when I had almost given up hope and suggested Lisa Weiss to write it with me. To top it off she then found my book a perfect home at Ten Speed Press.

Lisa Weiss, thank you for your wonderful words. You heard my stories, grew to know the players, kept the dates straight, made my recipes clear, and even learned a little Mandarin. Your lovely home and fantastic kitchen made recipe testing a pleasure, but the best part is that you've become my friend. And your coffee is still the most delicious anywhere.

Alice Waters, I am honored by your beautiful and touching foreword and treasure our friendship.

Allison Saunders, who came to us when we didn't know we needed her (thanks to Mary Risley), and then turned out to be invaluable. A simple thank you doesn't seem enough to let you know how much Lisa and I appreciate all your hard work, first testing and then typing recipes. Not to mention all the good cookies you brought us.

To Phil Wood and the entire team at Ten Speed Press: It was only in my wildest dreams that I could have imagined a group of people who were so excited and enthusiastic, who were so sensitive to my feelings and understood just how much this book has meant to me. In particular I'd like to acknowledge Lorena Jones, who believed in the book from the beginning and gently oversaw its production like a (patient) mother hen, and Aaron Wehner whose insightful comments got us on our way.

Amanda Berne, it wasn't an easy assignment, to come in at the end, immediately grasp what we were trying to do, and keep us on track. But with your infectious laugh, positive feedback, and good humor you've made some very difficult times less stressful. Also your respectful and caring demeanor has not gone unnoticed.

If it's true that we eat with our eyes then this book is a feast. Photographer Leigh Beisch made my recipes come to life. Thanks also to her assistant Lauren Grant and studio manager Shana Lopes. A special thanks to Sara Slavin for her stylish eye and creative use of props, and Karen Shinto with assistant Jeffrey Larsen for spot-on food-styling.

Thanks to Ed Anderson who took all the wonderful photos of me "in action," in the kitchen cooking and shopping in Chinatown, and since I rarely stand still he had his work cut out for him.

Jane Horn, thank you for your conscientious copy editing. A difficult job, but you made my stories and recipes consistent as well as clear. And to Carolyn Miller for her deft hand at proofreading.

To Catherine Jacobes, with her simple yet stunning design, who gave this book its modern feel yet still made it seem traditional.

For years, many of my friends have encouraged me to write an update of my story, but I owe a special thanks to Mary Risley who set everything in motion by putting me in touch with Jane Dystel.

Thank you to Jie Chen, Paul Denlinger, George Hsu, Bill Wu, and Jay Stone Sih for your counsel about Chinese culture, history, and language.

My friends Alex Ong, Bill He, and Sue Yung Li generously shared recipes. And a special thanks goes to my former sous chef at The Mandarin, Ah Lou, for showing me how he used to make the Beggar's Chicken, and Elizabeth Hu and Sharon Mark for their assistance (and translations).

FOREWORD
by Alice Waters

CECILIA CHIANG IS THAT RARITY in any culture, a true grande dame, a woman of real and lasting influence. She is the living repository of a vast body of cultural knowledge about food passed down from generation to generation; and she is the embodiment of a certain exquisitely commanding graciousness. I count it among my lifetime's greatest gifts of good fortune that we met so early in my own career as a restaurateur and became such fast friends. Because I have had the privilege of knowing Cecilia, I have gained an appreciation of both the intricacy and the immensity of Chinese culture. What is more, she has been a role model, a mentor, and an inspiration. Her cooking classes, her banquets, her company, and her contacts have all helped shape my aesthetics. It was through her that I first met important gastronomes like James Beard and Marion Cunningham. It was through her that I learned the ultimate reward of refusing to compromise when it came to quality. And most of all, in her I have had a shining example of the way in which food can be harmoniously and seamlessly interwoven with all of life.

Although I had known the outlines of Cecilia's biography from her own stories, it wasn't until we traveled together with Marion Cunningham to China in 1983 that I understood the full dimensions of her charismatic and nurturing personality. We traveled through Hong Kong and on to a tour of the mainland that culminated in Beijing. To be a part of that homecoming was an unforgettable demonstration of both her magnanimity and her magnetism. When we set out, Marion and I were taken aback by the quantity of Cecilia's luggage. Why so many giant suitcases? How many outfits could she possibly need? What we didn't realize until we arrived was that the suitcases were full of gifts for her Chinese relatives and friends: gifts of food, clothing, appliances—even a typewriter, if I remember correctly. And when we returned, the suitcases were refilled with gifts for her family and friends in America—and with the beautiful traditional dresses for which she is famous, for which she had been fitted in Hong Kong, and which had been made up for her while we were on the mainland.

Of course I knew before our trip to China that Cecilia spoke beautiful Mandarin and had great taste and that she would take us to amazing places and introduce us to wonderful friends, but what I had not expected was the reception she received. Wherever we went, when ordinary people heard her voice they would crowd around us to listen because she spoke Mandarin with an old-fashioned refinement of pronunciation, vocabulary, and diction that has all but disappeared in modern China. She was so interested in talking to people and telling them where we were from and the people who crowded around were so fascinated and awed by her demeanor that every encounter became a little drama. She was a living symbol of how much things had changed in only a generation.

Once during that trip, at a banquet she had arranged to be served to just the three of us at the Summer Palace, she was bitterly disappointed by the mediocre food and lackadaisical service. At first she was quietly embarrassed and saddened; but as the meal progressed, she became so angry that she finally stormed back to the kitchen and took charge, practically cooking and serving the rest of the meal herself. What had upset her so was that the cooks and waiters just didn't care; they weren't taking any pride in what she had planned to be a reenactment of a beloved part of her own cultural upbringing. Not that she was asking them to do anything she would not have done herself: Cecilia's fierce pride in her heritage and her work extends to everything she does. No job is beneath her, no task too lowly or too small. She is a ferocious scrubber of floors, scaler of fish, and peeler of tubers—and, at my house, a washer of dishes, no matter how hard I try to stop her.

We have traveled together in Europe, too, and I have been as proud to be in her company there as I was in China. Wherever she is, her extraordinary poise and her focused curiosity attract attention. Even in the heart of France, in Burgundy, Cecilia's connoisseur's instincts won her the dazzled admiration of no less a winemaker than Hubert de Montille, who was so deeply impressed with her acute judgments on his

Cecilia and Alice Waters, Chez Panisse 10th Anniversary party, Berkeley, October 1981.

recent vintages that it was she—not I—for whom he insisted on unlocking the inner sanctum of his underground wine library so as to pour us his most treasured vintages from decades ago.

But it is as the host at her own table that I love Cecilia the most. She is an orchestrator of the subtlest, most significant menus, utterly true to the particular moment in time—as you will see when you start to cook from this book. Inevitably, when I dine at Cecilia's I have to remember not to over-eat when the first dishes start to arrive. This is dif-ficult, to say the least, not only because they are so delicious, but because Cecilia is so eager to serve second helpings at any sign of genuine apprecia-tion from a guest. And every dish has a story, whether it be about the dish's role in tra-ditional medicine, or about its literary allusiveness, or about its sentimental associations or autobiographical context. This book is filled to the brim with these stories, and each one is a little revelation.

Many years ago, I was dining at The Mandarin one evening at sunset, admiring the glorious view of the Golden Gate, when Cecilia brought a big, lidded bowl to the table. The lid was lifted, releasing a seductive aroma and revealing a sparkling clear soup strewn with cilantro. At that precise moment, a 5.2 earthquake rolled through San Francisco. I will never forget the way the soup seemed to lift itself almost out of the bowl, only to fall back without having spilled a drop. I watched the soup gently lapping back and forth, the cilantro resembling nothing so much as seaweed in a tide pool, and thought, if I have to go in an earthquake, this would be the way. Such are Cecilia's powers.

INTRODUCTION
by Lisa Weiss

ALL THE WAY OVER TO CECILIA CHIANG'S HOME to talk with her about writing a memoir/cookbook together, I couldn't decide whether to address her as Madame Chiang, which is how she's often referred to in the press, or Cecilia. Even though I had met her on a number of occasions, I was frankly feeling a little intimidated. Maybe it was because I knew I would be in the presence of a Bay Area culinary icon, or perhaps it was because I instantly flashed back to 1971, when the regal and impeccably dressed Madame Chiang showed us to our table at The Mandarin, (where, incidentally, I had one of the best meals of my life). When she answered the door of her home, though, ever the gracious and intuitive hostess, it was as if she had read my mind. "Hello, hello. You must be Lisa. Please call me Cecilia."

It's hard for me to imagine there was ever a time when minced chicken in lettuce, hot-and-sour soup, and pot stickers were unfamiliar items on Chinese-American restaurant menus. But in 1961, when Cecilia opened her now-legendary San Francisco restaurant, The Mandarin, most Chinese restaurants in the United States served Cantonese cuisine. The Mandarin was the first Chinese restaurant in San Francisco to serve the authentic flavors of Beijing, Shandong, Sichuan, and Hunan provinces.

Not only did Cecilia Chiang introduce Americans to regional Chinese cuisine, hers was one of the few Chinese restaurants in San Francisco owned by a woman and one of the first to open outside of Chinatown, a move considered to be the culinary equivalent of suicide. That Cecilia defied the odds and became successful was as much from her sheer determination and will, as from the incredible response of her customers who were at first mildly curious, and then ultimately seduced by The Mandarin's gutsy food and refined service.

By 1968, when Cecilia moved The Mandarin from its original modest location on Polk Street to the architecturally stunning space at Ghirardelli Square, her restaurant had developed a national reputation. Everyone who was anyone dined at The Mandarin, and Cecilia's closely guarded guest book had celebrity names like Jackie Onassis, Paul

Newman, Sophia Loren, Danny Kaye, Rudolf Nureyev, Luciano Pavarotti, Janis Joplin, John Lennon and Yoko Ono, as well as scores of politicians and socialites. However, a more contemporary measure of success might be The Mandarin's appeal to people in the food world. In the 1970s, current and future culinary giants like James Beard, Julia Child, Marion Cunningham, Alice Waters, Jeremiah Tower, and Chuck Williams were revolutionizing America's culinary landscape. What they loved was the taste of her food. What they respected was its authenticity.

Cecilia with Julia Child, Hotel Cipriani, Venice, Italy, 1994.

I think Cecilia was as surprised as anyone at the direction her life had taken. I, for one, would never have suspected that the charming and elegant Madame Chiang who greeted us at the door of The Mandarin some 36 years ago had ever seen a day of sorrow or deprivation, much less enough to last a lifetime.

Born in 1920s China into a life of privilege, Cecilia was the seventh daughter of a very wealthy family of ten children (her mother gave birth to twelve). Sun Yun is her Chinese name, but while enrolled at a Catholic university in Beijing, one of her European professors gave her the name Cecilia.

Her childhood was idyllic, with servants for everything and fashionable homes in the city and country. War, invasion, and politics dramatically and irrevocably changed her life and that of her family, eventually forcing Cecilia, along with her husband and children, to flee China for safe haven in Tokyo. Some years later, on what was intended to be just a visit to a widowed sister in San Francisco, Cecilia ended up owning a restaurant there, which she named The Mandarin. She embraced a new life in the United States, where her incredible story begins and ends.

"Wow," was all I could think after many afternoons spent listening to Cecilia's story. ("Wow" is also one of Cecilia's favorite words.) But during all those hours and months together, we did more than sit and sip tea, pleasant as that was. While Cecilia was telling me her remarkable story, she was usually in the kitchen cooking.

I would watch her move with utmost efficiency in her small, well-organized kitchen, slicing as precisely as a surgeon, stir-frying as confidently as a master wok chef.

Observing her skills, I found it difficult to believe that this was a woman who really hadn't cooked until she moved to the United States, when she was forty. "We always had male cooks when we were growing up, and daughters weren't allowed in the kitchens," she explains. "And then my husband was very traditional, so we had cooks when we lived in Shanghai and Tokyo."

Although Cecilia and her sisters were not permitted in the kitchen, their mother was adamant that they all develop keen palates and know how good food should be prepared. This training served Cecilia well as a restaurateur. Just like her mother, she would scrutinize every dish that came out of the kitchen. But while Cecilia educated her chefs on the finer points of food, her chefs instructed her as to the ways of the kitchen; Cecilia, ever the eager pupil, learned how to fillet fish and chop vegetables. Before long, she was not only entertaining at home, she was teaching cooking classes at The Mandarin and at Williams-Sonoma.

Today, even at eighty-seven, Cecilia Chiang is still as eager to learn as she is to teach.

The first time we cooked together, it was in my kitchen and we decided to make her famous Mongolian lamb. She usually buys a half leg of lamb, slices off a pound or so, and freezes what she doesn't use. I suggested that we instead use lamb top round, which is a whole muscle cut from the top of the leg; it's tender and lean, and at about one-and-one-half pounds, perfect for four to six servings. When we got to work, she patiently showed me how to slice the meat across the grain and how to quickly shred an entire bunch of green onions in about two seconds flat (a trick she learned from her chefs). Next, she stirred together a marinade of soy sauce, oyster sauce, oil, and ground white pepper. Totally open to improvising, she then tasted the marinade and asked, "Do you have some fish sauce?" Not a typical Chinese ingredient, I thought, but I did have a bottle. It really did add more flavor.

We tasted as we cooked, adding a little more soy and pepper. When the lamb was done, we turned it all out onto a pretty platter and added a garnish of fresh cilantro sprigs. I was feeling pretty good about my cooking abilities as I dove into the lamb with my chopsticks. The tender meat was lightly napped with the salty-sweet sauce and the green onions had picked up a perfect amount of char from the griddle so that they were crisp, yet mellow. I looked to Cecilia for her reaction. "It needs more white pepper. Pretty good though, huh?"

"Yes," I thought, "your mother would approve."

SHOPPING WITH CECILIA
by Lisa Weiss

BACK IN THE EARLY 1970s, when I was first learning how to cook, I concentrated mainly on French and Italian cuisine. However, I'll never forget the day an acquaintance of mine told me I just had to try a restaurant at Ghirardelli Square where they served the best Chinese food imaginable. The restaurant was The Mandarin, and once I tasted Cecilia Chiang's food, I was hooked.

I took classes from Cecilia at both The Mandarin and Williams-Sonoma, and bought her book, *The Mandarin Way*.

Armed with Cecilia's recipes, I would head off to San Francisco's Chinatown or the Richmond District's Clement Street. I loved these excursions. The exotic smells, bustling streets, indecipherable signs, and small hole-in-the-wall places selling snacks and foods I'd never tasted before were intoxicating. Shopping in these markets was always great fun. But in the end finding ingredients, or rather making sense of all the labels was difficult, not to say exhausting.

Nothing compares to shopping an Asian market with Cecilia. The first day we went to the store together she said, "We need to get to the markets when they first open because Chinese people stay up late and the markets don't get crowded until late morning and then parking is too difficult." She was right. We got there at ten A.M., and by the time we left at eleven-thirty, it was difficult to maneuver our cart through the crowded aisles.

We all have our limits, however. As Cecilia stood before the snow peas, choosing only those that looked perfect, a young woman tried to move her aside. With an uncharacteristic flash of anger, Cecilia told her in Mandarin to wait her turn.

Things were a little better at the meat counter, where the butchers were friendlier.

"I want some pork belly, with skin," Cecilia said in English, pointing to a pink-and-white striped slab of meat. The butcher held up the piece for her inspection and she shook her head. "No, too fat." The butcher then pulled four others up for her to look at, all getting scowls. Finally, he showed her a pork belly that she liked. Again, in English, she said, "Thank you, thank you," and flashed her famous brilliant smile. Cecilia turned to me and said, "He only speaks Cantonese, but he respects me because I know what I want."

Cecilia's Pantry

THIS IS NOT MEANT TO BE a comprehensive glossary of Asian ingredients. For that, there are several terrific books out there. Two favorites are *Asian Ingredients*, by Bruce Cost and *The Asian Grocery Store Demystified*, by Linda Bladholm. Another helpful book is *Vegetables from Amaranth to Zucchini: The Essential Reference*, by Elizabeth Schneider, which is encyclopedic in scope and has descriptions, cooking, storage recommendations, and recipes for vegetables from all over the world.

What we've tried to do here is give you a list of the basic ingredients called for in this book, the ones that Cecilia keeps in her pantry and the brands she prefers. However, if an ingredient is used only once, you'll find a description of the ingredient included in cook's notes at the beginning of the recipe.

❊ ❊ ❊

Bean sauce—Made from ground, salted, and fermented yellow soybeans mixed with seasonings, is sold in jars as well as small cans (we like Szechuan brand), but be careful to get the kind that is labeled simply "bean sauce," not "sweet bean sauce" or "hot bean sauce," both of which will ruin the recipe.

Black bean sauce—A prepared sauce sold in a jar and made from salted black beans mixed with soy, salt, sugar, and depending on the brand, garlic or rice wine. Store in the refrigerator in its jar for up to 1 year.

Chili Oil—Variously called red-pepper oil, hot oil, or chili oil, this is a seasoning only, and not for cooking over heat. The best brands, sold in small glass bottles, are made by infusing a mixture of vegetable and sesame oils with chiles. They vary in heat, with those from China generally less intense than the brands from Southeast Asia. It's easy (and cheaper) to make your own and you can adjust the heat to suit your palate.

To make about 1 cup of chili oil, heat $3/4$ cup peanut or corn oil (not canola, which is flavorless) with $1/4$ cup Asian sesame oil in a small, heavy saucepan over medium heat. After 3 or 4 minutes, or when the oil registers 250°F on an instant-read thermometer, add $1/4$ cup dried red pepper flakes. Remove the pan from the heat (the flakes should be foaming slightly), stir, and cover. Let sit off the heat at room temperature for a couple of hours or overnight. Strain the oil through a fine-mesh sieve into a clean glass or plastic container, discard the red pepper flakes, and store in a cool, dark place.

Chili Paste—Made from a mixture of ground chilies with seasonings that may include garlic, ginger, and sesame oil, these thick sauces are found in an astonishing array in both Asian as well as American markets. Our "go-to" brand in these recipes is Lan Chi Chili Sauce with Garlic, but we also like Lee Kum Kee's Chili Garlic Sauce.

Dried Black Mushrooms—Common throughout Asia, and incomparable in flavor, dried black mushrooms can be purchased in all Asian markets. The best ones are small, about $1^{1/2}$ inches in diameter, and are grayish-brown with white "cracks" on the surface of the caps. Dried shiitakes are not the same and are not a good substitute. In this case, you get what you pay for, and a good way to judge quality is to select the ones that are most expensive. Large bags offered at a low price are always inferior.

Dried Chinese Red Dates—This small dried date with a red skin and a sweet, white flesh can be found in Asian supermarkets in vacuum-packed plastic bags. Some preparations require soaking and peeling.

Dried Lily Buds—These long, dried unopened day-lily flowers are also called golden needles, tiger lily buds, or lily stems. They're sold in plastic packages and should be velvety soft, golden yellow, and not brittle or brown. Always soak them for 20 to 30 minutes in warm water before cooking. Snip off the hard knobby ends before use.

Five-Spice Blend—Despite its name, this savory spice blend usually contains more than five ingredients, typically ground star anise, cloves, cinnamon, fennel seed, Sichuan peppercorns, and sometimes cumin, cardamom, coriander seed, and/or ground ginger. Prepared blends are readily available in any Asian market, as well as in the spice section of most supermarkets, but it's easier, cheaper, and far more flavorful to make your own mixture.

To make your own five-spice seasoning, in a dry skillet, put 2 tablespoons fennel seed, 8 whole star anise, 1 tablespoon coriander seed, 1 teaspoon cumin seed, 1 tablespoon white peppercorns, and 14 whole cloves. Stirring frequently, toast over medium heat for 5 to 8 minutes, or until the mixture is fragrant, taking care not to scorch the spices. Add 1 teaspoon ground cinnamon. When cool, transfer to a coffee grinder or food processor and whirr until finely ground. The seasoning will keep in a cupboard in a closed container for up to 3 months. Makes about 1/4 cup.

Gingko Nuts—Both unshelled and shelled fresh gingko nuts are sold in Asian markets. To remove the little ivory-colored shells, simply use a nut cracker. Shelled gingkoes are available in small vacuum packages.

Hoisin Sauce—This thick, sweet-spicy sauce, made from ground soybeans mixed with sugar, flour, and vinegar, and flavored with garlic and sesame oil, has become almost as common as ketchup. The quality of brands varies, but Ma Ling, Koon Chun, and Lee Kum Kee are all good.

Kosher Salt—Coarse and flaky, kosher salt is much cleaner tasting than regular table salt because it has no additives to make it free-flowing. Sea salt can be used in the same proportion as kosher salt. If substituting regular table salt for kosher salt, use half as much as specified.

Oil—Canola oil is a good, healthy all-purpose oil for wok or high-heat cooking. If you have a stove that really puts out a lot of heat, use peanut oil, which has a high flash point (meaning that it can reach a higher temperature without burning or smoking). Asian sesame oil, made from toasted sesame seed, is generally used either in salad dressings or as a finishing drizzle over cooked dishes just before serving. Any brand of sesame oil is best to buy in small bottles, as it can turn rancid quickly.

Oyster Sauce—A popular Cantonese condiment, oyster sauce is made from oyster extracts, salt, cornstarch, and caramel, and adds flavor to everything from noodles to stir-fries.It will keep indefinitely in the fridge. Hop Sing Lung and Lee Kum Kee are two good brands.

Sichuan Peppercorns—Also called Chinese pepper or wild pepper, these are reddish-brown flowerlike berries that have a tingly, spicy taste and a slight numbing effect on the tongue. Sichuan peppercorns are often infused in oil, or toasted and ground to use plain or in combination with salt and other spices.

Soy Sauce—When a recipe calls for soy sauce, we mean Kikkoman, which is a good and consistent brand for all-purpose cooking and dipping. Cecilia also likes to use premium soy sauce, which is lighter in color and more subtle than regular soy, perfect for dipping and sauces. For that, the brand we like is Lee Kum Kee. Sometimes Cecilia uses mushroom soy sauce, which has a nice rich, earthy flavor; among several good brands, Pearl River Bridge stands out.

Tofu—Also called dofu or bean curd, these familiar white soybean cakes can be found in every supermarket today. Some are sold submerged in water in packages, and others are sold in sealed boxes. There are several kinds: silken (or soft), firm, and pressed, often called "seasoned." The recipes in this book specify which kind you should buy.

If you can't find seasoned tofu, it's also easy to make your own. Halve a 14-ounce block of firm tofu crosswise and place both pieces in a saucepan. Cover with 1 cup of water, $^1/_2$ cup soy sauce, $^1/_2$ cup Shaoxing wine, 1 tablespoon brown sugar, 4 whole star anise, and 1 teaspoon of Sichuan peppercorns. Bring the liquid to a boil over high heat, then decrease the heat to medium-low and simmer, uncovered, for 30 minutes, adding more water if necessary to keep the tofu covered. Drain, discard the liquid, and keep the cooked, seasoned tofu refrigerated in an airtight container for up to 2 days.

Tree Ears—These mushrooms are most often sold dried in packages, although fresh tree ears show up occasionally in Asian produce markets. The best dried tree ears, also called wood ears, black fungus, mu-er, or cloud ears, are small; the large black and gray ones should be avoided. Soak them in warm water for 30 minutes before use; they expand considerably, so start with a large bowl and a generous amount of water. Any hard knobs should be snipped off.

Vinegar—Two kinds of vinegar appear most often in the recipes. **White rice** vinegar is made from rice wine diluted with water and is pleasantly mild. **Chinkiang black vinegar** is made from glutinous rice and malt and is rich, deep, and complex, much like balsamic vinegar (which can be used as a substitute).

Cecilia uses Marukan rice vinegar (plain, not seasoned) and Gold Plum or Koon Chun black vinegar.

Virginia Ham—The Chinese have a long history of preparing cured pork products, the most famous of which is their Yunnan ham. This hard, dry-cured ham is not imported to this country. Luckily, country hams from Smithfield, Virginia, are pretty close in flavor and texture. You can buy 1-inch slices in many Asian markets. The ham keeps forever well wrapped in the refrigerator. If it develops a little mold you can scrape it off.

White Pepper—When the Chinese speak of ground pepper they mean white pepper. In all our recipes we specify freshly ground white pepper because, as with all spices, the flavor is best when freshly ground in a pepper mill and far surpasses anything already ground in a jar. If you must use already ground white pepper, make sure that it is fresh. It loses potency after six months.

Wine—Shaoxing wine, made from rice, rice millet, and yeast, is used both as a beverage and in cooking. Its rich flavor and alcohol content is similar to dry sherry. The best brands are made by Pagoda. Some Asian markets, because of local liquor laws, carry only brands labeled as Shaoxing Cooking Wine, which is not meant to be consumed as a drink and has added salt. Dry sherry would be a better substitute.

Zha Cai or **Suan Cai Zha Cai,** or preserved mustard tuber, is authentically the main ingredient in the sauce for dan dan noodles. It's sold in Asian markets in bulk, in cans, or in vacuum packages. This very popular salted, cured vegetable adds a rich flavor (as well as nutrition) to all kinds of dishes, from soups to stir-fries.

Chapter 1

The Mandarin

IN 1960, MY HUSBAND, CHIANG LIANG, and I, and our two children, May and Philip, were living in Tokyo, where we had moved after our escape from China in 1949 just before the Communists assumed power. The last plane out of Shanghai, our home at the time, was going to Tokyo and we were lucky to get on it, so we went. Chiang Liang was a commercial attaché with the Nationalist Chinese Mission, which eventually became the Nationalist embassy, a post he assumed during the last days in China. With a few friends, we had invested in a Tokyo restaurant called The Forbidden City, which had become extremely popular with other Chinese expatriates living in Tokyo.

That year, I received a letter from my Number Six sister, Sun (who went by the English name Sophie when she moved to America), telling me that her husband, Bill Hoy, had succumbed to cancer. They had met in Shanghai in 1948, the year before the Communist takeover of China. Bill, an American-born Chinese (ABCs, as they're commonly referred to), was in China covering the civil war for his San Francisco newspaper (he published the only English-language paper in that city's Chinatown). After their marriage in 1948, she returned with him to San Francisco, settling in Chinatown.

Cecilia at The Mandarin at Ghirardelli Square, San Francisco, 1972.

It had been nearly twelve years since I had seen my sister. Sophie and I had always been close, and my heart broke for her. Through her letters over the years and our few phone conversations, she had confided that she had been unhappy for a long time. Most surprising, since Sophie was the funniest and most outgoing of my sisters, she'd found it hard to make friends. As she explained it, she spoke only Mandarin and the majority of Chinese people in San Francisco spoke Cantonese, so it was difficult to converse (the two dialects are as different as German and French). After her husband died, she was left penniless. On top of that, she had never applied for American citizenship. Her situation made it virtually impossible for her to get a visa to come to Japan and stay with me. Looking back now, I can see that she was depressed and had isolated herself. All I knew at the time, though, was that I missed her, and more than that, I wanted to be with her and help get her back on her feet.

Cecilia and Number Six sister, Sophie, Shanghai, China, 1947.

With Chiang Liang's connections, as well as with his encouragement, I got an expedited visa and was quickly able to book ocean passage to the United States. I left Japan secure in the knowledge that Philip and May would be well taken care of by their father and nannies. With a three-month visa and diplomatic passport in hand, I embarked on my first journey across the Pacific to America, a trip two weeks by sea and, culturally, light-years away from anything I had ever known.

✿ ✿ ✿

At the pier in San Francisco, I was met by a sweet, bespectacled official from the Nationalist Chinese Consulate named Lin Chien, who had been instructed by his embassy superiors to take good care of me for the duration of my three-month stay. He introduced me to his wife, and the three of us, along with my sister Sophie, became good friends, exploring San Francisco together.

A few weeks into my visit, on our way to lunch in Chinatown, I ran into two Chinese women I knew from Tokyo who had recently immigrated to the States. We chatted for a while and then they invited my sister and me to join them the next day for dim sum. I accepted, eager to help Sophie make more friends.

We met at the Lotus Garden, in those days one of only two dim sum houses in San Francisco. The bustling restaurant impressed me because I remember thinking, "*Har gow. Siu mai. Bao.* Mmmmm, this is good, something other than more sweet-and-sour pork and chow mein." But, after a few minutes of small talk, my reverie over the food was interrupted. The women got right to the point about something I realized later must have been on their minds from the moment they ran into me.

"Sun Yun," they said, addressing me by my Chinese name, "we want to open a restaurant here in San Francisco, but we need someone like you, a businesswoman who speaks some English and can help us negotiate a lease." They had already found an affordable restaurant space they liked on Polk Street, which just happened to be far removed from Chinatown.

Although a little voice kept telling me that my English wasn't much better than theirs, they persuaded me to talk to the landlord. Somehow, between his heavily accented Italian and my heavily accented Mandarin, we were able to strike a deal for a ten-year lease for $24,000. The only hitch was that someone needed to put up a $10,000 deposit. I wrote a check on the spot. To this day people ask me why I did such a generous thing for virtual strangers. Even now I'm not sure myself, but the only explanation I can come up with is because that's the Chinese way—if you can, you do.

Within just a few days, however, the women backed out of the deal. They both got cold feet—one citing that her husband forbade it, the other claiming it would be too much work on her own. "No problem," I said. "I'll just ask for my money back." That's where my lack of fluency in English came back to bite me. The landlord told me that the deal explicitly stated that I was obligated for the deposit, no matter the circumstance, except death. Since death was not an option, and I was embarrassed to admit to my husband that I had come to America and lost $10,000 of his money (a very large sum in those days), I decided I would try to make the best of it. First, I would make the restaurant a success, and then I would tell Chiang Liang.

Unfortunately, I hadn't counted on the fact that I needed to extend my visa and, of course, explain my reasons to Chiang Liang.

"Come home, Cecilia," he urged. "Don't throw good money after bad."

Lin Chien was supportive and helped me with the paperwork, but everyone else said I was crazy. After I'd gotten my new visa, even the clerk at City Hall, when I went to apply for a business license, said, "Lady, do you know seven businesses have opened and closed at that location in six years? You're crazy, but good luck." Sophie said, "You're too good-hearted, what are you going to do?"

Never one to turn down a challenge, I said, "Well, I guess I'm going to open a restaurant!"

Stubbornly, I ignored all the negative voices, and I don't know if I was just naive or overconfident, but for some reason I believed I could make the restaurant a success.

❈ ❈ ❈

Most Chinese restaurateurs were serving Americanized versions of Cantonese cuisine and certainly no one offered the deeply satisfying and flavorful dishes of my native northern China, much less the spicy food of Sichuan Province or the sophisticated dishes of Shanghai. Where were the fresh vegetables, feather-light dumplings, or rich soup broths I knew distinguished true regional Chinese cuisine?

In Chinatown, the only restaurant that impressed me was Johnnie Kan's. The food was typically Chinese-American, and while it might not have been authentic, it was quite good and well presented. What I really liked was that Johnnie Kan was a restaurateur, a charming host who greeted his customers at the door, spoke perfect English, and knew how to make his customers feel special. If you came through the door once, he made sure to remember you on your second visit. Also, his was the only restaurant in Chinatown that had tablecloths, carpets, and a full bar, and was constantly filled with Americans. All the others had Formica tables, linoleum floors, and fluorescent lights. I began to think that if I could create a restaurant with Western-style service and ambience and the dishes I was most familiar with—the delicious food of northern China—maybe my little restaurant would succeed.

But the first thing I needed to do was find a chef.

One misconception about me is that I must have grown up in the kitchen. The truth is, for most of my early life, I was really just a good eater.

I grew up in Beijing in a traditional upper-class household where the kitchen was off-limits to us children. My mother was a wonderful cook, even if—again in traditional fashion—she didn't actually do the cooking herself. We had two full-time chefs, both of whom spent many hours shopping with her (a challenge for my mother, as her feet were bound, making it impossible for her to stand for more then a few minutes at a time), as well as learning to prepare our meals to her exacting standards.

I learned, too, from my mother. Not how to cook exactly, but how good food, properly prepared, was supposed to taste. Perhaps because I'd been deprived of the experience growing up, once I left home I loved watching cooks at work. I intently observed street vendors make dan dan mian (a classic spicy Sichuan noodle dish) or xiao long bao (soup dumplings). In Shanghai, where Chiang Liang and I lived as newlyweds, I went to the markets with our cook. After shopping, as she moved about our kitchen preparing the meals, I took mental notes. I even instructed her at times as to how I thought her dishes needed to be seasoned. Now, I realize I was making corrections just as my mother had with her chefs.

Cecilia and husband, Chiang Liang, 1945.

For my restaurant, I knew I didn't want to hire just any Chinese chef, but, wanted someone versed in Mandarin cuisine, as well as someone who would be willing to work for a woman, almost unheard of in those days. I put a small ad in the local Chinese-language newspaper in San Francisco. After many interviews and a lot of anxiety on my part, I found a married couple from Shandong who had immigrated to the United States via Korea.

"We only cook northern home-style food," said the chef.

"That's what I want to serve in my restaurant. But can you make *jiao zi*?" I asked, referring to the dumplings I loved so much. "It's my wife's specialty," he said. "She can make 100 in an hour."

The next day, he brought in some of his wife's *jiao zi* for me to taste. The filling was light, with perfectly minced pork and cabbage. The homemade wrappers were thin, yet properly chewy, just as my mother would have liked.

"You're hired," I said. "Both of you."

After I found my chef, the next thing I did was have the restaurant's entrance door painted ruby red for good luck and affixed with brass Chinese letters that spelled out The Mandarin. Translated literally, *Mandarin* means Manchurian nobleman, and the three Chinese characters that spell out Mandarin are *fu* (good luck), *lu* (prosperity), and *sou* (long life).

*Cecilia at The Mandarin on Polk Street,
San Francisco, 1964.*

✿ ✿ ✿

Another misconception about me is that I'm an astute businesswoman. In truth, when I first opened the restaurant, I had no idea how to run it. Luckily for me, my friend from the consulate, Lin Chien, came to my rescue at just the right time.

My first few months as a restaurateur in America had been a disaster. Not knowing what people would like, I put 200 dishes on the menu at a time when we had no walk-in refrigerator, just a little icebox. Every day we had to throw out cases of food. Most of the ingredients we needed were unavailable, even in the Asian markets. We had to have them shipped from Taiwan, paying a premium for things like Sichuan peppercorns, sesame paste, sesame oil, and preserved vegetables. The chef and I made daily shopping trips, not just to Chinatown, but also to Japantown for fresh herbs like garlic chives, and to North Beach, San Francisco's Italian community, for eggplant.

One day, in a state of exasperation, I blurted out to Lin Chien, "What am I going to do? I'm losing money like crazy!"

"Madame Chiang, let me look at your records. I think I can help."

Even though we'd become friends, he continued to address me formally. I gave him my books, which my sister Sophie had been doing for me. The next morning he explained about food costs and factoring in rent and salaries for the staff.

"What staff?" I said. "I just have two cooks and two waiters. Besides the book-keeping, which my sister does, I do everything else."

Most days I arrived early to clean, shop, and prep, and then stayed until we closed to greet guests. I was obsessed with cleaning the restaurant, determined that my estab-lishment would be unlike many of the other Chinese restaurants that always seemed dirty to me. Many nights after the restaurant closed, or early in the morning before the chef arrived, I was in the kitchen scrubbing away the grease.

Suddenly I had a thought. I knew that Lin Chien's term of service in the United States was up, and he had been ordered by his government to return to Taipei. His wife loved her life in San Francisco, and did not want to leave.

"Lin Chien," I said, "come to work for me. You can manage the books and maybe take on some other jobs, too."

He told me he'd discuss it with his wife. Within the week he called and said, "I'd be honored, Madame Chiang."

"Okay, but you have to call me Cecilia from now on."

Lin Chien sold insurance during the day and did our books at night. I was left free to concentrate on the food and service at my restaurant. After being in the red for a while, we slowly began to make a little money. Through word of mouth, our busi-ness gradually began to grow. At first we had a mainly Chinese clientele, but slowly I noticed that more Americans coming in and requesting some of the dishes they'd been at first reluctant to try. Hot-and-sour soup had become really popular, and we had trouble keeping up with all the orders of *jiao zi*, which we were pan-frying to make pot stickers.

About a year after The Mandarin opened, the restaurateur Vic Bergeron (Trader Vic), a friend and one of my regular customers, brought in a man he introduced as Herb Caen. I didn't think much of it, but a couple of days after their dinner, I arrived at the restaurant as usual and the phone wouldn't stop ringing.

"My God, what's going on here?" I cried to no one in particular.

Finally, one of the calls was from a regular customer who told me that Herb Caen had said in his morning column that a "little hole-in-the-wall" joint on Polk Street had some of the best Chinese food east of the Pacific Ocean.

Herb Caen was a San Francisco "three-dot" columnist and from that day on, my little sixty-five-seat restaurant was full through several turnovers, often with lines out the door. I hired more waiters, busboys, and kitchen help. And I even found someone to clean the kitchen at night.

Excited, I called Chiang Liang and told him about my sudden success, but also admitted that I had no idea when I'd be able to return to Tokyo. Within the month, my husband came to San Francisco to see for himself this little restaurant that was keeping me in the States.

☼ ☼ ☼

I've had to make two difficult decisions in my life. The first was deciding to marry Chiang Liang when I was living away from home during the war and unable to get my parents' advice. The second was when I took out a $750,000 personal loan to move The Mandarin from Polk Street to Ghirardelli Square.

I find it funny that the question I'm most often asked is how I could have made the decision to leave my husband. Truly, I never made a conscious decision to do so. Looking back, I feel it was more like a series of small choices.

When Chiang Liang said he was coming to San Francisco, I couldn't wait to show him all that I'd accomplished. I planned a special evening for us. The restaurant looked beautiful, with ceiling fans, starched linens, and twinkling candlelight. The chef prepared two of my husband's favorite dishes, minced squab in lettuce and an elegant shark's fin soup.

We enjoyed dinner together and sat talking long after the restaurant closed. Finally he said, "Sun Yun, you've made the best of this little investment, but I think if you're going to stay longer, May and Philip should come live with you."

I was hurt that he had dismissed The Mandarin as insignificant. I think he expected a much grander restaurant because those were the kind he patronized in Shanghai and Tokyo. I realized we were going to go our separate ways. Our marriage was over.

"I think they should finish their studies at the American school in Tokyo and then come here for high school," I replied.

The following year, in 1962, May and Philip came to live with me in San Francisco. Chiang Liang visited at least twice a year. Although we never lived again as husband and wife, we never divorced, and remained good friends.

☼ ☼ ☼

As The Mandarin's business increased, Westerners were discovering there was more to Chinese food than chop suey. Dishes that had been a tough sell initially, particularly the spicy ones like sichuan shrimp and dry-shredded beef, were ordered frequently. This was the 1960s and the most adventuresome diners were usually young, in their twenties, and though they usually didn't have much money to spend, they loved the food.

One evening, just as I unlocked the door to open, I seated a young, scruffy-looking, blue-jean-clad group of five or six.

I went off to do something in the kitchen and their waiter came to me and said, "Boss Lady, those kids out there want Champagne." At the time we had a license to serve beer and wine, but no hard liquor.

"That's okay," I told him. "If you're worried they can't pay the bill, it's my problem, not yours."

"But, they're asking for Dom Perignon."

"Oh." That took me by surprise, but I said, "Well, I have a few bottles for special guests. I'll serve them myself."

They couldn't have been nicer, paid cash for their bill, and also left a 20 percent tip, unheard of in those days. I said to the waiter, "See, you never know. You can't just judge people by how they're dressed."

The group came in two more times and it always was the same: they ordered Dom Perignon, paid in cash, and left a generous tip. On their third visit, they came in just as we were about to close. Another diner said quietly, "Cecilia, do you have any idea who those people are? They're members of a rock band called Jefferson Airplane."

All I thought was that they must be successful if they could spend so much money.

That night they did something a little out of the ordinary. One of the members of the group handed me an envelope when he left and said, "This is for you, Madame Chiang. Open it when you get home. Oh, by the way, my name is Jack and we love your restaurant."

The next morning as I was making breakfast, I told Philip that a group had been coming into the restaurant and I found out that they were in a rock band called Jefferson Airplane.

"Mama, are you kidding me? They're famous. Wait till I tell my friends! Next time get their autographs."

It was then that I remembered the envelope that Jack handed to me. When I opened it, two hand-rolled cigarettes fell out. "What are these?" I asked.

Philip laughed so hard he could barely speak. "Mama, those are marijuana cigarettes."

I, too, laughed as I tossed them in the garbage. "Well, I guess it's the thought that counts."

❊ ❊ ❊

By 1966, May and Philip had been living with me for four years and were in their last year at Galileo High School (even though she was older, they both entered as freshmen). The Mandarin was doing really well. So well that Lin Chien was working for me almost exclusively, and many of my regular customers were complaining that the restaurant had become too crowded.

The problem as I saw it wasn't that we'd become too crowded. It was that we had no bar, which meant there was nowhere for guests to wait. Even if we'd had the room, we had no hard-liquor license, which was an exorbitant $75,000 at the time (if you could get one). We could only serve wine and beer, and in those days all anyone wanted was Manhattans and martinis. Luckily, there was a bar right next door.

But the complaints increased. One night, one of my best and most influential customers said, "Cecilia, we love your food but this place is just too damn small and I'm tired of waiting next door for a drink. If you can find a larger space, I can probably get some investors together."

I'd heard offers like that before and had dismissed them all. But, the very next day, I happened to drive past Ghirardelli Square, a new commercial development on the waterfront that had been generating a lot of publicity, and saw a huge sign advertising spaces for lease. This group of vintage brick buildings had housed Ghirardelli family's chocolate manufacturing plant. The family had sold their businesses to Golden Grain Macaroni, which had moved the chocolate factory across the bay. William Matson Roth, of the steamship line, bought the historic property and was turning it into a terraced, multi-use shopping center.

As soon as I got to the restaurant, I called the Ghirardelli leasing agent. I toured the space on the top floor of the Woolen Mill building and immediately fell in love with its brick walls and sweeping views of San Francisco Bay. Its huge size scared me—enough room for 300 seats. But, I told them I was very interested. For a couple of weeks I got the runaround. Finally, I went to see the leasing agent and he explained, rather apologetically, that the leasing company did not want a Chinese restaurant at the complex.

The red door at the original Mandarin on Polk Street.

"Why not?" I demanded. "I can bring in all my good reviews. My restaurant is busy all the time and I pay all my bills."

"I'm not sure how to put this, Mrs. Chiang, but many of the tenants are concerned about sanitation standards."

"What does that mean? Are they worried that my restaurant would not be clean?"

"Unfortunately, yes."

I was furious, but kept my temper when I realized that even I had been guilty of that same presumption about other Chinese restaurants.

"My restaurant is spotless," I insisted, "and to prove it I want you and your wife and anyone else you'd like to bring to be my guests at The Mandarin. You can call me an hour before you'd like to come in and I will show you my kitchen."

He took me up on my offer the next evening. I had the feeling things had gone well when he asked for four extra orders of pot stickers to go as they were leaving the restaurant. The very next day a messenger arrived with a rental agreement.

✿ ✿ ✿

There were many other obstacles besides dirty kitchens that needed to be addressed, not the least of which was the million-dollar price tag on the deal.

Before I signed the lease, I had three architects inspect the space and give me an estimate for what it was going to cost to build the restaurant. All the spaces at Ghirardelli were shells. Although nothing structural was needed, I had to put in a commercial kitchen and then design the dining rooms.

Lin Chien figured out what I needed in capital to open, plus the cost of architect's fees. He estimated the project to cost as much as $1,000,000. I nearly fell over in a dead faint.

He added that he thought I would be taking on too much risk, but suggested I speak to one of my regular customers, who his wife said was a loan officer at Bank of America. I made an appointment.

The first thing the banker said was, "You need how much? Are you sure?"

"Well, yes," I responded. "But I think I can come up with part of it, maybe $250,000."

"What kind of collateral can you offer?"

I was embarrassed to admit I wasn't sure what collateral meant, but guessed he was asking me what I could sell to raise money.

"Well I have three fur coats—one of them a valuable leopard, a twelve-carat diamond ring, Mikimoto pearls . . ."

"Cecilia, what am I going to do with those if you default on your loan?"

In the end, predictably, all of the people who had said they'd invest in a new restaurant did not come through. I made the decision to do it on my own. I sold some real estate I owned in Palm Springs—and my furs and jewels—to raise the $250,000. Then, I took on a $750,000 six-year loan for the rest. Just as when I opened the first Mandarin, everyone said I was crazy. And this time even Lin Chien, who had been my biggest supporter when I opened Polk Street, was among them.

✿ ✿ ✿

Of the three architects I interviewed, I was most interested in Lun Chan, a Chinese-American who specialized in oriental-themed restaurants. He'd designed several Trader Vic's and I was pretty impressed with his portfolio.

When he asked about my vision for the space I simply told him, "I have four 'no's: No gold. No red. No dragons. No lanterns." I didn't want my Chinese restaurant to be like any other.

I purposely didn't give him much to go on. When he came back with preliminary drawings that were beyond anything I could have ever imagined, I was floored. The sketches showed dining rooms that were dark, elegant, and understated, with the Woolen Mill's original exposed beams and brick walls.

I told him I loved his designs, but when I asked him how to proceed, his expression changed. I knew something was wrong.

"There's one small problem. Well, maybe it's not so small," he said. It turned out to involve Trader Vic, whom everyone called "The Old Man." Lun Chan continued, "The Old Man has signed me to an exclusive agreement that stipulates I can't work on any other oriental restaurants."

I couldn't believe I was just now hearing this, but tried to remain calm.

He continued, "I very much wanted to work with you because you have great taste and you clearly know what you want. Vic's a pretty difficult guy, but he speaks highly of you. My hope is that you will talk to him and get permission for me to take on your project."

I was never one to back down from a challenge, much less one wrapped in flattery. One Sunday evening, like most Sunday evenings, Vic came in with his private chef, as usual (Sunday nights his chef didn't have to cook). I approached him with my plan—that I wanted to move to a new location at Ghirardelli Square and have Lun Chan design the space. "But I know he's got an exclusive deal with you," I added.

Vic expressed surprise that I wanted to move into such an expensive location. He quizzed me about how I was going to pay for it. I explained I was taking out a loan that I thought I could pay back with the added income I expected from the bar and banquet business.

"You're a smart gal," Vic said. "I'll get back to you." He did the very next Sunday.

"Young Lady, I think you're making a mistake by taking on such a big investment. There's a huge difference between sixty-five seats and three hundred, but I have faith in you. I'll tell Lun Chan he can design your new restaurant."

✿ ✿ ✿

Three years remained on the Polk Street lease, but through a broker, I was able to sell the restaurant to a woman I had met only briefly. About six months after I opened Ghirardelli Square, I learned something interesting about the buyer. When some silver hot pots and chopsticks fell out of my chef's kitchen locker onto the floor right in front of me, I discovered that he was actually the new owner of the old Mandarin (he had bought the restaurant in someone else's name). He had been stealing items as well as food from my new restaurant to use at his place.

✿ ✿ ✿

Our opening party for The Mandarin, Ghirardelli Square, was a black-tie benefit for the San Francisco Opera Guild in June, 1968. If I was a nervous wreck in the hours before guests were to arrive, I was a woman possessed in the months leading up to the opening (a lot like my mother was in the months before New Year's). While Lun Chan was overseeing the interior construction, I made sure that every detail was perfect so The Mandarin would be the most beautiful Chinese restaurant in the country, if not the world.

Not only did I personally interview each of our seventy employees, I made two trips to Hong Kong to purchase some very special blue-and-white rice-patterned porcelain china I'd fallen in love with in San Francisco Chinatown. In those days, the United States had no relations with Communist China. But Hong Kong was an international free port, so it was possible to get goods there (including opium and cocaine, I was told) from the mainland. The crates arrived with all the porcelain carefully wrapped and cocooned in straw in the furniture. Not one piece had broken in transit.

I designed the waiters' uniforms, which were copper velvet with satin trim, as well as the carved rosewood frames for some of my antique paintings. Aside from ivory chopsticks and custom ashtrays, we also had other special touches, like crystal wineglasses and special little round cruets for soy sauce that looked like perfume bottles. Last but not least, I had to make sure that I looked stunning for opening night, so I wore a custom-tailored emerald green cheongsam (a traditional Chinese dress) with Charles Jourdan stiletto pumps.

Lin Chien, who was now my general manager with the support of several accountants, was already having fits over the money I was spending. "Cecilia, you're going to be broke before we ever even sell a dinner!" he moaned.

"I know, I know," I replied. "But first impressions are important, and I want to make sure people are talking about this restaurant for days to come. Don't worry so much."

Even though I was so scared I wasn't sleeping very well, I hoped my reassurances would let him have a good night.

✲ ✲ ✲

Opening night was the party of my dreams. The restaurant looked beautiful—dark and romantically lit like an old temple that had existed for centuries. I loved hearing the oohs and aahs from guests as they came through the doors. Everyone who was anyone in San Francisco turned out, including Herb Caen, whose items in his columns had first put us on the San Francisco restaurant and social map.

My sister Sophie came with May and Philip. The one family member we missed was Chiang Liang, who sent his regrets.

Chiang Liang did come to The Mandarin later that year, while visiting for the Christmas holidays. I think he was taken by surprise.

"Wow, Sun Yun, I'm impressed. This is quite a change from that other little matchbox of a place. Where did you get the money?"

I had never asked him to help finance Ghirardelli because truly it was his money that was the initial investment for Polk Street. I explained about the Bank of America loan, and thought about how I had done all this on my own.

✲ ✲ ✲

Every once in a while, when I would stop to think about it, I was amazed at how my life turned out. As a young girl I hadn't even been allowed in the kitchen, and here I was, a restaurateur.

Although we had some typical problems to work out—like finding sturdier dinnerware when after a few months all my beautiful porcelain dishes had been broken—we made money from the day we opened. Lin Chien's worries (and mine) were put to rest.

✲ ✲ ✲

Herb Caen continued to be one of my best customers. He often brought celebrities with him for dinner, which I would then read about in his column. And just like the first time he wrote about The Mandarin, each subsequent mention was followed by an immediate increase in reservations.

One Wednesday night, Herb came in for dinner with John Lennon and Yoko Ono. Sure enough, on Friday morning I read a little blurb that said that the three of them had dined at Cecilia Chiang's The Mandarin.

Saturday morning after their dinner, I got a call from John saying how much he had enjoyed meeting me, as well as dining at The Mandarin. He also wanted to make reservations for four people on Tuesday of the following week, and said Herb Caen would be with them again. After I put him on the books, he added that he had a favor to ask. A friend of his, a musician, was flying into San Francisco that afternoon from London and needed some cash since all the banks were closed.

"His name is Paul and I told him to ask for you. Give him $250, feed him a good meal, and we'll square up when I come in on Tuesday."

I said I'd be glad to.

In the late afternoon, after our lunch rush, a distinguished black man carrying a suitcase and a musician's instrument case came in and asked for me. "I'm Cecilia Chiang," I replied.

"John Lennon told me to speak to you, Madame. I've just arrived from London."

"Come, have something to eat, you must be hungry."

He seemed to relish his meal and ordered several things to take back with him to his hotel room. When he requested a check, I said, "John Lennon is picking up your tab and he also asked me to give you this." I handed him an envelope with the cash. He thanked me and told me to thank John for him. "Of course," I answered. "Have a good trip and enjoy San Francisco."

Tuesday came and went and Herb and John Lennon were no-shows, but then the following day they did come—Herb Caen and his wife, Maria Theresa, along with John Lennon, Yoko Ono, and another person. I assumed we had just gotten the dates mixed up and didn't say anything.

When they were getting ready to leave and pay the bill, I turned to John and said, "Your friend Paul was here on Saturday and I gave him the cash and fed him as you asked. You'd think he hadn't eaten in a while, he ate so much food!"

John just looked at me as if I had spoken in Chinese. He turned to Herb and said, "Look's like he's struck again!"

I was completely confused until John said to me, "Cecilia, this bloke has been following me around the United States and every time I'm written up in a newspaper, he calls afterward and pretends to be me."

I felt really foolish. "But he sounded just like you," I said. "And he seemed so nice."

"Yes, that's his trick, of course. How much did he take you for?" I told him and he immediately reimbursed me. "Sorry about that, you know."

It was just coincidence that John and Yoko came in to the restaurant on Wednesday. On Thursday, Herb Caen had another item to mention in his column.

✿ ✿ ✿

About a year after we opened, I heard a familiar, "Young Lady, sit down." It was, of course, Vic. "Have a drink," he ordered. "You work too hard."

Vic Bergeron had been a regular at Ghirardelli Square on Sunday nights, just as he had at Polk Street.

"Young Lady, I was pretty worried that your food was going to suffer when you moved here, but I have to admit that it's even better than before. How do you do it?"

"Three things," I replied. "I have a new chef from Hong Kong. I have new equipment in the kitchen that allows us to make more special dishes like Tea-Smoked Duck. And I have more suppliers who find me special ingredients these days."

"Would you give me your recipe for that duck?"

"No, Old Man. It's a secret!"

Vic Bergeron just smiled at me.

✿ ✿ ✿

Five years after we opened The Mandarin at Ghirardelli Square, we made the loan officer at the Bank of America a very happy man. Lin Chien and I wrote out a check for the last of our loan payments.

One year after that, in 1974, I opened The Mandarin in Beverly Hills. Even though I took out a loan for that restaurant, the amount was for less than half of what I had borrowed before, and I paid it back it in two years.

FAMOUS RECIPES from
THE MANDARIN

One of the biggest challenges I faced when I opened The Mandarin on Polk Street was writing my first menu. When I opened the Forbidden City in Tokyo with a group of friends and family, we were one of only a few Chinese restaurants in that city and we knew that there were lots of other of expatriates from China who, like us, missed the cuisine of our homeland. We were right, and our very large (400-seat) restaurant with its very large menu of dishes from all regions of China was a hit from the beginning.

So I knew that we wouldn't have trouble attracting Chinese customers who would recognize many of the regional dishes on our menu, but what about Americans who didn't know *jiao zi* from wontons? And how would they like peppery hot-and-sour soup when they were used to bland versions of egg-drop soup? But what did I know about American tastes when it came to Chinese food? All they were used to, at least that I could see, was nearly unrecognizable versions of Cantonese cuisine—like egg foo yong made with canned mushrooms and bean sprouts with gloppy brown gravy, or celery and canned bamboo shoots stir-fried with little pieces of chicken and called chop suey.

My first menus were large, almost ridiculously so, with 200 dishes listed for a 60-seat restaurant. But I viewed those early menus as an experiment. I needed to find out what my customers liked. Every night I would help my non-Chinese patrons order and suggest things they might want to try. "Do you like eggplant? I have some fresh I think you'd enjoy." "If you like dumplings, I'll bring you an order of pot stickers to try."

I also always made a point to find out how they liked the dishes afterward. If I saw any food returned to the kitchen uneaten, I would ask them if they'd like me to bring them something else.

Initially, it was our Chinese customers who kept me in business the first year, but slowly I began to see more and more of the same American faces. "Are you back for some of the pot stickers?" I'd tease after they were seated. "I noticed you really liked that bok choy last time. I'll bring you some tonight."

As we began to get busy, I was able to pare down the menu. I was getting to know my customers' tastes, but more than that, I was proud to feel that I was also educating them as to just how delicious and complex Chinese cuisine could be. Even though the majority of the dishes on my menu were from the northern China region of Beijing, where I had grown up, I also included a great many from the three other major culinary regions of the country: Shanghai, Sichuan, and yes, Canton.

Eventually of course I got to know my customers' tastes, as many of the dishes became hugely popular, both at the first Mandarin on Polk and then at The Mandarin at Ghirardelli Square. They are the dishes that made The Mandarin famous and the recipes for which I still get requests. They're also, maybe not coincidentally, my personal favorites.

Pot Stickers

guo tie

THESE HUMBLE DUMPLINGS WERE responsible for putting The Mandarin on the map. We became famous for many Chinese dishes, but pot stickers took on a life of their own. Common throughout China, they're dumplings generically called *jiao zi*, which can be prepared many different ways—steamed, boiled, pan-fried, deep-fried. Fillings range from pork to beef, or lamb in Muslim provinces. In Beijing, *jiao zi* are usually pan-fried and served during the New Year's holidays.

I think homemade wrappers are best, but frankly, they're so much work I'd never dream of doing it now. There are so many good-quality wrappers available commercially.

✿　✿　✿

Pot sticker wrappers, unlike wonton wrappers, are round rather than square and tend to be a little thicker. They usually are sold, depending on the manufacturer, 48 to a 12-ounce package. This recipe makes 25 dumplings, so you can double the filling recipe given here or deep-fry the extra wrappers to use in a salad.

To freeze the pot stickers, place on a baking sheet with space between them so they don't stick together; freeze for an hour or so, then put them in a ziplock plastic bag. You can cook pot stickers straight from the freezer by increasing the steaming time to 8 minutes and letting them brown after the water has evaporated.

Cecilia does a clever "box" pleat that I found almost impossible to describe. Any method that works and is easy for you is fine. One important tip, use a nonstick skillet to brown the dumplings, otherwise you'll find out in a hurry why they're called "pot stickers." —L.W.

Makes 25 dumplings

2 cups napa cabbage, rinsed, cored, finely chopped, and squeezed of excess water

2 teaspoons minced green onion, white and light green parts only

1 teaspoon minced fresh ginger

1 pound lean ground pork

1 1/2 teaspoons kosher salt

1 tablespoon Asian sesame oil

Flour, for dusting

25 pot-sticker wrappers

1 large egg, beaten

Peanut oil, for pan frying

Dipping sauce

3 tablespoons premium soy sauce

2 tablespoons rice vinegar

Dash of chili oil and/or pinch of minced fresh ginger (optional)

TO MAKE THE FILLING, mix the cabbage, green onion, ginger, pork, salt, and sesame oil together in a bowl with your hands until well combined.

TO ASSEMBLE THE DUMPLINGS, lightly dust a rimmed baking sheet with flour and set aside. Keep the wrappers moist under a slightly damp towel; have a small bowl of water handy for sealing the filled dumplings. For each pot sticker, place 1 tablespoon of the filling in the center of a wrapper. Dip a finger in the water and moisten all around the edges of one side of the wrapper. Fold the wrapper in half to form a triangle that encloses the filling and press together. With your finger, dab a little egg on the two opposite points of the long side of the triangle. Bring the two points together so they overlap and press to seal. Repeat with the remaining filling and wrappers. If not frying and eating the dumplings right away, they should be refrigerated, loosely covered with the damp towel, and cooked within 1 hour. Or, they may be frozen.

TO MAKE THE DIPPING SAUCE, whisk together the soy sauce, rice vinegar, chili oil, and ginger in a small bowl; mix well. Set aside.

TO COOK THE DUMPLINGS, heat a large nonstick skillet over high heat until a bead of water dances on the surface and then evaporates. Cover the bottom of the skillet with a thin film of peanut oil and swirl to coat. Arrange some of the dumplings in the skillet in a single layer, being sure to not overcrowd. Pan-fry on high heat until the bottoms are golden brown, about 2 minutes (skip this if cooking frozen pot stickers). Pour enough water over the pot stickers to create $1/2$ inch of liquid. Cover the pan, reduce the heat to medium-high, and steam for 5 minutes (or 8 minutes if frozen). If cooking frozen pot stickers, uncover and let them brown after all the water has evaporated. Transfer the pot stickers to a platter and serve with the dipping sauce.

Chongqing Spicy Dry-Shredded Beef

gan bian niu rou si

A FEW DAYS AFTER ARRIVING IN CHONGQING, Sichuan Province, after our "long walk" from Beijing, my Uncle Ting's cook served us this dish. At the time I thought I'd never tasted such a wonderful balance of heat and flavor. In 1996, when George Chen asked me to help him create the menu for his San Francisco restaurant Shanghai 1930, I remembered this dish from The Mandarin, one I hadn't put on the menu of any other restaurant since. George loved it, but felt that it was too labor-intensive. I reworked the recipe to make it easier to reproduce in a restaurant kitchen. The result is a dish that is still popular with Shanghai 1930 regulars, as well as with my friends when I serve it at home.

✿   ✿   ✿

Although it might seem a messy and unnecessary step, frying the beef slices first in hot oil results in a texture that transforms this dish from simple to sublime. —L.W.

Serves 6 to 8 as part of a Chinese meal and 4 to 6 as a Western-style entrée

1¹/₂ pounds flank steak

2 to 3 cups peanut or corn oil, for deep-frying

3 garlic cloves, minced

1 teaspoon peeled minced fresh ginger

5 whole dried red chiles

5 celery stalks, sliced diagonally ¹/₈-inch thick

1 carrot, peeled and cut in ¹/₂-inch dice

¹/₂ teaspoon freshly ground black pepper

2 tablespoons soy sauce

1 teaspoon chili paste or chili oil (page 5)

So the beef is easier to slice, freeze it for 30 minutes or so to firm it up. Slice it diagonally against the grain into ¹/₈-inch-thick strips. Cut them crosswise into 2- or 3-inch pieces.

Line a plate or small baking sheet with paper towels and have it ready near the cooktop. In a large, flat-bottomed wok or wide, deep saucepan, heat the oil over high heat until it registers 350°F on a deep-fry thermometer. Carefully slide the beef into the oil, and using a long chopstick, quickly stir the pieces to separate them. Stir and cook for 15 seconds; with a mesh strainer, scoop out the pieces and spread them out on the paper-lined plate to drain. Reserve the cooking oil.

Heat another pan over high heat until a bead of water dances on the surface and then evaporates. Add 2 tablespoons of the reserved oil from the other pan and swirl to coat the pan. Add the garlic and ginger and cook, stirring continuously, for 15 seconds. Quickly add the chiles, celery, carrot, black pepper, soy sauce, and chili paste, and stir until well combined. Toss in the cooked beef and stir until the meat is glazed with the sauce, about 15 seconds longer.

Turn the beef mixture out onto a platter and serve hot.

Prawns "à la Szechwan"

gan shao ming xia

IF I WERE TO GIVE A MORE ACCURATE ENGLISH NAME to this dish it would be Sichuan Shrimp. I guess I thought Prawns à la Szechwan sounded fancier when I wrote the first menus at The Mandarin. But that was at a time when the only fine-dining restaurants were primarily French. The name for the dish stuck, and when we moved to Ghirardelli Square, Prawns à la Szechwan remained one of our best sellers.

✿　✿　✿

My husband, Dan, who loves spicy food, but isn't too crazy about shrimp, thought this was one of the best dishes we tested. His only suggestion was that it could be spicier, so add more red pepper flakes if you're so inclined. Consider serving the shrimp as an hors d'oeuvre, skewered on toothpicks. —L.W.

Serves 6 to 8 as part of a Chinese meal and 4 to 6 as a Western-style entrée

1 pound medium shrimp, shelled, tails removed, and deveined

2 teaspoons kosher salt, plus a pinch for the wok

2 teaspoons cornstarch

3 tablespoons plus 2 teaspoons peanut oil

2 tablespoons Shaoxing wine

2 tablespoons soy sauce

2 tablespoons sugar

1/4 cup ketchup

2 teaspoons Asian sesame oil

2 teaspoons minced garlic

2 teaspoons minced fresh ginger

2 teaspoons red pepper flakes

Thinly sliced green onions, for garnish

In a bowl, gently mix the shrimp with 2 teaspoons of the salt to coat well. Cover the shrimp with cold water and slosh them around a few times. Drain well and transfer the shrimp to a clean bowl. Mix the shrimp with the cornstarch and 2 teaspoons of the peanut oil. Set aside for 5 minutes.

TO MAKE THE SAUCE, whisk together the wine, soy sauce, sugar, ketchup, and sesame oil in a small bowl until well combined. Set aside.

TO COOK THE SHRIMP, heat a large wok over high heat until a bead of water dances on the surface and then evaporates. Add the remaining 3 tablespoons of peanut oil and a pinch of salt and swirl to coat the pan. Add the garlic, ginger, and pepper flakes, stirring constantly for 10 seconds. Toss in the shrimp and stir-fry until they are just pink, about 1 minute. Pour in the reserved sauce, bring the liquid to a boil, and toss to coat the shrimp well. Immediately remove the pan from the heat, as you don't want to overcook the shrimp.

To serve, turn the shrimp out onto a platter, sprinkle with a few green onion slices, and serve hot.

Cecilia's Minced Squab in Lettuce Cups

sheng chao ge song

I CAN'T EVEN IMAGINE HOW MANY times I've given out this recipe. The problem for me, though, is that too often the recipe isn't right. Either the writer has changed the ingredients or the restaurant cook has decided to add a little more of this or that. This is my version and I've tested it several times for this book to make sure that it's just the way I want it.

☼ ☼ ☼

One change that does have Cecilia's approval is to substitute boned chicken thighs for the squab. No matter which you use, the texture of this dish is important, so make sure the meat is not finely ground.

To trim the lettuce, cut off and discard the bottom core of the head of lettuce. Put the lettuce in a large bowl, fill the bowl with enough ice cold water for the lettuce to be fully submerged, and soak for at least 30 minutes. Trim off the ragged edges from the leaves with scissors so they form, neat circles. —L.W.

Serves 6 to 8 as part of a Chinese meal and 4 to 6 as a Western-style entrée

6 dried black mushrooms

1 pound bone-in squab

2 tablespoons Shaoxing wine

1 tablespoon soy sauce

1 teaspoon oyster sauce

2 tablespoons peanut oil

1/4 cup finely diced Chinese sausage (*lop chong*) or Virginia ham

1/3 cup (5 ounces) drained and diced canned water chestnuts

2 teaspoons (about 2 stalks) minced green onions, white part only, plus additional, thinly sliced, for garnish

1/2 teaspoon freshly ground white pepper

2 tablespoons toasted pine nuts

6 to 8 crisp, trimmed iceberg lettuce leaves

In a small bowl, soak the dried mushrooms in hot water to cover for 15 minutes. Drain and chop them finely. You should end up with about 1/3 of a cup.

On a cutting board, use a cleaver or sharp knife to carefully remove the bones, tough tendons, and extra fat from the squab. Mince the remaining meat and skin and set aside until ready to use; you should have 6 ounces.

TO MAKE THE SAUCE, whisk together half the wine with the soy and oyster sauces in a small bowl.

TO MAKE THE FILLING, heat a large wok over high heat until a bead of water dances on the surface and then evaporates. Add the oil and swirl to coat the pan. Add the squab, and quickly stir the meat to break it apart. Cook, stirring constantly, until a bit of pink remains, about 1 minute. Toss in the mushrooms and stir to combine well. Add the sausage, water chestnuts, and green onions and cook for 30 seconds more. Pour in the reserved sauce, bring the liquid to a boil, and toss to coat. Sprinkle with white pepper and remove the pan from the heat.

Turn the squab mixture out onto a serving platter and scatter with pine nuts and sliced green onions. To serve, place a bit of the squab mixture in a lettuce leaf and eat while the mixture is still warm.

Sichuan Spicy Eggplant

yu xian quie zi

WHEN I FIRST CAME TO CALIFORNIA in the early 60s, I was surprised to find that in a land of such abundance, the choice of vegetables in the markets was so limited. I found it particularly strange that in Chinese restaurants most of the vegetables were canned. The fresh vegetables were mainly carrots and broccoli. One day while shopping in San Francisco's Japantown, I came across some lovely, slender violet eggplant, like the kind grown in China. I was inspired to serve this Sichuan recipe, and it became one of our best sellers.

✿ ✿ ✿

Asian eggplants have thinner skins, fewer seeds, and sweeter flesh than the Western globe eggplant. When fried, the smaller, denser Asian eggplant absorbs less oil. It's important though, to make sure your oil is at 350°F. If the oil is not hot enough, the eggplant will be too oily no matter which variety you use. For the same reason, I like to fry in two batches, so the temperature of the oil doesn't drop too much. —L.W.

Serves 6 to 8 as part of a Chinese meal and 4 to 6 as a Western-style entrée

1¹/₂ tablespoons Shaoxing wine

1¹/₂ tablespoons soy sauce

1 tablespoon Chinkiang black vinegar or good-quality balsamic vinegar

2 teaspoons chili paste

1 teaspoon sugar

2 thinly sliced green onions

2 to 3 cups peanut or vegetable oil, for deep-frying

2 or 3 small Asian eggplants (about 1 pound total), stems trimmed, quartered lengthwise, then cut crosswise into 2-inch wedges

1 tablespoon peanut oil

¹/₄ pound ground pork

TO MAKE THE SAUCE, whisk together the wine, soy sauce, vinegar, chili paste, sugar, and green onions in a small bowl until combined.

Line a plate with paper towels. In a large flat-bottomed wok or a wide, deep saucepan, heat the oil over high heat until it registers 350°F on a deep-fry thermometer. Carefully slide half of the eggplant pieces into the hot oil and fry them until golden brown, about 2 minutes. Transfer eggplant to the plate to thoroughly drain. Fry the remaining eggplant.

Heat a large skillet or wok (if you have another one) over high heat until a bead of water dances on the surface and then evaporates. Add the 1 tablespoon of peanut oil and swirl to coat the pan. Add the pork and a bit of the reserved sauce and stir constantly with a spoon, breaking the meat apart as it cooks. Continue to cook until the pork begins to brown, 1 to 2 minutes. Add the eggplant and the rest of the sauce, bring the liquid to a boil, and toss until all the ingredients are well combined, about 30 seconds more.

Remove the pan from the heat, turn the eggplant mixture out onto a serving platter, and serve immediately.

Mandarin Crispy Chicken Salad

liang ban ji si

I ALWAYS CHUCKLE TO MYSELF WHENEVER I see "Chinese Chicken Salad" on a menu. It seems like every restaurant (even the fast food chains) offers some variation of the salad that we first served at The Mandarin. Truly, there is no "real" Chinese chicken salad. In China, lettuce was imported and rare, and salads were things that were pickled. I came up with the idea for this salad simply as a way to use up iceberg lettuce. We had plenty left over after we trimmed the outer leaves of the heads to serve with minced squab. In the 1960s, everyone loved salads made with iceberg lettuce, and it became a very popular dish in San Francisco, but it was the number-one seller at The Mandarin in Beverly Hills, where it seemed that all our customers were watching their weight and that anything with lettuce back then was "low-cal."

✿　✿　✿

This salad is all about crunch. Cecilia says that originally the waiters at The Mandarin tossed the salad tableside, so that all the ingredients would retain their crispiness.

The recipe calls for fried rice-stick noodles, which are also called bean thread or cellophane noodles, and are usually sold in 2-ounce bundles. You can fry them ahead of time and keep them in a ziplock bag for up to 2 days, or fry them before you fry the chicken in this recipe.

Make this recipe easier by using leftover chicken or a roasted chicken purchased from the deli. —L.W.

Serves 4

1 large egg, lightly beaten

Cornstarch

2 boneless, skinless chicken breast halves

2 to 3 cups peanut or vegetable oil, for deep-frying

1/2 large head iceberg lettuce, cored and shredded

3 green onions (white part only), shredded

1 1/2 cups (about 7 ounces) finely chopped lightly salted roasted peanuts or cashews

2 tablespoons toasted sesame seed

2 to 3 cups deep-fried rice-stick noodles (see page 36)

1 bunch chopped fresh cilantro, plus fresh cilantro sprigs for garnish

1/2 teaspoon Asian sesame oil

Kosher salt

Freshly ground black pepper

For the dressing

2 teaspoons dry mustard

1/4 cup warm oil (reserved from the frying, above)

2 teaspoons Five-Spice Mix (see page 6)

Set a wire rack over a plate and keep it nearby. Put the beaten egg in one shallow bowl and the cornstarch in another. Dip a chicken breast in the egg, letting the excess drip off, and then dip it in the cornstarch, turning until well coated. Dip it once more in the egg, and then rest it on the rack. Repeat with the other chicken breast. Refrigerate for 1 hour.

continued

Line a plate with paper towels and have it ready near the cooktop. In a large, flat-bottomed wok or wide, deep saucepan, heat the oil over high heat until it registers 350°F on a deep-fry thermometer. Add the chicken and cook until golden on both sides, about 3 minutes per side. Transfer to the paper-lined plate to drain. For the dressing, set aside ¼ cup of the oil from the wok in a small bowl to cool slightly from hot to warm.

TO MAKE THE DRESSING, whisk the mustard powder with the reserved warm cooking oil in a small bowl; whisk in the five-spice mix until well combined.

TO ASSEMBLE THE SALAD, put the lettuce, green onions, nuts, sesame seed, rice sticks, and cilantro in a large salad bowl. Slice the chicken breast into ¼-inch-thick strips and add to the salad. Pour over the dressing, add the sesame oil, and toss until all is well combined. Season to taste with salt and pepper. Serve the salad garnished with sprigs of cilantro.

Frying Rice-Stick Noodles

To fry rice-stick noodles, heat 2 or 3 cups of peanut or vegetable oil in a large, flat-bottomed wok or wide, deep saucepan to 350°F on a deep-fry thermometer. Break the noodle bundle apart and drop a handful of the noodles into the hot oil. They will puff up and expand immediately. Turn the noodles over with tongs or a slotted spoon so that all the noodles are cooked. Once they're puffed, immediately transfer them to a plate lined with paper towels to drain. Repeat with the remaining noodles.

Beggar's Chicken

jiao hua ji

CHUCK WILLIAMS, ONE OF MY OLDEST AND DEAREST FRIENDS and the founder of Williams-Sonoma, loves this dish, both for its flavor and dramatic presentation—especially the sound the hammer makes when it cracks the crust. I've combined techniques from two talented chefs and come up with what I think is the most delicious recipe of Beggar's Chicken.

☼ ☼ ☼

You can buy pottery clay at any artist or ceramic supply store, but be sure to pick the softest one you can find. If the clay is too stiff and difficult to work with, mix in a bit of warm water until well incorporated. It's best rolled out on a smooth surface (as opposed to a wooden cutting board). You can also place a sheet of parchment paper on top of the clay as you're rolling it out to prevent it from sticking.

While this recipe is great for entertaining because it can be made ahead and makes a dramatic presentation, be careful not to cook it too far ahead—time it so you bring it to the table 15 minutes (30 minutes max) after it's been removed from the oven. The clay retains an amazing amount of heat, and the chicken continues to cook. —L.W.

Serves 6 to 8 as part of a Chinese meal or
4 to 6 as a Western style entrée

1 small chicken (2^1/2 to 3 pounds), with head, feet, and the first 2 wing joints removed

1 gallon water

1 cup kosher salt

For the stuffing

10 to 12 small dried black mushrooms

1 (8-ounce) can sliced water chestnuts, drained

½ cup sliced bamboo shoots

1-inch thick piece (about 1^1/2 ounces) Virginia ham, sliced ^{1}/8 inch thick

1 bunch green onions, white part only, cut in half lengthwise and sliced on the bias into 1^1/2-inch strips

5 thin slices peeled fresh ginger

For the marinade

1 teaspoon five-spice powder (page 6)

2 teaspoons Asian sesame oil

2 teaspoons granulated sugar

2 teaspoons oyster sauce

1 tablespoon soy sauce

2 tablespoons water

2 tablespoons mushroom soy sauce

1 (5-pound) box moist pottery clay

2 (20-inch) square pieces aluminum foil

1 large brown paper grocery bag, opened up and cut into 1 (20-inch) square

continued

For the sauce

3 tablespoons soy sauce

2 tablespoons oyster sauce

2 teaspoons Asian sesame oil

2 teaspoons sugar

¼ cup Delicious Chicken Broth
  (page 57)

2 teaspoons cornstarch dissolved in
  1 tablespoon water

Trim the chicken of any excess fat. In a large plastic bag or container, cover the chicken with the water and salt, making sure it is fully submerged. Brine for 3 hours, drain, rinse the chicken well, and pat it dry. Transfer it to a cutting board or plate.

Preheat the oven to 450°F.

In a small bowl, cover the mushrooms with boiling water and soak until softened, about 15 minutes. Drain the water off the mushrooms, gently squeeze them of any excess liquid, and remove and discard their stems. Transfer the mushrooms to a clean medium bowl. Add the water chestnuts, bamboo shoots, ham, green onions, and ginger and toss to combine all ingredients well.

TO MAKE THE MARINADE, in a small bowl, whisk together the five-spice powder, sesame oil, sugar, oyster sauce, soy, water, and mushroom soy. Rub this mixture on the inside and outside of the chicken, being sure to coat the surface evenly. Fill the cavity of the chicken with the stuffing, packing it tightly. Tie the legs together with kitchen string and tuck in the wings.

Arrange both pieces of aluminum foil (one atop the other) in a diamond shape on a counter. One corner of the foil should be pointing directly toward you. Place the chicken, breast side up, in the center of the foil, with the head and tail facing east and west. Using the top piece of foil first, wrap the chicken in it, by tightly crimping the edges and creating a tidy seam. Repeat this process with the second piece of foil. Turn the chicken upside down and place it in the center of the brown paper bag. Wrap the bag neatly around the chicken, tightly folding the edges to create a top seam and trimming any excess paper as needed. Your goal is to have a tidy and well-sealed package. Turn the parcel over and place it in the middle of a lightly oiled roasting pan. The paper bag seam should now be on the bottom.

On a smooth surface, using a rolling pin, roll out the clay into a thin round, about ¾ inch thick and big enough to fully cover the chicken. Don't worry if there are holes, as you can easily patch them after the clay is on the chicken. You should have some clay left over.

Carefully drape the clay over the top and sides of the chicken and tuck it tightly around the sides, being sure to patch up any holes or tears in the clay. It is very important to have as tight of a seal as possible. Transfer the pan to the oven and cook for 1 hour at 450°F. Reduce the heat to 350°F and cook for 1½ hours more. Remove the pan from the oven and let the chicken rest for 15 or, at most, 30 minutes.

TO MAKE THE SAUCE, just before you are ready to serve, in a small saucepan whisk together the soy, oyster sauce, sesame oil, sugar, and chicken broth. Over medium heat, bring the mixture to a boil and then whisk in the cornstarch slurry. Heat it over low heat until warm and slightly thickened.

With a mallet or the butt end of a large knife, carefully crack the shell (the clay will be very hot). Using scissors and being mindful of hot steam, cut open the paper bag. Carefully lift out the foil-wrapped chicken, transfer it to a rimmed platter, and unwrap each piece of foil individually.

Carve the chicken and drizzle the warm sauce over the chicken and serve with a bit of the stuffing.

Mu-Shu Pork with a Hat

he cai dai mao

WHEN I WAS IN COLLEGE IN BEIJING I would go with three of my friends to a nearby restaurant that served a wonderful version of Mu-Shu Pork—a Beijing specialty. As a bonus, they offered free soup with any entrée, making a very filling meal for any students who were on a budget. They prepared their Mu-Shu Pork in almost the same way as our cook did at home (one of the things I loved about it): the egg was cooked as an open omelet that was placed like a little hat or beret on top of the platter of stir-fried pork. We would tear the omelet into pieces and enclose them inside the pancakes with the sauce and pork mixture. When I made Mu-Shu Pork at The Mandarin, we served it the more traditional way, with the cooked egg mixed into the jumble of vegetables and pork, I really prefer this more home-style version.

✿　✿　✿

This is not a difficult dish to execute, but it is important to have everything prepped.

Mu shu wrappers, which are like crepes, can be purchased fresh or frozen at Asian markets. They're also sold as Peking doilies or Mandarin pancakes. The wrappers dry out quickly and need to be kept covered at all times with a damp kitchen towel. Thin flour tortillas will do in a pinch and don't need to be covered. —L.W.

Serves 4 to 6 as part of a Chinese meal and 2 to 3 as a Western-style entrée

8 ounces pork loin

2 tablespoons cornstarch

4 tablespoons Shaoxing wine

4 tablespoons plus 2 teaspoons peanut or vegetable oil

3/4 cup (about 1 ounce) loosely packed dried lily buds

3/4 cup (about 1/2 ounce) loosely packed dried tree-ear mushrooms

2 1/2 tablespoons hoisin sauce

1/4 teaspoon sugar

5 large eggs, lightly beaten with a pinch of salt

2 to 3 mu shu wrappers per person

1/8 teaspoon kosher salt

1 pound bean sprouts

2 tablespoons premium soy sauce

1 1/2 teaspoons Asian sesame oil

6 green onions (white part only), cut into 2-inch pieces and shredded, for garnish

So the pork is easier to slice, freeze it for 30 minutes or so to firm it up. Slice the frozen meat diagonally against the grain into 1/4 by 1/4 by 2-inch strips. In a small bowl, toss the pork, cornstarch, 2 tablespoons of the wine, and 1 teaspoon of the peanut oil and stir to coat well. Set aside.

Place the dried lily buds in a small bowl and mushrooms in a medium bowl, generously cover both with very hot tap water, and let them soak until soft, about 30 minutes (the tree ears expand quite a bit, so they require a larger bowl and perhaps more water). Once

continued

softened, drain off the liquid for both and return them to their respective bowls. Rinse the mushrooms to remove any grit or sand, cut or tear off any tough stems, then cut the mushrooms into small (1-inch) pieces. Set both bowls aside.

TO MAKE THE SAUCE, heat a teaspoon of the peanut oil in a small saucepan on high until hot and shimmering. Add the hoisin sauce, 1 tablespoon of the wine, and sugar; stir until thoroughly combined and heated through. Transfer the sauce to a small serving bowl and set aside.

Just before serving, make the omelet. Heat a nonstick skillet over medium-high heat. Add 1 teaspoon of the peanut oil and swirl to coat the pan. Add the eggs and swirl to make sure they're spread evenly in the pan. Cook until set, pushing the cooked eggs from the outer rim of the pan to the center, letting the liquid run onto the pan bottom. Try not to cook the eggs too long or they will get tough or brown. It may only take 1 to 2 minutes. It's best to remove the pan from the heat as soon as the eggs have set and let the residual heat of the pan finish the cooking. Transfer the omelet to a plate while you steam the wrappers and stir-fry the pork and vegetables.

TO STEAM THE WRAPPERS, fill the bottom of a steamer with water and bring to a boil over high heat. Just before you stir-fry the pork, put the mu shu wrappers on a rimmed plate that will fit in a steamer tier and then place the plate on the tier over the boiling water. Cover and steam until the wrappers are soft and warm, about 5 minutes. Carefully lift the plate out of the steamer tier and cover with a damp towel.

TO COOK THE PORK, heat a large wok over high heat until a bead of water dances on the surface and then evaporates. Add 2 tablespoons of the peanut oil and a pinch of salt and swirl to coat the pan; add the pork. Using tongs or chopsticks, toss to coat the pork in the hot oil, stirring frequently until the pork appears glossy and slippery, about 1 minute. Remove the pan from the heat and transfer the pork to a bowl or plate.

Return the pan to high heat, add the remaining 2 tablespoons of peanut oil and a pinch of salt and swirl to coat the pan. Add the lily buds and bean sprouts and stir constantly to coat in the oil. Add the remaining 1 tablespoon wine, soy sauce, sesame oil, and tree ears; cook about 1 minute, stirring and tossing constantly. Toss in the reserved pork and stir until well combined. Remove from the heat and transfer to a platter.

To serve, top the pork with the omelet. Place the bowls with the sauce and the green onions alongside. If your steamer is attractive, rest it on a plate and place it directly on the table. Otherwise, remove the wrappers from the steamer, wrap them in a clean, damp cloth to keep them moist, and place on a serving platter. For each serving, have your guests spread a little sauce on a wrapper, tear the omelet into pieces, and top with more sauce. Spoon on some pork mixture and sprinkle with the green onions. Folding a mu shu pork wrapper is similar to folding a burrito that's open on one end: for the bottom, fold one-third of one side of the wrapper up over the filling, then fold the two sides over each other to create an envelope that's open at the top.

Sichuan Dry-fried Green Beans

gan bian si ji dou

THIS DISH OF SPICY twice-fried green beans was our most popular vegetable at The Mandarin from the day I put it on the menu. There is just something about it that appeals to many people's tastes: spicy chiles, crunchy yet tender beans, and pebbly meat mixed with garlic and ginger. I know that I quickly fell in love with this dish the first time I tasted it in Chongqing, even though I hadn't yet become accustomed to the chile peppers that were everywhere in Sichuan. At Betelnut in San Francisco, chef Alex Ong tells me that they go through four to five cases of beans a day. Wow, that's a lot of beans!

✿ ✿ ✿

What makes this dish unique (and authentically Sichuanese) is the flavor of zha cai, *salted, cured mustard greens, sometimes labeled as preserved mustard tuber or Sichuan preserved vegetable.* —L.W.

Serves 6 to 8 as part of a Chinese meal and 4 to 6 as a Western-style entrée

1 tablespoon soy sauce

2 teaspoons Shaoxing wine

2 teaspoons chili oil (page 5) or 1 tablespoon chili paste

2 to 3 cups vegetable oil, for deep-frying

1 pound green beans, trimmed and cut in 2-inch pieces

1 tablespoon peanut oil

1 teaspoon minced garlic

1 teaspoon minced fresh ginger

¼ cup (about 1 ounce) finely chopped *zha cai*

¼ pound ground pork

TO MAKE THE SAUCE, whisk together the soy sauce, wine, and chili oil in a small bowl until well combined and set aside.

Line a plate with paper towels and have it ready near the cooktop. In a large, flat-bottomed wok or wide, deep saucepan, heat until the oil over high heat until it registers 350°F on a deep-fry thermometer. Carefully drop the green beans into the hot oil and fry until the skins just begin to blister, about 2 minutes. Scoop the beans out of the oil with a slotted spoon and transfer to the plate.

Heat a large skillet or another wok if you have one over high heat until a bead of water dances on the surface and then evaporates. Add the peanut oil and swirl to coat the pan. Toss in the garlic and ginger and cook until fragrant and slightly golden, about 20 seconds. Add the *zha cai* and a little of the sauce and continue to cook, stirring frequently, about 20 seconds more. Add the pork and stir constantly, breaking the meat apart with a spoon. Continue to cook until the pork begins to brown, 1 to 2 minutes. Add the reserved beans and the rest of the sauce and toss until all ingredients are well combined and heated through, about 30 seconds more. Remove the pan from the heat, turn the beans out onto a platter, and serve immediately.

Hot-and-Sour Soup

suan la tang

TO THIS DAY, just like when I was a school girl in Beijing, a satisfying lunch for me usually consists of a steaming bowl of clear broth with bits of meat or tofu and sometimes noodles or dumplings. Spicy and vinegary hot-and-sour soup is still my favorite comfort food. Unfortunately, many restaurant versions today have become so heavy handed with seasonings and gloppy with cornstarch thickening that I barely recognize it anymore. This authentic Sichuan soup should have a pleasant balance of tingle, pucker, and lightness on the tongue.

✿ ✿ ✿

Cecilia says the "hot" in the soup should come from freshly ground white pepper, never chili oil, and the "sour" should be a well-balanced but healthy dose of good-quality vinegar, preferably Chinkiang, a Chinese black rice vinegar. For the bamboo shoots, if you live near an Asian community you can usually find them fresh, but canned ones are acceptable if you rinse them in cold water a couple of times to remove the "tinny" taste. —L.W.

Make about 8 cups

3 or 4 dried black mushrooms, stems removed

4 ounces pork loin

8 cups Delicious Chicken Broth (page 57) or
 Double Delicious Chicken Broth (page 58)

1/4 cup sliced bamboo shoots, fresh, or canned
 and rinsed, cut in 1/4-inch julienne strips

4 ounces firm tofu, cut in julienne strips

1 teaspoon kosher salt

2 teaspoons ground white pepper, or more to taste

2 to 4 tablespoons Chinkiang black vinegar

1 to 2 tablespoons white vinegar

1 tablespoon soy sauce

1 large egg, lightly beaten

2 teaspoons Asian sesame oil

2 tablespoons chopped fresh cilantro

In a small bowl, soak the dried mushrooms in hot water to cover for 15 minutes. Drain and slice the caps 1/8 inch thick. Set aside.

So the pork is easier to slice, freeze it for 30 minutes or so to firm it up. Slice the frozen meat diagonally against the grain into 1/4 by 1/4 by 2-inch strips.

In a large saucepan or wok, bring the chicken broth to a lively simmer over high heat; add the pork strips and cook 2 minutes. Add the mushrooms, bamboo shoots, and tofu. Let the broth return to a simmer, cook 1 minute, and skim off any foam. Stir in the salt, pepper, vinegars, and soy sauce.

Slowly pour in the beaten egg, stirring gently as you add it, until wisps of egg are visible in the broth. Remove from the heat. Season to taste with more salt, pepper, and vinegar.

To serve, ladle the soup into individual bowls, or into a tureen if serving at the table. Drizzle each serving with sesame oil and sprinkle with chopped cilantro.

Glacéed Bananas

ba si xiang jiao

ON SPECIAL OCCASIONS my mother's chefs would make this Beijing dessert, which is quite a production, but really not too difficult if you're organized. Bananas are coated in a batter, quickly fried in hot oil, dipped in caramel, and finally plunged into ice water so that the caramel forms a crackled glaze. The combination of cold, shatteringly crisp coating against hot, soft banana is irresistible.

✧ ✧ ✧

This is not the easiest of desserts to pull off, but it can be a fun and dramatic conclusion to a dinner party. You need to have six things ready: the batter for the fruit, a deep-fry-candy thermometer, a wok or deep fryer with oil heated to 375°F, sugar and water for making the caramel in a medium skillet or sauté pan, a serving bowl with ice cubes and water, plus a platter lightly filmed with a little oil for the cooked fruit.

Apples cut into 6 wedges can be substituted for all or half of the bananas. —L.W.

Serves 4 to 6

1 tablespoon unbleached all-purpose flour

2 tablespoons cornstarch

2 large egg whites, lightly beaten

3 cups peanut or vegetable oil, for deep-frying

1 tablespoon vegetable oil, plus a little to film the platter

1 cup sugar

3 tablespoons water

5 firm, ripe bananas

TO MAKE THE BATTER, whisk the flour and cornstarch in a large bowl. In a small bowl, whisk the egg whites briefly. Add them to the flour-cornstarch mixture, stirring until almost smooth.

Have a large serving bowl filled with water and ice ready. While you make the caramel, heat the peanut oil in a large flat-bottomed wok or deep fryer over high heat until it registers 375°F on a deep-fry thermometer.

TO MAKE THE CARAMEL, heat 1 tablespoon of vegetable oil with the sugar and the water in a heavy-bottomed saucepan over medium-high heat. Stir the sugar with the water until dissolved, bring to a boil, decrease the heat to medium, and cook until the syrup registers 300°F on a deep-fry thermometer. Decrease the heat to to low so the caramel stays warm.

Lightly film a serving platter with vegetable oil. To fry the bananas, peel them and cut each diagonally into 4 pieces. Using tongs, dip each piece into the batter so they're well coated, drop into the hot oil, and fry in batches for 30 seconds, or until light amber. Using a slotted spoon, transfer the bananas to the oiled platter. When all the fruit is fried, place them in batches in the pan with the caramel, turning to coat them well, then immediately move them to the oiled platter.

Serve the caramel-coated bananas by plunging them into the bowl of ice water as soon as they're coated in the warm caramel, and then bring them to the table.

Chapter 2

The Seventh Daughter

I STILL HAVE MANY MEMORIES OF MY CHILDHOOD IN BEIJING, though I have to admit that they're beginning to blur together, maybe because of my age, yes, but also because my early years were happily uneventful. A peaceful calm existed within our home—I never once heard harsh words uttered between my parents—yet, I see now how that serenity was deceptive. It masked and protected us from the roiling turbulence that occurred in twentieth-century China, turbulence that would eventually tear our family apart.

Considering the size of our family, we all got along remarkably well. My mother, Sun Shueh Yun Hui, gave birth to twelve children—nine girls and three boys—over the course of twenty-four years, all of us about two to three years apart. My parent's firstborn child was a boy who died before he was a year old. Next were two girls, followed by a second son, then four more daughters (two of whom were twins), and then their third son. I was next, the Seventh Daughter, and then came daughters Number Eight and Nine, though Nine, the baby of the family, died of meningitis when she was five. All told, ten healthy surviving children. I was born in 1920, (the Year of the Monkey on the Chinese lunar calendar) when my mother was thirty-eight, and seventeen years after the birth of my oldest sister.

Cecilia, age 12, Beijing, China, 1932.

From left: Sun (Number Six), Zhen-ji (brother), Teresa (Number Five), Qiao (Number Three), Ling (Number Four), Ning (Number One), Yi (Number Two) with Ning's daughter, Father, Jin (Number eight) Cecilia (Number Seven), Mother, Yi's husband; at home in Beijing, China.

In the early part of the twentieth century, it was not uncommon to see large Chinese families, but what was rare was that my mother had given birth to all my father's children. He had no concubines, which because of his upper-class social status and traditional upbringing made him an exception amongst his peers. My mother would have considered it impolite to discuss such personal things, but my brothers and sisters and I sensed it was a point of pride for her and for my father as well.

Born in 1878, my father, Sun Long Guang, was a gentle, scholarly man, who retired from his engineering job with the railway when he was fifty so he could tend his beloved gardens, read, and listen to music. My father was quite progressive in many ways, perhaps the result of his schooling in France, or the fact that at the beginning of the twentieth century, after the overthrow of the Qing dynasty, many intellectuals of his generation had been trying to bring Western liberal ideas and modernization to China. As a small example, contrary to the rules of etiquette at the time, he was not hesitant to express his affection and admiration for my mother. This may seem like nothing, but Chinese men were taught to never show pride in their own or their families' accomplishments, considering it boastful, and were even expected to dispute any compliment.

However, if a friend of my father's were to say something flattering about my mother, my father would graciously accept with a simple "thank you." He even went so far as to extend his own compliments at home when we were gathered around the family dinner table. To her, he might say something like, "Yong Hui, you are such a good cook, and this meal was delicious!" Or, to us it might be, "Children, your mother manages the household money so well. We are all very lucky!"

And manage she did. She was also well educated (at home by tutors, as were most upper-class young women of her time). When she was only fourteen or fifteen, she had been forced to take on the enormous responsibility of looking after the finances of her family's textile and flour mills upon the early death of her parents. Because she never discussed what had happened (nor did any of us ever ask), I've always assumed her parents and siblings had died of opium addiction, which was very common in nineteenth-century upper-class societies, but still considered shameful.

My mother was very much a woman of her generation, bound both figuratively and literally to the old customs. As she tottered around our house, directing the servants, overseeing the nannies, and instructing the cooks, I can't help but think that if her tiny, four-inch-long bound feet must have been a constant—and very painful—reminder of her dutiful link to ancestral tradition.

Supposedly, the only disagreement my father and mother ever had (which had happened before I was born, and which had been divulged to me by my two older sisters only upon my solemn promise that I was never to bring it up in my parents' presence) was over the binding of my Number One sister's feet. In 1903, when my sister Ning was born, most females in China were still having their feet broken and wrapped in bandages according to a thousand-year-old custom, so that they resembled lotus buds, or "golden lily blooms." Binding would usually begin between five and seven years of age, when a young girl's bones were still fairly soft and malleable. The toes were folded down under the ball of the foot and the arch folded in half, then the whole foot was wrapped tightly in gauze bandages so it would essentially stop growing. The smaller the foot, the more desirable the woman, and thus the more marriageable she would be. It was an unbelievably painful and lengthy process, and often girls died from the resulting infection.

As my sisters told the story, when my mother said to my father that the time had come to call the foot binder for five-year-old Ning, my father absolutely forbade it.

"But Yung Xiao" (my father's "unofficial" or familiar name, for which there is no Western equivalent), "what man of means would want to marry a woman with the shovel-sized feet of a peasant farmer?"

To which he replied, "Yong Hui, I would rather support all my daughters until the end of their days than have them suffer the way you have. I want my daughters to be able to walk about in the world on the feet God gave them."

I guess that must have been the end of the discussion, because none of my father's daughters had bound feet. We ran, danced, played tennis, and ice-skated. By the 1930s, except in all but the most rural areas, the custom of foot binding became a thing of the past.

✿ ✿ ✿

When I was four years old, our family moved from my parents' hometown of Wuxi, near Shanghai, to Beijing, the capital of China. In those days it was highly unusual for people to travel between towns even a few kilometers apart, much less uproot an entire family with ten children and move from one province to another. My parents, however, were drawn to the capital because of its intellectual and cultural offerings. In Beijing, they could indulge their passions for opera, music, and fine dining, as well as send their children to the best private schools and universities. An added incentive was that my father's two sisters had settled there, and he wanted all our families to be near one another. I can only imagine what a spectacle it must have been loading up the boxcars full of furnishings and belongings, plus the six motorcars carrying my parents, nine siblings, nannies, servants, dogs, cats, and birds for the big trek to Beijing.

I still clearly recall, as if it were yesterday, the sense of security I felt whenever the rickshaw boy who took us to and from school every day pulled up in front of the enormous red gates to our walled compound in Beijing. Our home was one of many *siheyuan*, or courtyard houses, which, with their perimeters of high walls, formed a maze of narrow alleys called *hutongs* that branched out from the Imperial Palace. In a prestigious neighborhood to the east of the capital, ours was larger than most. Although I was too young to remember the house in Wuxi, I knew our old home paled in comparison to the Beijing house, which, in fact, it wasn't a "house" at all. It was a palace—an actual palace–that took up an entire city block and had been built in the sixteenth century for a minister to one of the last emperors of the Ming dynasty.

It had fifty-two rooms and six bathrooms in seven parallel buildings, each separated by elaborately landscaped courtyards with raised beds filled with an enormous variety of trees, shrubs, and flowers. Once past the red entrance gates, you were met by another wall before you entered the first courtyard (it was considered good *feng shui* to not see the interior of the house upon entrance). The first building housed the male servants, and in the last were the female servants, next to the kitchen. In the other buildings were the children's quarters (with rooms for their nannies), guest lodging, and then the three main buildings with my parents' bedroom, the formal living rooms, and the dining room—the most important room of our house.

Though she was short, wide, and hobbled by her deformed feet, my mother ruled our house like a general. But it was in the kitchen—and by extension, of course, the dining room—that she was truly a force to be reckoned with.

Both Old Cook, who came with us from Wuxi and specialized in the Shanghai food of my parent's native province, and Young Cook, whom my parents hired in Beijing and who cooked northern-style dishes, knew without question who was boss. While my mother was so short she needed a stool to stand on to see into the pots cooking on the stove, she ran the kitchen with absolute authority. Like all upper-class Chinese women of her time, she did not actually cook. (There were times, though, that I would find my mother seated at the dining table—she could not stand for long—stringing beans, or pleating dumplings.) Instead, she instructed her chefs as to how she wanted things done. This included pickling meat and drying vegetables, as well as making her own soy sauce, a few bottles of which contained shrimp roe—though those are the ones she brought out only for special occasions. My mother, however, was different from most of her peers because not only was she constantly in the kitchen overseeing the chefs, she had impeccable taste, a point almost everyone who had ever eaten at our table agreed upon.

In fact, the true definition of punishment for any of her children was to be denied her food (which became really clear to me later during some very difficult circumstances). Early on, my siblings and I learned that one of the things she demanded was punctuality. If we were late arriving to the dinner table without a good explanation (she was autocratic, but not unreasonable), we would be forced to spend the entire meal in the corner, driven crazy by the aromas of soy, ginger, garlic, and spices—truly more hungry than humiliated.

My mother was a perfectionist and endlessly critical, something that became a bit of a family joke. In the back seat of the car, on the way home from a meal at a restaurant or the home of friends or family, we children couldn't wait for my to mother start in.

"Well, that was a good dinner." Pause. We counted the seconds. "But, not their best. The *bao* dough was much too thick." Another pause. "The meat was also too chewy and too salty." Although there was a part of me that felt a little bad for the cooks who were on the receiving end of my mother's barbs, I listened intently to all of her criticisms and then usually smiled in secret agreement with her.

We all waited for the next assault, the harshest criticism of all. "And the soup. It had no flavor and was cold by the time they served it." The worst thing you could say about a Chinese meal is that someone screwed up the soup.

✿　✿　✿

In American homes, most family interactions tend to take place in the kitchen, but in upper-class Chinese homes such as ours, the kitchen was strictly off-limits to all but senior family members—no children allowed. There was no such thing as gathering around the TV in the den, either. Our family life took place in the dining room. On weekends, it was common for my parents to entertain, both for lunch and dinner, but on weekdays we routinely gathered in the dining room, morning and night, around the huge circular rosewood table that my mother designed to seat fourteen people. For banquets and large family gatherings, the dining room accommodated one or two other tables that could be brought in for the occasion.

Mornings, as in most busy households, were choreographed chaos, with everyone going in different directions and trying not to be late. Usually my older sisters Ning, Yi, and Qiao, and brother Xiu Ji, were usually already out of the house and on their way to school by the time my sisters, twins Ling and Qin, Sun, and Jing, and brother Zhen Ji, and I had been roused at six A.M., dressed, and ushered into the dining room by our nannies. The baby of the family, Number Nine daughter, was usually already there with my mother, who doted on her probably because she was her last child. (She was also the only one of her children that she ever really got to spend time with, since by the time she was born, the rest of us were all grown or well on our way to independence.) We were served breakfast, typically rice congee—a kind of rice porridge—with assorted condiments such as sausage, dried fish, thousand-year eggs, pickled vegetables, and fermented bean curd. As soon as we finished, we were rushed outside where the rickshaw drivers were waiting to whisk us off to school.

Unlike our breakfasts, family dinners were more leisurely, and somewhat predictable. Unless my parents were going out to the opera or dining with friends, most nights the family ate together. Promptly at six-thirty, my father would sit down at the dining room table so my mother could bring him his *jiu cai* ("little wine dishes") to nibble while he sipped his glass of French vermouth or Spanish sherry. All of us children had been warned by our mother not to disturb him during his end-of-the-day ritual. As a young child, I remember watching silently from the adjacent room as she lovingly placed the *jiu cai* dishes in front of my father. "Wow!" I thought. In a traditional Chinese household such as ours, the servants did everything for us, so to see my mother serving my father was pretty unusual. At the time, I thought my mother was worried that my father was too thin and that people (only those unfamiliar with her culinary talents, of course) would think she was a terrible cook. But now, looking back, I can only believe that her simple gesture of serving him his *jiu cai* actually spoke volumes about the fondness between them. Once my father had finished his *jiu cai*, the rest of the family was permitted to join him at the table for dinner.

✿ ✿ ✿

One dinner stands out. Perhaps it was because on that particular evening the discussions were more animated than usual, but more probably because in a family with so many children—and as a seventh daughter—it was the first time I remember feeling noticed and special.

It was in the fall of 1932 and I was eleven years old, just beginning junior high. It was an evening that began the same way as all others. As soon as we were all seated, platters and bowls magically began to appear, borne aloft by the two or three servants who seemed to live somewhere in that huge room. On this particular evening, there were only five or six dishes, typical when we were just family, with no guests joining us. The food was placed before us at intervals in the vast center of the table.

My older siblings were allowed to reach for food directly from the platters, while we younger ones were restricted to pointing to what we wanted, so that the servants could retrieve our portions. (Taking something from the platter ourselves was strictly forbidden. My mother would have banished us without dinner for such an infraction.)

Above all, no one, including our older brothers and sisters, was permitted to take anything until our parents had been served, and we were not allowed seconds until every last morsel on our plate had been consumed. "Each grain of rice represents a drop of sweat," my mother admonished us, meaning that someone had worked very hard in the field to harvest the rice and nothing should go to waste. (I was quite surprised to learn after I came here that American mothers encouraged their children to eat with the caveat, "Finish your food, children are starving in China!")

Another rule of my mother's was that the younger children were not supposed to speak at the table unless spoken to, while our older siblings, considered adults, were able to converse freely with our parents.

I was obediently quiet, but all ears, as my oldest sister, Ning, "the beautiful one," chatted on and on with my mother about her upcoming wedding plans. She had been matched with a young man from Wuxi. Qiao, Number Three sister, and the one with the "voice of a bird," kept interrupting to complain that the costumes for the opera she was to perform in the following weekend hadn't been sewed correctly and made her look fat. Meanwhile, I could tell my mother was distracted by her continuing annoyance with her first daughter-in-law, Quan-Quen, who, against all house rules, was yet again late for dinner. I could see that her husband, my older brother Xiu Ji, was trying to ignore our mother's displeasure and was engrossed in a conversation with my father about politics, the ongoing skirmishes between the warlords, and the recent invasion of Manchuria by the Japanese. Zhen Ji, Number Three son, who was only two years my senior and on the cusp between the age when he could speak at the table and needed to be quiet, unexpectedly shocked us all into silence by stating that Chiang Kai-shek and his Nationalists were in trouble because they didn't have enough manpower to fight both the warlords and the Japanese.

"Besides that, I've heard at school that the Communists have moved to Jiangxi Province and are starting to gain strength by recruiting the peasants," he proudly added, but almost shocking himself in the process with his boldness.

"Yes, Zhen Ji, I'm concerned that if Chiang has to fight the Communists again, which he must do to preserve the Republic, he will lose," my father replied. From that time on, my brother had crossed the line to adulthood, at least in terms of dinner-table protocol.

I kept trying to keep up with all the conversations, but I was young, and apart from the family drama that captured my attention, I was actually more interested in the food. The first dish set on the table was a platter of cold items that I'm sure, though I don't really recall, must have included chilled spiced beef and marinated radishes or pickled cabbage. The next dish that I do remember was one of my favorites: chicken steamed and served with a wine sauce, called Drunken Chicken, another of my mother's Shanghai specialties. We could always expect one or two vegetables, maybe sautéed mushrooms or spinach, and rice of course, as well as a whole fish, which that evening was fried carp with a light sauce of ginger and leeks. What I'll never forget, though, was the heady aroma of my mother's red-cooked pork wafting into the dining room from the kitchen. When the platters of pork were placed before us, it was all I could do to keep from serving myself. I behaved, of course, and when the nuggets of pork belly glistening with their glaze of soy, wine, and rock sugar melted on my tongue, I felt that I had been amply rewarded for my patient restraint.

"A wonderful meal," I thought, "but where is the soup?" Usually, it was put on the table steaming hot toward the end of the dinner—the Chinese always serve soup at the conclusion of the meal, rather than at the beginning. Just as I had that thought, the servants brought in steaming pots of broth and individual bowls of noodles, and it dawned on me that it was someone's birthday. The Chinese don't celebrate birthdays the way Westerners do, with parties, cakes, presents, and singing "Happy Birthday." I was always astonished that with so many children, my mother could keep track of our family milestones, yet at least twelve times a year, we acknowledged birthdays with bowls of noodles.

It never failed to amaze me to see such perfectly arranged noodles. Later, I learned that my mother had taught her chefs the trick of draping the cooked noodles over a pair of chopsticks so they were neatly aligned before they were carefully transferred to waiting soup bowls. On that evening the noodles were brought into the dining room piled high with a mixture of stir-fried bamboo shoots, pork, and cabbage. At the table, the servants ladled some rich meat broth into each bowl.

Um-ma, my mother, deftly scooped up a tangle of noodles with her chopsticks so that the longest strand cleared the bowl and said, "Long life, Lao Chi (Old Number Seven, which is what my mother affectionately called me), long life." Everyone at the table repeated her gesture. "Long life, Number Seven, we wish you a very long life!" And, so it was that I would never forget my twelfth birthday, September 18, 1932.

SOUPS

Except for a few months of my life when I was forced to endure horrible hardship, I don't think I've ever gone a day without soup. In fact, I could probably say those days of deprivation were probably defined less by my lack of a soft bed, warm room, or even of a bath, and more by my craving for a nourishing broth. Longtime friends say they would assume that they'd arrived at the wrong house if the aroma of chicken simmering with ginger wasn't wafting from within. To this day, even though I eat out several times a week, a simple soup of a few vegetables or dumplings made with the broth of a flavorful yellow chicken gives me a deep-down comfort like nothing else can.

The soups I've chosen to include in this chapter are all the kind I like to make and eat, which means that they are easy to prepare and have pure flavors with just a few ingredients. The recipes may seem simple, but they are elegant enough to serve Chinese style as a palate cleanser between courses or at the conclusion of a dinner, or Western style, as a first course. I can't stress enough, however, the importance of using the best ingredients you can find. If you rely on only a few ingredients, they must be of pristine quality.

To that end, I've included my very easy recipe for chicken broth, one of the fundamentals of the Chinese kitchen, and the basis for all of my soups. The flavor of the broth is the first thing you taste in a soup, so it must be delicious. If you have made broth before, you'll be pleasantly surprised to learn that you don't need a lot of vegetables, nor must you skim it constantly. All you do need is a really flavorful chicken.

Delicious Chicken Broth

qing dun ji tang

I CAN'T COUNT THE NUMBER OF TIMES I've heard even good cooks say that making broth is too much of a bother, and they don't have any problem substituting canned broth in recipes. Not that there's anything bad about canned broth—there are some pretty good ones on the market. It's just that it is so easy (and often a lot cheaper) to make a delicious broth, salted and seasoned to your liking. And what else can you do in the kitchen that yields such high returns? With a delicious broth on hand, you have the basis for countless soups, sauces, stir-fries, and slow-cooked dishes—like Chinese money in the bank.

✵　✵　✵

I absolutely love the frugality of Cecilia's chicken broth, made with the least amount of effort and the fewest ingredients. It's also one of the best-tasting broths ever, as good as the one made by my husband's Grandma Rose, the standard by which I measure all chicken broths.

Cecilia has a few secrets, the first of which is to buy a good, fresh "yellow" chicken at the Asian market. At several Asian markets I could find chicken labeled "yellow chicken." An organic, free-range stewing hen (or fryer), preferably still with head and feet (which lend a gelatinous quality to the finished broth), will certainly be tasty even though the result may not be quite the same. I also have to note here that chicken broth made with this generic "yellow chicken" is an amazing, almost fluorescent, if not lemon, yellow, with an intense chicken flavor to boot. It's worth a trip to the nearest Chinatown to find it.

Cecilia's second trick is to cook the chicken very slowly for a few hours to extract as much flavor as possible from the bones and meat "so all goodness goes into the liquid," as her mother used to say.

Her final secret went against everything I knew about making broth: she doesn't remove all the fat. Although Cecilia blanched the chicken first to get rid of impurities and then skimmed the broth during the first half hour she only skimmed it a few times more during the remaining hours of cooking.

Consider this less a recipe and more a procedure. It's not exact and can be doubled or tripled.
—*L.W.*

Makes about 8 cups

1 whole "yellow" or organic chicken, with head and feet attached (about 4 pounds)

2-inch piece unpeeled fresh ginger, lightly smashed

1 tablespoon kosher salt

Rinse the chicken well under cold running water. Put it in a small stockpot or large saucepan with enough cold water to cover it by at least 2 inches. Bring to a boil over high heat, let it cook 3 to 4 minutes, then quickly transfer it to a colander to drain.

Rinse the chicken again with cold water to remove all traces of scum and clean out the stockpot.

Return the chicken to the pot, add the ginger and salt, and enough cold water to cover it by several

continued

inches. Bring the liquid to a boil over high heat. Decrease the heat to medium-low to maintain a simmer and cook for 4 to 5 hours, skimming off fat and foam frequently during the first 30 minutes, and then occasionally the rest of the time. Strain and refrigerate for up to 4 days.

DOUBLE DELICIOUS CHICKEN BROTH—If you really want to make your soup special and have the time, make Delicious Chicken Broth as previously directed, and chill it in the refrigerator. Skim off the fat and repeat the entire recipe for Delicious Chicken Broth, but, for the long (4- to 5-hour) simmer, use the chilled broth instead of water. If there's not enough liquid to cover the chicken then add some water (or even canned chicken broth).

Three Simple Soups Made from Delicious Chicken Broth

I'VE GROUPED THESE THREE RECIPES TOGETHER to demonstrate how easy it is to make a delicious soup with a good, homemade chicken broth as a base and adding just a few ingredients. Don't let the simplicity of these recipes fool you into thinking they might be bland. On the contrary, they're extremely flavorful, but only if you use real Virginia ham, sweet corn cut off the cob, supremely fragrant sesame oil, and even freshly ground white pepper.

TOFU AND SPINACH SOUP
bo cai dou fu tang

Makes 6 (1-cup) servings

4 cups Delicious Chicken Broth (page 57)

8 ounces silken tofu, diced and gently squeezed to rid it of some of its water

2 cups (about 2 ounces) loosely packed fresh baby spinach leaves

1/2 teaspoon kosher salt

Asian sesame oil, for drizzling

In a small saucepan, bring the chicken broth to a boil over high heat. Add the tofu, decrease the heat to medium, and simmer until the tofu is heated through, about 5 minutes.

Add the spinach and salt to the broth, stir, and remove from the heat.

To serve, ladle the soup into individual bowls, and drizzle each with a little sesame oil.

WINTER MELON AND HAM SOUP

hou tui dong gua tang

Makes 6 (1-cup) servings

2-ounce piece Virginia ham, about 1 inch thick

1/4 winter melon, about 1 pound

4 cups Delicious Chicken Broth (page 57)

Freshly ground white pepper

2 tablespoons chopped fresh cilantro, for garnish

Slice the ham into 1/8-inch-thick strips and set aside.

TO PREPARE THE WINTER MELON, remove and discard both seeds and rind. Cut the flesh into 1-inch squares that are approximately 1/4 inch thick. Bring a saucepan of water to a boil, drop in the winter melon, and cook 5 minutes. Drain, rinse the melon in cold water, and set aside.

In a saucepan, bring the chicken broth to a boil over high heat. Add the winter melon, decrease the heat to medium-low, and simmer 10 minutes. Add the ham and simmer 5 minutes more.

To serve, ladle the soup into individual bowls, season with white pepper (the ham should provide enough salt), and sprinkle with cilantro.

MINCED CHICKEN AND SWEET CORN SOUP

yu mi ji li tang

Makes 6 (1-cup) servings

4 large egg whites

1 tablespoon cornstarch

6 ounces boneless, skinless chicken breast, coarsely chopped

4 cups Delicious Chicken Broth (page 57)

2 cups very fresh sweet white or yellow corn kernels (cut from 2 large or 4 small ears)

1/4 cup diced (1/4 inch) Virginia ham

Kosher salt

Freshly ground white pepper

2 tablespoons chopped fresh cilantro, for garnish

Whisk 2 of the egg whites with the cornstarch in a bowl until combined. Add the chicken and stir to coat well. Set aside.

In a saucepan, bring the chicken broth to a boil over high heat. Add the corn and cook 5 minutes. Add the chicken and ham and cook 2 minutes longer, then add salt, to taste. Remove the saucepan from the heat. Whisk the remaining 2 egg whites and drizzle into the hot soup so that the whites form wispy trails.

Ladle the soup into individual bowls, grind over white pepper, and sprinkle with cilantro.

Stuffed Cucumbers in Double Delicious Broth

huang gna qian rou tang

I'VE ALWAYS LOVED CUCUMBERS and think that they've gone underappreciated as a cooked vegetable. Here, they're stuffed with a savory mixture of ground pork and black mushrooms, steamed until they are crisp, but tender, and served in an intense, clear chicken broth. The soup is fresh and delicate and the cucumber cups can be made ahead and steamed just before serving, making a great dinner party dish.

☼ ☼ ☼

We found that the microwave does a fine job with these. Because all microwaves cook at different rates, cut into one of filling mixtures to make sure it's done all the way through. —L.W.

Makes about 24 cucumber cups

8 ounces ground pork

8 dried black mushrooms

1 tablespoon minced green onion, white part only

1 tablespoon finely chopped fresh cilantro, plus additional leaves, for garnish

1 teaspoon peeled, minced fresh ginger

1 teaspoon Shaoxing wine

1 tablespoon kosher salt

1 tablespoon soy sauce

1 teaspoon Asian sesame oil

Freshly ground white pepper

2 English cucumbers, peeled

8 cups Double Delicious Chicken Broth (page 58)

Asian sesame oil, for drizzling

In a bowl, soak the dried mushrooms in hot water to cover for 15 minutes. Drain, then squeeze the excess moisture from the mushrooms, remove and discard the stems, and cut the mushrooms in ¼-inch dice. Put in a medium bowl and add the pork, green onion, cilantro, ginger, wine, salt, soy sauce, sesame oil, and pepper until it's well combined. To taste the mixture for seasoning, sauté a tablespoonful.

Cut each cucumber crosswise into 12 rounds, each ¾ inch thick. With a melon baller or spoon, scoop out the seeds, leaving a little bit of flesh on the bottom of the rounds (so the filling doesn't leak out), forming little cups.

Fill the cucumber cups generously with the pork mixture, mounding it in the centers. Place the filled cups on 1 or 2 glass pie plates or baking dishes. You can prepare the cucumber cups to this point up to 8 hours ahead; store, covered with plastic wrap, in the refrigerator until needed.

Cook the cucumber cups, covered with plastic wrap, in a microwave on high for 4 minutes, or 5 to 6 minutes if the mushrooms are cold from the refrigerator. Check the filling to make sure it's cooked all the way through, cooking them longer if necessary. Heat the chicken broth in a saucepan on the stove over high heat and decrease to a low simmer.

To serve, divide cucumber cups among 8 soup bowls, then ladle over the broth. Garnish with a few cilantro leaves and a drizzle of sesame oil.

Spareribs with Daikon Soup

pai gu lou bu tang

MY MOTHER USED TO MAKE THIS simple, affordable, and nutritious soup frequently during Beijing's cold winters. It's one of my favorites and is a great example of thrifty Chinese home cooking—you'll never find it served in a restaurant. Often, when I know that I'm going to be out for the day, I'll make the broth for this soup in the morning or even the night before. When I get home, I add the daikon radish just before serving. Along with a bowl of rice (from the rice cooker), it makes for a quick, nourishing supper.

✿ ✿ ✿

Daikon radish, which can be quite sharp when eaten raw, develops a sweet flavor when cooked. The size of the radish doesn't matter in terms of flavor or freshness. Look for smooth, slightly shiny skin and, if they're attached, fresh-looking green tops. If you do have the fresh tops, they can be sautéed and served along with the soup.

To roll-cut the daikon radish, begin by cutting off a diagonal piece from the end of the radish. Roll the radish a quarter turn, then make another diagonal cut about 1 1/2 inch up from the last. Continue rolling and cutting so you end up with large triangular pieces. —L.W.

Makes 8 servings

1 1/2 pounds meaty pork spareribs, trimmed of excess fat and cut in half lengthwise, then in half again lengthwise

2-inch piece unpeeled fresh ginger, smashed

3 cups (about 1 pound) daikon radish, peeled and roll-cut into 1 1/2-inch pieces

1 tablespoon kosher salt

Freshly ground white pepper, for finishing

Fresh cilantro leaves, for garnish

Premium soy sauce, for dipping

Put the spareribs in a large saucepan or Dutch oven and add enough water to cover the meat by 2 inches. Bring the liquid to a boil over high heat, skimming off any fat and foam that rises to the top. Add the ginger, decrease the heat to medium-low to maintain a simmer, and cook for 1 hour. Add the daikon radish, cover the pot, and continue to simmer, decreasing the heat if necessary to maintain a low simmer, until the daikon is tender and translucent, 15 to 20 minutes more. Pull out and discard the ginger. Add the salt and stir to combine well.

To serve, ladle the soup, including some of the spareribs, into individual bowls. Season each with white pepper and sprinkle over a few cilantro leaves. Serve with small individual bowls or one communal bowl of soy sauce for dipping the spareribs.

Long-Life Noodle Soup

shi jin chang shou tang mian

WHETHER THEY'RE THICK OR THIN, in soup, stir-fried, or simply sauced, long noodles—noodles that have not been cut—are served at almost every Chinese birthday, anniversary, or New Year's celebration because they symbolize long life. To support the theory that eating long noodles can bring you a long life, I offer myself (and many in my family) as proof that there must be something to our superstitions. This recipe is one of my favorite ways of serving the noodles, the way my mother did, in a soup bowl and topped with a mixture of stir-fried vegetables and meat, with broth ladled over all. It is endlessly, and deliciously, variable.

☼   ☼   ☼

I'd never eaten fresh bamboo shoots until I had them at Betelnut in San Francisco. What a revelation fresh ones are. Not only are they crunchy, they are incredibly sweet and delicate. For this recipe we used one large bamboo shoot, about one pound before it was trimmed. Look for bamboo shoots that are heavy and free of soft spots, mold, or cracks. If they smell at all sour, pass them by.

I found its prep was much like the way I pare an artichoke. The key is using a very sharp knife and having a kitchen towel to rest the shoot on so it doesn't slip. Cut off about 1 inch from the tip and then cut into the shoot, about ¹⁄₂ inch lengthwise. From there, start cutting off the outside leaves, working your way around until you reach the pale inner core of the shoot. Cut off about ¹⁄₂ inch from the bottom of the shoot and set this trim aside to add to the broth for flavoring. The shoot should now be a rough, cone-shaped cylinder. Cut that lengthwise into ¹⁄₈-inch slices, then stack and cut the slices into matchsticks. You can store sliced bamboo shoots in the refrigerator, wrapped in a paper towel in a plastic bag, for up to 1 day. —L.W.

Makes 6 to 8 servings

8 ounces pork loin

1¹⁄₂ teaspoons cornstarch

1¹⁄₂ teaspoons Shaoxing wine

3 tablespoons canola, safflower, or peanut oil

2 cups (about 8 ounces) fresh winter bamboo shoots, trimmed and cut into ¹⁄₄ by ¹⁄₄ by 2-inch matchsticks

2 cups thinly shredded napa cabbage

2 tablespoons premium soy sauce

¹⁄₂ teaspoon kosher salt

2 tablespoons Shaoxing wine

¹⁄₄ teaspoon sugar

8 cups Delicious Chicken Broth (page 57)

1 pound fresh ¹⁄₈-inch-wide Chinese noodles

Kosher salt

Freshly ground white pepper

continued

So the pork is easier to slice, freeze it for 30 minutes or so to firm it up. Slice the frozen meat diagonally against the grain into 1/4 by 1/4 by 2-inch strips. In a small bowl, stir the cornstarch with the wine, then add the pork and toss so the strips are well coated.

TO COOK THE VEGETABLES AND THE PORK, heat a nonstick wok or skillet over high heat until a bead of water dances on the surface and then evaporates. Add half of the oil and swirl to coat the pan. Add the bamboo shoots and cook, stirring continuously, for 2 minutes, or until the bamboo shoots begin to color on the edges. Add the cabbage and cook 15 seconds, then add 1 tablespoon of the soy sauce and the salt. Cook 1 minute longer, or until the cabbage is wilted; transfer the mixture to a plate.

Add the remaining oil to the pan. Add the pork, stirring constantly, and cook until the pork has lost its raw color, about 30 seconds. Stir in the wine and remaining soy sauce, and a couple of pinches of sugar. Taste for seasoning and set aside.

Bring the broth to a simmer over high heat in a large saucepan and add the trimmed ends of the bamboo shoots. Decrease the heat to a simmer while you cook the noodles. Bring another large stockpot of water to a boil over high heat. Cook the noodles until tender, about 4 minutes; drain.

To serve, place equal piles of noodles in individual bowls. Season the broth with salt and pepper to taste, then ladle some broth over each bowl of noodles (leaving behind the bamboo shoot trimmings) and top with some of the stir-fried mixture.

Shark's Fin Soup

ji si yu chi tang

THE FIRST THING ALICE WATERS SAID TO ME when I told her I was writing this cookbook was "Cecilia, you're going to include your recipe for shark's fin soup, aren't you? I adore it and no one makes it like you do." Usually reserved for banquets and special occasions, shark's fin is extremely expensive and considered a delicacy in China. It's prized not only for its texture, but also for its subtle, briny flavor. I love it too, but it's quite a production so I rarely make it except once in while for New Year's. But how can I disappoint my old friend? Alice, this recipe is for you.

✿   ✿   ✿

Use whole shark's fin for the most authentic tasting and aesthetically pleasing results, otherwise you'll end up with odd-sized pieces. Don't be tempted to use canned or pre-soaked and softened shark's fin. It will not yield the same flavor and texture.

To prepare the shark's fin: Rinse 4 ounces of dried shark's fin under cold running water and, using a small bristle brush, carefully clean off any dirt or grime. The strands of the fin are very delicate, so this process requires a gentle hand. In a medium bowl, soak the fin in a generous amount of cold water for 24 hours. Change the water and soak for another 24 hours. Drain the water and discard. Keeping the fin in one piece, carefully peel off the skin and discard it.

Place the peeled shark's fin on a rimmed plate or bowl that will fit inside a steamer tier. Fill the steamer bottom with a generous amount of water, bring it to a boil, and then place the bowl with the fin above it. Cover and steam for 3 hours. Carefully lift the plate out of the steamer tier and set aside until ready to use.

Be sure to use Double Delicous Chicken Broth (page 57) and the best quality ham you can find to make this special soup. —L.W.

Serves 6 to 8 as part of a Chinese meal and 4 to 6 as a Western-style entrée

3 cups Double Delicious Chicken Broth (page 58)

1 (2-ounce) piece Virginia ham (about 3 inches by 1 inch)

4 ounces shark's fin, soaked and steamed

For garnish

2 tablespoons finely shredded Virginia ham

1 cup fresh bean sprouts, ends trimmed, quickly blanched in boiling water and rinsed well under cold water, optional

Chinkiang black vinegar or balsamic vinegar (optional)

In a large saucepan, bring the chicken broth and Virginia ham to a boil over medium heat. Reduce the heat and simmer for 30 minutes. Add the shark's fin and cook on low for 20 minutes.

To serve, ladle the warm broth into bowls and divide the shark's fin evenly among them. Garnish each bowl with a pinch of ham, a few bean sprouts, and a dash of vinegar, if you like.

Easy Sizzling Rice Soup

guo ba tang

EVEN I STILL GET A KICK OUT of hearing the sizzle made by the hot rice cakes when they're plopped into the steaming liquid. Rice cakes, or *guo bah*, are made from rice that has cooked for a long time until it has become dried and hard, then fried so that it puffs up. After I sold the restaurant, I never made this soup at home because it was too much trouble to make the rice cakes and set up a fryer to cook them just before serving. One day, I discovered prepared rice cakes and decided to try them. Wow! So easy, and now I make this soup all the time, to the delight of my dinner guests.

✿ ✿ ✿

The key to ensure that the rice sizzles when it's dropped into the soup is to have both the rice cakes and the broth very hot when they're brought to the table. Rice cakes are a typically frugal Chinese method for using rice that has been overcooked and hardened on the bottom of the pot. Short of having overcooked rice on hand, it's not difficult to make your own if you can't find commercial rice cakes. —L.W.

Makes 6 (1-cup) servings

5 or 6 dried black mushrooms

1 large egg white

2 teaspoons cornstarch

3 ounces boneless, skinless chicken breast, cut into 1/2-inch dice

6 (2-inch) square commercial rice cakes

6 cups Delicious Chicken Broth (page 57) or Double Delicious Chicken Broth (page 58)

1/2 cup sugar snap or snow peas, stringed and cut diagonally into 1/2-inch pieces

3 ounces medium shrimp, shelled, deveined, and tails removed, cut into 1/2-inch pieces

2/3 cup water chestnuts, drained and finely diced

Kosher salt

Freshly ground white pepper

In a bowl, soak the dried mushrooms in hot water for 15 minutes. Drain, thinly slice, and set aside.

Whisk the egg white a little to break it apart and then combine it with the cornstarch. Add the chicken breast and stir so it's well-coated. Set aside.

About 20 minutes before you want to serve the soup, preheat the oven to 350°F. Put the rice cakes on a baking sheet and bake 10 minutes. In a large sauce-pan, bring the chicken broth to a boil over high heat. Decrease the heat to medium-low to maintain a simmer and add the mushrooms. Cook about 2 minutes, decrease the heat to low so the broth is barely at a simmer, then add the chicken (if the broth is simmering too hard the coating will slip off the chicken). Cook 2 minutes more; add the sugar snap peas, shrimp, and water chestnuts. Cook 2 minutes and then remove from the heat. Season to taste. Transfer the hot soup to a heated tureen or large serving bowl and put the rice cakes on a heated platter.

To serve, immediately drop the rice cakes into the soup and listen to the sizzle. Ladle the soup into bowls, making sure to include rice in each portion.

Chapter 3
Love and Marriage, Chinese Style

"GREAT QUESTION!" I said out loud the first time I heard Tina Turner's "What's Love Got to Do with It?" on the radio. Love, I've come to believe after all these years, is a wonderful thing, but it can make relationships very complicated.

When I was young, most marriages in China were still being arranged, either through the services of a professional matchmaker, or, informally, through family and friends.

My parents' marriage was arranged by one of my mother's aunts, since both her parents had died before she was of marriageable age. My parents, in turn, arranged marriages for my Numbers One, Two, and Three sisters, (Ning, Yi, and Qiao). Although we were living in Beijing at the time, the three men they were matched with came from Wuxi, the town near Shanghai where my parents grew up.

I know it's probably difficult for anyone in this day and age to even imagine a third party conspiring with one's parents (or uncles or aunts) to negotiate a life-long partnership with someone not of their choosing. But some of the best, most long-lasting relationships I've known have been arranged.

Usually a great deal of effort goes into aligning couples who come from similar social and economic backgrounds. The Chinese, cautious by nature as well as superstitious, also

Cecilia's parents in courtyard of Beijing home, 1928; this photo was found after the Red Guard destroyed the house.

add another layer of scrutiny to potential matches: the *ba zi*, a written record of the year, month, day, and hour of an individual's birth that enables a matchmaker to determine the couple's compatibility based on ancient, sophisticated, and complicated astrological charts.

By all appearances, my three older sisters seemed happy with their husbands. My parents seemed content that they had indeed arranged satisfactory matches for their daughters, particularly when the first of their many grandchildren began to arrive.

"One big happy family!" That's what my mother would invariably clap her hands and exclaim every time she asked for an extra table to be brought into the dining room to accommodate the grandchildren at one of our New Year's celebrations.

The happiness of our ever-expanding family was tempered when my older brother, Xiu Ji, fell in love during his first year of college with a beautiful but spoiled and hot-tempered girl named Wu Quan-Quen. My mother hoped his ardor would be short-lived, so, against her better judgment, she gave in to his relentless pleas that she allow my sisters to buy gifts for him to present to Quan-Quen in an effort to win her favor. However, after a year, when it became obvious that his feelings for her had only increased, Um-ma finally requested to see Quan-Quen's *ba zi*. To her utter dismay, she discovered that the girl her adored son had fallen in love with was a fire sign, as was Xiu Ji—a match destined for difficulty, if not outright failure. But it was too late. My mother was unable to break her son's heart.

Wu Quan-Quen seemed to enjoy playing with my brother's feelings. It wasn't until seven stormy years later that they wed, in a lavish ceremony given by my parents. In China, it's customary for the parents of the groom to host the wedding, and then the wife moves in with her husband's family. When Quan-Quen came to live with us, the constant tantrums she threw disrupted our entire household. The situation only reinforced my mother's belief that the old ways were best.

✿ ✿ ✿

Carefully wrapped in tissue paper and stashed in a drawer at my home in California is a tiny shoe, no more than three inches long, so small you would think it belonged to a child, except that the heel is elevated and the toe pointed. The inside is made of quilted cotton and the outside, black-and-red silk. The shoe belonged to my father's older, Number One sister, You Lei, who had intricately embroidered the silk with gold and green images of dogs, birds, and flowers with trailing vines.

Sun You Lei was a tiny woman, probably no more than eighty pounds, known throughout Wuxi for her petite stature as well as her beautiful porcelain skin and perfect almond eyes. According to family legend, when the matchmaker went to present the potential groom, Mr. Xu, with my aunt's carefully drawn up *ba-zi*, plus two photographs, one of her face and the other of her full length, he asked only to see one of her "golden lily" shoes. The matchmaker had wisely anticipated this request of Mr. Xu's, because not only was my aunt famous in Wuxi for her beauty, she was also famous for her bound feet—her exceptionally small three-inch feet.

"I don't need to see photographs and I don't care if she's pockmarked and hunchbacked," he supposedly exclaimed when presented with Sun You Lei's shoe. "The woman who can fit into this extraordinary slipper is the woman I want to marry!"

Marry they did. My Aunt and Uncle Xu went on to have eight children who, in Old World tradition, also had arranged marriages. None of my five girl cousins, however, had bound feet. Maybe it was because in the early twentieth century the practice had started to fall under criticism as being barbaric. I think the more likely reason is that women who had the tiniest feet were admired for their ability to tolerate great pain, and my Uncle Xu didn't want that for his own daughters.

✿　✿　✿

The Number One son in my father's family, his older brother, Sun Qui Bou, whom we all called Big Uncle, was born in 1870. His was an arranged marriage, of course, but he did not follow the custom for any of his five children. I'm not sure why, but it may have been that when his wife died and their older children reached marriageable age, he simply didn't want to be bothered. My father was very close to his brother as well as his two sisters. When my uncle's wife died, the whole family grieved with him. I was only eight or nine at the time.

Big Uncle left the care of his two younger children to my mother, with the older three already off to college. and she embraced them as if they were her own. Our large family became even larger. Suddenly we had to bring in not one, but two extra tables for New Year's. My mother continued to clap her hands and exclaim, "Just one big happy family!"

My twin sisters, Ling and Qin, and I became quite fond of our cousins, particularly Big Uncle's Number One son, Sun Li-Ji, who was attending college with my oldest brother Xiu-Ji and often came home with him to sleep at our house. We nicknamed him Bamboo Brother because he was so tall and thin. He became best friends with my older brother Xiu-Ji who was about his same age.

When we were in our teens, my younger sister, Jing (Number Eight), and I shared a room next to our parents' bedroom. One night we were kept awake by a loud conversation between them. It was such a rare occurrence for either of our parents to raise their voice that Jing and I froze in astonishment. Then our natural teenage curiosity kicked in, and within seconds we both had our ears to the wall.

While much of what they said was unintelligible, when we deciphered the words Ba-Da Hutong we knew we were on to something very juicy. Even though Jing and I were naive, we knew immediately what it meant because the Ba-Da Hutong was infamous. It was the street in Beijing where all the courtesan houses were located. Chinese courtesans were like geishas, women who were educated from the time they were very young in the art of entertaining men. To call the women prostitutes would be inaccurate as well as misleading. Although sexual relationships existed, the women generally did not trade sex for money. Any woman who worked there was shunned, almost reviled, in polite Chinese society. The conversation got even juicier when we thought we heard the words "Qui Bou." Big Uncle? Had we heard correctly?

For three nights, Jing and I tuned into the soap opera on the other side of the bedroom wall. That first night we learned that Big Uncle had been visiting the same courtesan house for several years and had confided to my father that he had fallen in love with one of the women—Chrysanthemum Number Four—and wanted to marry her.

"A-ya! What is he thinking? A courtesan? He must be going crazy with grief!" Our mother tried to whisper, but her voice increased in decibels with each sentence.

"Yun Hui, his wife has been dead for years now. It's natural for him to want female companionship."

We couldn't hear her reply.

The second night, my father told my mother that he was asked by Qui Bou to accompany him to the house so my father could meet the woman.

"A-ya! You are a respectable man. What if someone sees you go there?"

"If they see me go there, then they're probably going there, too, and it won't matter. Qui Bou is my older brother and I need to show respect. He wants my approval."

The third night we stayed up to a very late hour waiting for my father to come home.

On and on our mother questioned our father. "Tell me about the house. Were there antiques? Was it well kept? What did the women look like? How many women were there? Did they all have lotus feet? Do the women sing or play *pee-ba* (Chinese cello)? Did you eat? What did they serve? How was the tea?"

At last he said, "Yun Hui. The woman is young and pretty, but her feet are large. The service was very good, but the tea was hastily prepared. However, Qui Bou seems to care a great deal for her, so I gave him my blessing." That was the last time we heard anything about that subject from our parents' room.

A few weeks after the end of our nightly "entertainment," my mother announced that we would all gather to welcome Big Uncle's new wife into the family. Of course, in a family as big (and as gossipy) as ours, nothing was secret for long. We all knew it was coming and had even heard that Big Uncle's Number One daughter had expressed her displeasure out loud, saying that her father's new bride was only after his money.

The very next afternoon, Uncle Qui Bou arrived at our house with the very beautiful courtesan Qui Yen (Chrysanthemum Number Four). Her name was a dead giveaway in terms of her occupation, but she was introduced to us as Yun Gu, which meant "Aunt Cloud," a name much more vague but respectable. I remember at first being entranced by her beauty. She was tall and thin, with porcelain skin and full, naturally red lips. What impressed me the most about her, however, was her manners. After she was introduced by Big Uncle, she immediately lowered herself on one knee and bowed to my mother, demonstrating her humble subservience.

"Thank you for allowing me into your family," she said. She then quickly rose to pour a cup of tea that one of the servants had brought in upon her arrival and offered it to my mother, another symbolic but necessary gesture of respect.

Big Uncle died several years later, apparently quite happy and content. Chrysanthemum Number Four, or Auntie Cloud, not only remained faithful to him to the end, but dutifully and graciously attended every holiday banquet and family event. A few days after his funeral, however, when Bamboo Brother and his other four siblings began the process of going through the family belongings, they discovered that the house had been hastily ransacked of all valuables. None of us ever saw Auntie Cloud again.

✿　✿　✿

Often in the afternoon before dinner, I would catch my mother in a moment of solitude out in the garden if the weather was warm, or inside, near a fireplace, during the cold months. Um-ma's head would be back, glasses off, eyes closed, blissfully unaware that any of us were near. Her *ya tou* would be seated alongside her on a little stool, devotedly massaging her legs. After years of binding her feet, my mother suffered terribly and forever with bad circulation and excruciating pain in her legs.

Ya-tou translates literally as "slave." Our *ya tou* came to live with us when she was a toddler, about the same age as Jing, my younger, Number Eight, sister. My mother named her Dong-Zhi, which means "winter is here," probably because Um-ma got her during the winter months, somewhere around our Christmas time.

Because there were no orphanages in China, it was common, particularly for female children of destitute mothers, to be offered in servitude to well-to-do families. I know how horrible it sounds, but for many children, it was their only opportunity to escape a future of poverty and deprivation. I'm not so naive as to think there weren't abusive situations, but in our own *ya-tou*'s case, my mother seemed to adore her. In many ways she treated her almost like another daughter, with a couple of obvious exceptions: when she was old enough she was expected to work, and she didn't attend school.

When Dong-Zhi was young she slept in one of the rooms near us, and was watched over by one of our nannies. When she was older, she moved to the female servants' quarters. She had no chores when she was young, but my mother kept Dong-Zhi close by her side, so that she could teach her to perform personal tasks.

In many ways, my mother would have been considered disabled. Because of her bound feet, she was unable to walk more than short distances without help and could not stand more than a few minutes. She truly came to depend on her *ya tou*. Dong-Zhi became the only one in the household who attended to Um-ma's wardrobe, wash the gauze bindings for her feet, and help her in the bath. She also accompanied my mother on shopping excursions, helping to carry her packages. But chores weren't all that filled her day. Often, when I came home from school, I would find the two of them huddled over a book, with my mother patiently teaching her *ya-tou* to read and do calligraphy.

Looking back, I have to admit that as a girl, I felt a little jealous of the relationship my mother shared with her *ya tou*. I knew that Dong-Zhi truly loved my mother and was devoted to her. Mine was the only mother she'd ever really known. But at the same time, I had wished that my mother would spend time with me the way she did with

Dong-Zhi. With her own daughters, Um-ma was warm, but distant and very formal. With her *ya-tou* she shared an intimacy that I envied.

All that changed sometime during my first year of college. I remember riding my bike home from classes one day and, coming into the courtyard, found a distraught Dong-Zhi running from the main house into the servants' quarters. I tried to stop her to find out what was wrong, but she just ignored me and I heard the door slam shut behind her.

As I walked into the house, I could hear Um-ma's muffled but raised voice in the kitchen, although I couldn't make out what she was saying. Obviously something terrible had happened. My Numbers Five and Six sisters were having a charged conversation in the dining room when I walked in.

"What's happened?" I asked them. "I just saw Dong-Zhi running out of here, crying."

I could hear voices again from the kitchen, and this time I heard the voice of Young Cook, Xiao Ling, arguing with my mother—and they weren't talking about dinner.

Sophie said, "Um-ma is angry because her *ya tou* is going to have a baby."

"You mean she's pregnant?" It took a few seconds and it was a silly question, but then I put it all together.

✲ ✲ ✲

I don't know which was worse for my mother: the thought of losing her extremely devoted *ya tou* or losing her extremely talented cook (whom she had spent years working with and who was like a member of the family). Immediately after the argument in the kitchen, my mother dismissed Young Cook and he moved out, while Dong-Zhi was confined to the servants' quarters. All I know for sure is that for days after the blow-up, she seemed to agonize over the problem and what to do about it. It was obvious that my mother wasn't herself. At dinner, she was short-tempered and tense, and then, afterward, she would withdraw to her room.

It was a strange time for all of us. Her absence was a very visible and sad reminder of what had occurred. But, what really seemed to bother everyone most (and which no one wanted to admit) was the absence of Young Cook from the kitchen.

How we missed his *jiao zi* and buns! And where were the green-onion pancakes? Young Cook, who was from Beijing and had worked for our family since we moved from Shanghai, was a master at making feather light, melt-in-your-mouth steamed breads, noodles, and dumplings.

Um-ma had remained largely silent for two weeks. Finally, one night at dinner, after a simple but delicious meal of soup, steamed fish, and spinach (minus any noodles), she cleared her throat, which caused us all to put down our chopsticks almost in unison.

"I'm very happy to announce that Dong-Zhi and Xiao-Ling have married and found a house to live in together. Xiao-Ling will continue to cook for us so that he can support Dong-Zhi and their future family."

I looked at my sisters, then my father, and we all cast quick glances at one another. My father smiled and cut the tension at the table by saying, "I wish both of them long, prosperous, and healthy lives."

Although it had taken her a while to figure out what to do, Um-ma had wisely come up with a solution that resolved a very difficult situation in the best possible way for everyone. My mother was in an awkward position. She knew it was out of the question for her to allow Dong-Zhi (in spite of their close relationship) to remain in the household, because the other servants needed to know that such indiscretion or misbehavior would not be tolerated or condoned. But by making sure Dong-Zhi and Young Cook married and had a place to live, their child would be assured of a legitimate future. And, by allowing Young Cook to keep his job, Um-ma was able to keep the rest of her family extremely happy.

While I never knew if love played a part in the relationship between my mother's *ya-tou* and Young Cook, I did know, without a doubt, that love was at the core of my mother's relationship with Dong-Zhi. In fact, love had a great deal to do with it. An image sticks out in my mind of Um-ma bouncing Dong-Zhi's laughing baby boy on her knee, smiling like a proud grandmother.

APPETIZERS AND LITTLE DISHES

Appetizers, or hors d'oeuvres, are not a common component of everyday Chinese meals, where four or five dishes come to the table at approximately the same time and there is never a first course. Soup is often served last, and rice is a side dish. Banquets, however, are a different story and always begin with a platter of cold sliced meats and vegetables.

In the late 1940s, when my husband and I were living in Shanghai, we went to nightclubs and cocktail parties, where I had my first taste of food designed solely to be served with drinks. "Wow," I thought when I tasted a bite of tiny crispy fried shrimp. "These are like the *jiu cai* my mother used to serve my father!" How fun and how glamorous it seemed.

Then in the early 1960s, when I opened the first Mandarin, hors d'oeuvres with drinks were de rigueur, but because we were limited in space it wasn't until I opened The Mandarin at Ghirardelli Square in 1968 that I was able to serve what I still thought of as *jiu cai* to accompany drinks in the bar.

The recipes I've chosen for this chapter are tantalizing preludes to dinner. None are difficult and all can be made in advance to a certain point, so that you can finish them right before serving.

Star-Anise Peanuts

wu xiang hua sheng mi

HUA SHENG MEANS "FLOWERING PEANUTS," probably so named because of the blossom shape of the star anise. They were a favorite of my father's and made frequent appearances as part of his nightly *jiu cai*, or "little wine dishes." They're a little salty, a little sweet, a little crunchy, and very addictive. Allison Saunders, who tested many of the recipes for this book, ate so many of them during the test, we probably should offer a disclaimer on the yield.

☼ ☼ ☼

Both Asian markets and natural food stores often carry shelled raw peanuts, both skin-on and skinless. You can skin peanuts yourself, if you need to. When you put the shelled peanuts in the saucepan with the water as you proceed with this recipe, skim off the loose skins that float to the top. Do this two or three times, continuing to remove any loose skins as they cook. If you'd like a stronger star anise flavor, feel free to add a few more to the cooking liquid.
—L.W.

Makes about 3 cups

12 ounces skinless shelled raw peanuts

6 whole star anise

2 tablespoons kosher salt

1 tablespoon soy sauce

2 teaspoons sugar

In a saucepan, add the peanuts and enough water to cover them generously. Bring to a boil over high heat, decrease the heat to medium-low and simmer, skimming off the foam with a slotted spoon.

After about 5 minutes (or when the foaming stops), stir in the star anise, salt, and soy sauce. Cook 30 minutes more, adding more water as needed to keep the peanuts moving freely in the liquid. Stir in the sugar, and cook 5 minutes more, or until the peanuts are soft, but still have a little resistance when you bite them.

Remove the pan from the heat and let the peanuts cool in the liquid. Drain, transfer to a covered container, and refrigerate for up to 5 days.

The peanuts can be served chilled or at room temperature.

Mini Spring Rolls

xiao chun juan

I OFTEN MAKE THESE FOR COCKTAIL PARTIES, and they disappear almost before I can scoop them out of the fryer. Fortunately, they can be made ahead and frozen so that I can prepare several recipes' worth and then have them ready on a moment's notice. They don't need to be defrosted. The filling I use in this recipe is one of my favorites: it's simple and packs a lot of flavor with just smoky ham and cabbage.

✿ ✿ ✿

Cecilia and I are able to buy small, 4-inch-square spring-roll wrappers at our local Asian markets. If all you can find are the large size, cut them smaller. Yellow Chinese chives are even sweeter and more delicate, though any kind of chive will work in this recipe. —L.W.

Makes 24 spring rolls

3 ounces thinly sliced good-quality smoked ham

1 tablespoon vegetable oil

3 cups thinly shredded napa cabbage (inner leaves only)

$1/4$ teaspoon kosher salt

24 (4-inch-square) spring-roll wrappers

1 cup (2 ounces) loosely packed yellow or green Chinese chives, cut into 2-inch pieces

Peanut or vegetable oil, for frying

Dipping Sauce

3 tablespoons premium soy sauce

$1^1/2$ tablespoons rice vinegar

Dash of chili oil (page 5), or to taste

TO MAKE THE FILLING, julienne the ham by cutting it into thin ($1/8$-inch) strips, then cutting the strips into 2-inch-long pieces. Set aside.

Heat a large sauté pan or wok over high heat until a bead of water dances on the surface and then evaporates. Add the oil and swirl to coat the pan, then add the cabbage and cook, stirring, for 1 minute. Add the ham and cook, stirring, 30 seconds. Stir in the salt, and transfer the mixture to a bowl. Make a well in the center to drain; let cool.

TO ASSEMBLE THE SPRING ROLLS, drain off the liquid from the cooled filling. Put the wrappers on a work surface and cover with a damp kitchen towel. Have both a little bowl filled with cold water and the yellow chives ready nearby. Place a wrapper on the work surface so that one corner points toward you. Dip a finger in the water and run it around the perimeter of the wrapper. Place about $1/4$ cup of filling in a line parallel to your body on the bottom third of the wrapper. Line up a few chives on top, then fold up the lower pointed end over the filling, tucking the filling in snugly. Fold in the end and then roll up into a tight cylinder. If the pointed end doesn't stick, dab it with a little more water. The assembled spring rolls can be frozen at this point for up to 1 month.

TO MAKE THE DIPPING SAUCE, stir together the soy sauce, vinegar, and chili oil in a small bowl. Line a plate with paper towels. Heat the oil in a wok filled no more than halfway with oil to 375°F. Fry the spring rolls until crisp and golden, about 1 minute (or longer for frozen); using a slotted spoon or mesh strainer, transfer to the prepared plate to drain.

To serve, cut the spring rolls in half diagonally and place on a platter with the dipping sauce.

Pork Riblets with Sweet-and-Sour Sauce

wu xi pai gu

WHEN WE FINALLY HAD A COCKTAIL LOUNGE at the Ghirardelli Square Mandarin, we wanted to accompany drinks with little nibbles to take the edge off the appetites of our customers as they waited for their tables. The only problem was that people got so filled up on appetizers that they ordered less at the dinner table. These ribs were especially popular, so we decided to make them in smaller portions, thus was born the riblet.

✿ ✿ ✿

You can ask your butcher to cut the slabs of ribs lengthwise into three even strips or just once in half so that the riblets are a little longer. You can also toss the ribs with the sauce instead of serving it on the side. If you do, use two teaspoons of cornstarch mixed with one tablespoon of water to thicken the sauce. —L.W.

Makes 24 to 36 riblets; 1 cup dipping sauce

1 slab baby-back pork ribs (about 2 pounds), cut lengthwise into 2 or 3 strips

2-inch piece unpeeled fresh ginger, halved lengthwise and lightly smashed

2 green onions, cut into 2-inch lengths

2 tablespoons Shaoxing wine

3 tablespoons soy sauce

1 tablespoon mushroom soy sauce

4 whole star anise

1 tablespoon kosher salt

2 tablespoons sugar

Sweet-and-Sour Sauce

1/3 cup white vinegar

1 teaspoon Shaoxing wine

1/3 cup ketchup

Juice of 1 lemon

3 tablespoons sugar

1 teaspoon cornstarch mixed with 2 teaspoons water

TO MAKE THE RIBLETS, cut between the ribs of each strip to create small bite-size pieces. Place the riblets into a large saucepan and cover with water. Bring to a boil over high heat, cook 2 minutes, then drain rinse with cold water. Clean the saucepan, return the ribs to the pan, and add enough water to barely cover them. Bring to a boil, decrease the heat to medium-high and skim off the foam.

Cook 5 minutes. Add the ginger and green onions and decrease the heat to medium-low. Cook 40 minutes, or until the meat is tender when pressed with a chopstick (add water as necessary). Add the wine, both soy sauces, and star anise; simmer another 20 minutes. Season with salt, remove from the heat, and stir in the sugar. The riblets can be made ahead and refrigerated, covered, for up to 3 days.

TO MAKE THE SWEET-AND-SOUR SAUCE, stir the vinegar, wine, and ketchup together in a small saucepan and cook over medium heat for 1 minute. Add the lemon juice and sugar and cook for about 20 seconds. Stir the cornstarch mixture into the sauce and cook, stirring, for about 2 minutes or until thickened.

Serve the riblets on a platter with a bowl of sauce.

Red-Cooked Chicken Wings

hong shao ji chi bang

IF THE ONLY ASIAN-STYLE CHICKEN WINGS you've tried are the kind with a sticky-sweet glaze, the subtle richness of these will surprise and delight you. Red-cooking is a technique where meat or poultry is braised in a fragrant liquid that includes soy sauce, ginger, wine, and sometimes spices. The liquid is often referred to as a "master sauce." Not only does it imbue the food with a beautiful reddish-brown color, it can be reused several times, becoming more flavorful. I also love to eat the leftover jellied sauce right from the refrigerator—it's that good!

✿　✿　✿

In Asian markets you can find whole chicken wings, but they also often sell them separated into three pieces: the drumstick or "drumette," the middle joint, and the wing tip. For this recipe look for just the middle joints of the wings, which connoisseurs of chicken wings will tell you is the tastiest part.

The sauce can be skimmed of any visible fat, frozen for up to 2 months, and used up to three more times to red-cook whole chicken or chicken parts, or even small birds like game hens.

Rock sugar, a common ingredient in red-cooked dishes, is a crystallized mixture of sugar and honey. Cecilia says it gives the dish a nice glaze. It's sold in Asian markets in 1-pound boxes. —L.W.

Makes 24 wings

2¹/₂ pounds chicken wings, middle joints only

3-inch piece unpeeled fresh ginger, halved lengthwise and lightly smashed

¹/₂ cup soy sauce

¹/₄ cup mushroom soy sauce or dark soy sauce

2 tablespoons Shaoxing wine

1 chunk of rock sugar or 1¹/₂ tablespoons granulated sugar

Sesame seed, for garnish

Rinse and drain the chicken wings. Put them in a large saucepan and cover generously with water. Bring to a boil over high heat, decrease the heat to maintain a low boil, and skim off any foam. Cook 5 minutes, then add the ginger, both soy sauces, and the wine, and cook for 20 minutes. Decrease the heat, add the sugar, and simmer 5 minutes longer.

Remove from the heat and let the wings cool to room temperature in the liquid. At this point, they can be served or refrigerated in their cooking liquid in a covered container for up to 5 days.

To serve, place the wings on a platter, drizzle with a little of the cooking liquid, and sprinkle with sesame seed. The wings can be served chilled from the refrigerator with their jelly still clinging to them.

Shandong Asparagus

liang ban lu sun

I'VE BEEN PREPARING THIS DISH from the northern Chinese province of Shandong since I opened the first Mandarin. Actually, before that we served it at my restaurant in Tokyo, The Forbidden City. The preparation is simple and can be done in advance, and is wonderful served as a small plate or hors d'oeuvre.

✧　✧　✧

While many people seem to prefer pencil-thin asparagus, Cecilia seeks out the fatter asparagus spears at the market; she feels they have more flavor. You can blanch the spears ahead of time, refrigerate them overnight, and then toss them with the dressing just before serving, or up to one hour ahead. If you dress them too far in advance, the asparagus loses its color. —L.W.

Serves 4 to 6

1¼ pounds large asparagus spears

1 tablespoon Asian sesame oil

1½ tablespoons soy sauce

1 teaspoon sugar

2 tablespoons toasted sesame seed, for garnish

Have a bowl of ice water ready near the cooktop. To prepare the asparagus, snap off the tough ends and roll-cut the spears into 1½-inch pieces (see Spareribs with Daikon Soup, page 62).

Bring a large pot of water to a boil over high heat. Drop in the asparagus and cook until they are crisp-tender, 1½ to 2½ minutes, depending on their thickness. Remove from the heat.

Drain the asparagus and plunge them into the ice water to stop the cooking. Drain again and pat the spears dry with a clean kitchen towel. Put them in a bowl and set aside at room temperature for up to 4 hours, or refrigerate overnight.

For the dressing, mix the oil, soy sauce, and sugar in small bowl until the sugar dissolves. Just before serving or up to 1 hour ahead, toss with the blanched asparagus. Garnish with a sprinkling of sesame seed.

Shanghai-Style Shrimp

you bao xia

I USED TO MAKE THIS VERY QUICK AND EASY stir-fry when we lived in Shanghai and could get the most incredibly sweet small shrimp. The shells and part of the tails are left intact to add flavor to the shrimp, and you can just suck the meat from the shells. Or, do as the Chinese do, and eat the shrimp, shells and all. Provide your guest with napkins and a bowl for the empty shells. The hardest part of the recipe may be finding a market that carries medium shrimp. Americans always think bigger is better, but in this case, the smaller shrimp make perfect morsels for nibbling before dinner with cocktails.

✿ ✿ ✿

When buying shrimp, ask your fishmonger for 31 to 35 or 36 to 40 count, an industry designation as to how many shrimp there are in a pound. As with all seafood, the fresher, the better. Previously frozen shrimp (which is usually all that's available) are perfectly fine if they haven't sat in the fish case too long after defrosting. This dish is meant to be prepared quickly, taking no more than 3 minutes total cooking time, so have all the ingredients ready near your stove. Cecilia likes them hot from the oven, but they're still good at room temperature. —L.W.

Makes 24 shrimp

24 medium shrimp (about 3/4 pound)

2 tablespoons peanut or canola oil

1 teaspoon Shaoxing wine

Kosher salt

1 teaspoon peeled, minced fresh ginger

1 green onion, white part minced to make
    2 teaspoons, green part thinly sliced on
    the diagonal

2 teaspoons sugar

Rinse and drain the shrimp, and pat them dry with paper towels. For each, snip off about half of the tail with kitchen scissors, remove the legs, and leave the shell on. Collect the prepared shrimp in a bowl and have them ready near the cooktop.

Heat a wok or large skillet over high heat until a bead of water dances on the surface and then evaporates. Add the oil with a pinch of kosher salt and swirl to coat the pan. Add the shrimp and, using a spoon or spatula, toss to coat them in the hot oil. Add the wine, and toss the shrimp between each addition; add the ginger, the minced white part of the green onion, sugar, and another pinch of salt. Cook about 2 minutes, stirring continuously.

To serve, turn the shrimp out onto a platter, sprinkle with a few green onion slices, and serve hot or at room temperature, but not chilled, which I think diminishes their flavor.

Stuffed Mushrooms

mno gn qian rou

IT SEEMS EVERYONE LOVES THESE little hors d'oeuvres, and I can't even guess how long I've been serving them. They're simple to put together and the ingredients easy to come by. They also can be made early in the day of your party and popped in the oven right before serving.

✿ ✿ ✿

To test the meat mixture for seasoning, sauté a bite-size piece first. Choose mushrooms with tightly closed caps and no exposed gills, a sign of age. —L.W.

Makes 24 mushrooms

1/2 pound ground pork or beef

1 teaspoon minced fresh ginger

1 tablespoon minced green onion, white part only

1/4 cup finely chopped fresh cilantro

1/2 teaspoon kosher salt

1/4 teaspoon freshly ground white pepper

2 teaspoons Asian sesame oil

2 teaspoons soy sauce

24 medium (about 1 1/2-inch-diameter) domestic white mushrooms

Small fresh cilantro leaves, for garnish

TO MAKE THE FILLING, combine the pork with the ginger, green onions, cilantro, salt, pepper, sesame oil, and soy sauce in a bowl, mixing until well combined.

Pop out and discard the stems from the mushrooms and fill the cavities with generous mounds of the meat mixture. Place the stuffed caps in a baking dish or on a small rimmed baking sheet. To make ahead, the mushrooms can be covered with plastic wrap at this point and refrigerated for up to 8 hours before baking.

Preheat the oven to 375° F. Bake the mushrooms, uncovered, 8 to 10 minutes, or until the meat is cooked through and the mushrooms are slightly softened. Serve hot from the oven or at room temperature, garnished with small cilantro leaves.

Crispy Meatballs

zha wu xian xiao wan zi

YOU CAN FIND MEATBALLS in every province of China, prepared in many different ways. I've had meatballs as big as baseballs in braised dishes, and tiny ones no bigger than small marbles in soup. They can be steamed, poached, or fried. One famous preparation, Pearl Balls, involves rolling meatballs in glutinous rice and then steaming them so that the translucent white grains look like tiny porcupine quills. At the bar at The Mandarin, we would serve these bite-size crispy fried meatballs along with the pork riblets with a sweet-and-sour sauce.

✿ ✿ ✿

At home as an easy appetizer with drinks, dip meatballs (and riblets too) in a toasted mixture of ground Sichuan pepper, salt, and star anise. —L.W.

Makes about 20 meatballs

1 pound ground pork butt

1/3 cup (about 5 ounces) drained and finely diced canned water chestnuts

1 1/2 tablespoons finely minced green onions

1 tablespoon finely minced fresh ginger

1 1/2 teaspoons kosher salt

1/2 teaspoon freshly ground white pepper

1 teaspoon soy sauce

1 1/2 teaspoons Asian sesame oil

2 to 3 cups peanut or vegetable oil, for deep-frying

Sweet-and-Sour Sauce (page 81)

In a large bowl, using your hands, gently mix the pork, water chestnuts, green onions, ginger, salt, white pepper, soy sauce, and sesame oil until well combined. Shape the pork mixture into 1-inch balls, packing the mixture a bit so that it will hold together when cooked.

Place the meatballs in a single layer on a rimmed plate (like a glass pie plate) that will fit inside a steamer tier (depending on the size of your steamer, you might need to cook the meatballs in several batches). Fill the steamer bottom with a generous amount of water, bring the water to a boil over high heat, and place the tier with the plate of meatballs above it. Cover and steam until the meatballs are firm to the touch and mostly cooked through, about 15 minutes. Carefully lift the plate off of the steamer tier and set it aside until the meatballs have cooled completely.

Have a plate lined with paper towels near the cooktop. Fill a wok no more than one-third full with the peanut oil. Heat the oil over high heat until it registers 350°F on a deep-fry thermometer. Carefully add the meatballs to the hot oil in batches, being sure not to overcrowd them, and fry until crispy, about 1 minute. Lift the meatballs out of the oil with a slotted spoon and transfer to the waiting plate. Repeat this process for as many batches as needed. To serve, arrange the meatballs on a platter with a bowl of Sweet-and-Sour Sauce alongside and serve hot.

Chapter 4

Bicycles

I THREW A PARTY FOR MY FIFTIETH BIRTHDAY and invited about a hundred of my good friends and family to celebrate with me at my new home on the water in Belvedere, California, a small waterfront town north of the Golden Gate Bridge. The year was 1970, and The Mandarin at Ghirardelli Square had been open for almost two years. As I drank and ate and laughed with the most special people in my life, I remember stopping for a moment to appreciate my good fortune. After all, here I was in America, celebrating my birthday! I could not believe it. Plus, I was a successful businesswoman running a critically acclaimed San Francisco restaurant, my children were living here with me, and I owned a home on the water in Marin County, one of the most desirable and beautiful places in the world. What could be better?

Immediately after I blew out the fifty candles on my cake—a Western custom I'd learned to look forward to—the boisterous crowd suddenly grew quiet as my son, Philip, and daughter, May, wheeled a shiny new red Schwinn into the room.

"Mother," Philip said, "May and I know how much you enjoyed your bicycle when you were a girl in China, and we thought you would enjoy bike riding again here in California. Happy birthday!"

I was uncharacteristically speechless.

Cecilia at The Mandarin at Ghirardelli Square, San Francisco, 1972.

"Also, you've been working so hard lately and we thought you needed a little exercise, a little something fun to do outside of the restaurant," May added.

After several awkward seconds of silence on my part, a weak "thank you" was all I could manage. My eyes moistened, but I still couldn't speak.

Anxious to get back to their conversations and cake, or maybe uncomfortable with my obvious emotion, the guests quickly dispersed.

With a mischievous grin Philip turned to me quietly and added, "Besides, Umma, you're starting to get a little chubby."

Not in the least bothered by his little tease, I stared at that red bicycle and then started to cry for joy in earnest.

✿ ✿ ✿

When I was still in junior high, several of my female classmates had started riding bicycles to and from school. It wasn't until the moment that I watched my friend Mei Li gracefully climb onto her bike and pedal away that I made up my mind that my rickshaw days were going to be numbered. Mei Li, whose name meant "beautiful," was truly that. Though at times I had envied her for her looks as well as her long legs, what I envied most on that particular chilly fall day was her freedom. There I was, chafing under layers of clothes and stuffed into the back of our covered rickshaw with my younger sister, Jing, so that we could barely move, while a smiling Mei Li blithely pedaled past us wearing just a quilted vest over her cheongsam, hair flying in the wind.

I had always been something of a tomboy and prided myself on my athletic abilities. Watching Mei Li, it suddenly occurred to me that learning to ride a bike could be my new challenge. Not only that, and perhaps more significantly to me at the time, I realized that a bicycle could also be a way for me to have a little independence. For as long as I could remember, every waking moment of my fourteen-year-old life had been accounted for. From the time our nannies woke us up, fed us breakfast and packed us in our rickshaws for school to the time we arrived home again, had dinner with our parents, and our nannies tucked us into bed, we were never alone. Our mother always knew where we were and what we were doing.

For the remainder of the forty-minute trip home, with the rickshaw boy pulling us as fast as his speedy legs would allow, I began to hatch my plan. I knew I needed to be clever, because almost as soon as I made up my mind to get a bike, I could hear my mother's response, "Daughters in this family do not ride bicycles." The first and most important step would be to get my father to plead my case.

☆ ☆ ☆

Unlike my friends, as well as their brothers and sisters, none of us Sun children were afraid of our father. While most boys kowtowed to their fathers in obedient deference, and girls received only minimal acknowledgment (if any at all) from them, our father always seemed approachable.

Um-ma, on the other hand—our barely five-foot mother—cast such a large and dominant shadow over our lives that, while I wouldn't exactly say we were afraid of her, we were definitely intimidated by her. Where my father was relaxed, accepting, and eager to engage in conversation, my mother was busy, critical, and often inaccessible. But at the risk of making her sound cold and aloof, in her defense I need to add that she was also a warm, loving, and generous woman who just happened to be a perfectionist, responsible for the running of household that consisted of a husband, ten children, some twenty-odd servants, and numerous animals.

Though I never once heard my mother raise her voice in anger, she didn't need to. We all wanted to live up to her high expectations and everyone, except probably our father, lived in fear of disappointing her. Our servants, of course, feared for their jobs, but we children lived for her approval. For the most part, we had to make do with knowing we were doing well if we didn't receive any criticism, since compliments were rarely given. It was simply assumed that of course we would do as we were told, get good grades in school, and generally behave in a manner that would make our parents proud.

Twentieth-century China saw a great number of changes, but none so radical as the role of women in society. Continuity of tradition was of utmost importance to my mother's generation (those women born in the latter half of the nineteenth century). My mother was brought up in the same strict traditions as her own mother and all the women who preceded her for hundreds of years.

☆ ☆ ☆

For an entire week I plotted my strategy.

Timing was important. First, I needed to make sure my father had particularly enjoyed his evening's *jiu cai* (small wine dishes served before dinner) and was in a

Cecilia and sisters, Beijing, 1928.

good mood. I had observed that on most nights, he had just one glass of wine and two or three little dishes, then simply retired to the parlor after dinner to read quietly. Occasionally, however, if the *jiu cai* were his favorites, he would ask for another glass of wine and then be very talkative after dinner.

In addition to the timing of my request, it was important that I anticipate all my mother's objections, which would demonstrate to my father that I was serious and had given my request much thought. He would respect my preparation.

After her initial and arbitrary response about Sun daughters not riding bikes, I figured my mother's second argument would be, "But you don't even know how to ride a bicycle." This would be easy (and fun) to take care of. I would ask my older brother, Zhen-Ji to teach me before I approached my parents.

Finally, and probably most importantly, I had to put on a good argument as to why I should have a bicycle. This part of my case had to be strong. Obviously, I couldn't just tell the truth and say because it looked like fun. I was at a loss until I realized that my sister Jing would still be in middle school a few months from now when I began high school. My school would be a thirty-minute ride in the opposite direction from hers, and we'd be starting and getting out at different times. My mother hated waste of any kind—including wasted motion—so I reasoned that the rickshaw boy shouldn't have to ride an extra hour a day just to get the two of us to and from school. I was sure this would be the one point Um-ma would have the hardest time denying.

✿　✿　✿

For a couple of weeks, after Zhen-Ji taught me at school to ride on a borrowed boy's bike (how I got on that bike in my cheongsam I'll never know), I patiently waited for the right opportunity. One evening I hit the jackpot in terms of timing, because not only did my father really seem to enjoy his *jiu cai*, he lingered over it, and even asked for a third glass of wine. This was going to be my night. All during dinner I silently rehearsed my lines, then accompanied my parents to the parlor afterwards.

As they settled into their chairs, I boldly blurted out "Ah-ba, Um-ma, I would like to make a request." There, I thought to myself, I said it!

"Yes, of course, Lao-chi, what is it?" my father asked.

"I would like to ride a bicycle to school."

My mother quickly said, "Girls in this family do not ride bicycles."

"I know Um-ma, but many of the girls in our school are riding now."

"Who cares about them? No Sun daughter rides a bicycle. Besides, you don't even know how to ride a bicycle."

I was ready for this one. "Yes, I do. I learned at school," which was the truth, carefully edited to keep Zhen-Ji out of it.

I could see my father paying close attention, and maybe it was wishful thinking on my part, but I thought I saw a slight smile cross his face.

My mother pursed her lips. "But you have the rickshaw. Most children would be grateful to have someone take them."

"I am grateful, Um-ma, but"—and here I played my trump card—"soon I'll be going to a new school that will be far from Jing's. How will the rickshaw boy be able to take us both? It would take him a very long time."

My mother seemed to be thinking carefully about her response when my father spoke up.

"Number Seven daughter has made a great deal of sense, Yun Hui. She's obviously thought this out very carefully."

"But Yung Xiao, young women should not be so active. It doesn't look right. What will people think?"

My father looked sweetly at my mother and said, "Yun Hui. Times are changing, and what didn't look right when you were young, now is acceptable. Girls today ice skate, row boats, and dance and no one thinks badly of them for it. I believe it would be fine for our Number Seven daughter to have a bicycle."

Like the good wife she was taught to be, my mother did not put forth any more argument once my father had given his decision.

❊ ❊ ❊

The very next day Zhen-Ji went with me to help me choose my bicycle. The bicycle we chose was sturdy and new, but boring and black. I wanted a zippy red bike, but Zhen-Ji felt I shouldn't get one that stood out. I guess he worried for my safety—a young woman riding alone in the city—and didn't want it (or me) to attract too much attention.

All through high school I rode my bike, rain or shine, sleet or snow, over gravel and over pavement. I loved my bicycle, and at one point I even showed off to my parents how I could ride up and down the stairs in the courtyard of our house. My father laughed, and I even got a smile out of my mother.

When I began to make the daily trip to Fu-Jen Catholic University, farther away than my high school, I had to retire my old bike, which was looking pretty worn, and replace it with a new one. Off I went by myself and found a shiny, new red Schwinn. After four years of riding, I could handle any attention I or my bike might attract.

❊ ❊ ❊

In 1937, the Japanese finally made their way into Beijing. Although the city had been bracing for their arrival and subsequent occupation of the capital ever since the invasion of Manchuria in 1931, I think everyone was taken by surprise by the speed at which our circumstances changed. It seemed as if overnight food became scarce. Luckily for our family, our shrewd and wise mother was not surprised at all, and in fact, had been preparing for the occupation for years. Unbeknownst to her children at least, she had been stashing easily hidden valuables, such as jewelry and gold pieces, and then, as the Japanese moved closer, foodstuffs like rice, soy sauce, and dried vegetables, as well. For a time we ate better than most because we had enough money to pay extra as the prices went up. Eventually though, almost all of the fresh food, the meat and fish and vegetables, went to feeding the Japanese army, leaving little for the residents of the city. Our servants had to travel farther and farther to outlying areas to find food and then finally, as we all grew hungrier, the few remaining servants understandably fled.

I tried to continue my college studies, but as our situation at home grew more dire, I was spending less time at school and more time on my bicycle, pedaling some days as much as forty or fifty miles, determined to find something, knowing that what I brought home to the family might be the only food we would eat.

One day, on my way back home, I passed the market of Kao Ming, one of Um-ma's favorite merchants. It made me sad to see his once glorious and thriving market now shuttered and dark, but for a small light in a side window. I had found quite a few decent vegetables and some fresh dofu that day, but we were still in need of some oil. I rapped on the door and Kao Ming himself greeted me.

After a brief exchange of pleasantries, I asked him if he had any food or cooking oil to sell. "Yes," he replied. "Do you have a bottle for the oil?"

I handed him the clean beer bottle I always carried with me for just such an opportunity. He returned from his back room with a full bottle of peanut oil. I couldn't wait to show Um-ma. I handed him one of the small gold pieces my mother had given to me and said, "Thank you very much. My parents will be very happy."

Kao Ming bowed and thanked me and then pulled out a cloth bundle.

"Give this to your mother with my best wishes."

Inside the bundle were a dozen carefully wrapped eggs.

When I arrived home I proudly put all my treasures, except the eggs, on the dining room table for my parents to see.

"One more thing," I said. "I forgot these." I brought out the eggs.

My mother broke into a huge smile and turned to my father and said, "See, Yong Xiao, I told you that bicycle was a good idea!"

POULTRY

It would be hard to overstate the importance of poultry in the Chinese diet. Throughout the country, in every province, you'll find whole birds that are roasted, steamed, fried, smoked, and simmered in broth. Nothing goes to waste. Chicken feet are especially prized; chicken and duck fat is rendered for cooking. Young hens are valued for their eggs and then, when old and tough, are relegated to the soup pot for broth.

Birds are also symbolic. At New Year's, a whole chicken or duck represents family unity and rebirth. At weddings, they symbolize the phoenix, or bride. Eggs dyed red are passed out at birth to signify fertility.

When I first came to the United States, I was surprised to find chicken at the supermarket already cut up and packaged in plastic. "How am I supposed to know if it's fresh?" I thought. In China, many people raise their own birds, and not only in rural areas. You'll even find chickens scratching little patches of land behind someone's home in the city. My mother always kept a few chickens, for eggs, and would also go to the market and choose a couple of live chickens for dinner.

Old habits are hard to break. I still prefer to buy my chicken and ducks at an Asian market. I use whole fowl, head and feet still attached, in my chicken broth.

To me, short of going to an Asian market to buy poultry, nothing tastes better than a freshly killed bird. Its flesh is tender, sweet, and succulent. Today, in many urban Chinatowns, it's not unusual to find markets that still sell live poultry, and good butchers sell fresh parts. If you're buying packaged breasts, legs, or wings, first look at the pull date and get the ones that are most recent. Check the package: if there is a lot of pink-red juice in the bottom it might indicate that the parts have been frozen and defrosted. Look for skin that is glossy white or yellow and has no shriveled edges, discoloration, or bruising.

Kung Pao Chicken
gong bao ji ding

I'M CONVINCED THAT ANYONE WHO has eaten in a Chinese restaurant in the last thirty-five years must be familiar with this dish. It's probably become almost as well known as fried rice and chow mein. When I opened the first Mandarin in 1961, though, I still had to explain that it was a spicy stir-fry of chicken, sweet bell peppers, fiery chile peppers, and peanuts. The peanuts identify it as authentically Sichuan, which is where the dish originated. The name loosely translates as "hot firecrackers," because *pao* sounds like "pop, pop, pop."

✿ ✿ ✿

Sometimes you can find packages of shelled and skinned raw peanuts in Asian markets, but if not, the peanuts will need to be blanched first to remove the skins.

I like to use a mixture of red and yellow bell peppers for color, but Cecilia uses green peppers, which are traditional. Use whichever color pepper you prefer. —L.W.

Serves 6 to 8 as part of a Chinese meal and 4 to 6 as a Western-style entrée

¹/₂ cup (about 3 ounces) shelled raw peanuts, preferably skinned

2 cups plus 2 tablespoons peanut oil, for frying

1 tablespoon Shaoxing wine

1 tablespoon soy sauce

6 (or more to taste) whole dried red chile peppers, tops trimmed and seeded

Pinch of kosher salt

1 pound boned chicken thighs, trimmed of excess fat and cut in 1-inch-square pieces

1 green bell pepper, seeded and cut in 1-inch-square pieces

To skin the peanuts, fill a small saucepan halfway with water and bring to a boil over high heat. Drop the peanuts into the boiling water and blanch, 1 to 2 minutes. Drain and transfer the peanuts to a bowl; set aside. When cool enough to handle, rub off the skins with a clean kitchen towel.

Line a small plate or bowl with paper towels. In a medium saucepan, heat 2 cups of the peanut oil over high heat until it registers 350°F on a deep-fry thermometer. Carefully pour the peanuts into the hot oil and fry them until golden brown, about 1 minute. Using a slotted spoon, transfer the peanuts to the prepared plate.

TO MAKE THE SAUCE, mix the wine and soy sauce. Set aside.

Heat a large wok over high heat until a bead of water dances on the surface and then evaporates. Add the remaining peanut oil and swirl to coat the pan. Toss in the chiles and a pinch of salt, stir to coat in the oil, and cook for about 1 minute, or until the chiles have darkened in color. Add the chicken and cook, stirring constantly, over high heat until the pink just disappears, 3 to 4 minutes. Add the green pepper, stirring for 1 minute. Pour in the reserved sauce, bring to a boil, and stir to coat the chicken. Remove from the heat, top with the peanuts, and mix well. Turn the chicken out onto a platter to serve.

Bon Bon Chicken

chen du bang bang ji

MANY CHINESE DISHES ARE named for sounds, like *pao* ("firecrackers"), and *bon* (or *bong*) for the chopping sound made when preparing the chicken for this dish. Whatever the name, this Sichuan dish is a dish of contrasts: cool cucumbers, tender chicken shreds, and rich, spicy sesame sauce.

✿ ✿ ✿

The method Cecilia uses for poaching chicken is one I use every time now when I want chicken for salad. For both aesthetic as well as practical reasons, in Chinese cooking all ingredients should be cut the same size. —L.W.

Serves 6 to 8 as part of a Chinese meal or 4 to 6 as a Western-style entrée

1¹/₂ pounds boneless, skinless chicken breasts

¹/₄ cup Shaoxing or dry white wine or vermouth

2 green onions, cut in 2-inch lengths and lightly smashed

6 (¹/₈-inch-thick) slices fresh ginger, smashed

1 teaspoon whole black, white, or Sichuan peppercorns

1 pound English or Japanese cucumbers, peeled

1 teaspoon kosher salt

2 tablespoons Asian sesame paste

3 tablespoons premium or regular soy sauce

1 tablespoon Chinkiang black vinegar

1 tablespoon sesame oil

2 teaspoons chili oil (page 5)

1¹/₂ teaspoons ground Sichuan peppercorns

1 teaspoon peeled, minced unpeeled fresh ginger

1 large garlic clove, minced

2 teaspoons sugar

Kosher salt

2 tablespoons finely chopped fresh cilantro, plus a few sprigs for garnish

TO POACH THE CHICKEN, put the breasts in a large saucepan with water to cover by 2 inches. Add the wine, green onions, ginger, and peppercorns. Increase heat to high; as soon as the liquid boils, cover and remove the pan from the heat. Let it sit 30 minutes or up to 2 hours. Remove from the broth and pull it into shreds that are about ¹/₃ inch thick. Strain the broth and use it to thin the dressing, or refrigerate or freeze it for another use.

TO PREPARE THE CUCUMBERS, cut them lengthwise into quarters and then crosswise into 2-inch lengths. (The important thing is to make the cucumber pieces about the same size as the shreds of chicken.) Set aside.

TO MAKE THE DRESSING, combine the sesame paste, soy sauce, vinegar, sesame oil, chili oil, ground Sichuan pepper, ginger, garlic, sugar, salt, and cilantro by hand with a whisk or in a food processor. Use immediately, or store, covered, in the refrigerator for up to 5 days.

To serve, arrange the cucumbers on a platter with the chicken on top. Thin out the dressing with some of the reserved cooking broth or water, if necessary. Pour the dressing over the chicken and garnish with cilantro.

Velvet Chicken

fu rong ji pian

AT THE MANDARIN, WE USED TO SERVE two versions of this luscious dish. In one, chicken breast meat is minced by hand into a fluffy paste, mixed with egg whites, and then poached in oil at low temperature. It's quite tricky to master, and because only two of our chefs could make it, we used to prep a limited number of portions on any given night. In the other version, which is easier to prepare (and the one I like to make at home), instead of mincing the chicken, the breast meat is very thinly sliced, coated in egg white, and poached in low-temperature oil. The term "velvet" in the recipe title refers both to the plush texture of the finished chicken, as well as the cooking technique. Velvet Chicken, which I had growing up in Beijing, is a peculiarly delicate dish for northern China, where the cuisine tends to be gutsier. It has a subtle beauty and snowy white color. I like to add tiny cubes of Virginia ham, both for the extra flavor as well as the touch of color.

✿ ✿ ✿

Some recipes for velveted meat that will be stir-fried and finished with a sauce call for oil to be heated to 270°F. In this recipe, in which the chicken gets a quick toss in a wok just to warm it through, it's important that the oil not go over 180°F or the egg white coating will slip off the meat into unattractive clumps. —L.W.

Serves 6 to 8 as part of a Chinese meal and 4 to 6 as a Western-style entrée

1 pound boneless, skinless chicken breasts

1 large egg white, lightly beaten with a splash of vegetable oil

2 cups peanut or vegetable oil, for deep-frying

1 tablespoon water

2 teaspoons cornstarch

1/2 teaspoon kosher salt

1/2 teaspoon sugar

1/4 cup finely minced Virginia ham

1/2 teaspoon Asian sesame oil

1/2 teaspoon Shaoxing wine

Pinch of freshly ground white pepper

Using a sharp knife, cut and scrape out the tendon of each chicken breast and remove the fillet or "tender" (reserve for another use). So the chicken is easier to slice, freeze it 20 minutes or so, until it's semi-firm. With your knife almost parallel to the cutting surface, slice the chicken crosswise into paper-thin slices (1/8 inch thick or less) and transfer them to a bowl. Pour the beaten egg white mixture over the chicken and stir so that all pieces are well coated. Cover the bowl with plastic wrap and marinate in the refrigerator 1 hour.

Line a plate with paper towels and have it ready near the cooktop. In a large, flat-bottomed wok or wide, deep saucepan, heat the oil over medium-high heat until it registers 180°F on a deep-fry thermometer. Carefully add the chicken to the pan, stirring with a long chopstick or spoon to separate the pieces. Cook 1 to 2 minutes, or until the chicken is about 90 percent white with just a little pink remaining, but not browned. Using a slotted spoon, scoop the chicken out of the oil and transfer to the prepared plate. Discard all but 2 tablespoons of the oil.

In a small bowl, whisk together the 1 tablespoon water with the cornstarch, salt, and sugar. Set aside. The recipe can be done to this point up to 2 hours ahead. Using the same pan as for the chicken, heat the 2 tablespoons reserved peanut oil over medium-high heat and swirl to coat the pan. Toss in the chicken and the ham and stir constantly 15 seconds to heat through. Pour in the cornstarch mixture and stir to coat the chicken. Quickly drizzle with the sesame oil and wine, then sprinkle with white pepper. Remove the pan from the heat

Turn the chicken out onto a platter and serve immediately.

Drunken Chicken

shanghai zui ji

WHEN I WAS A YOUNG GIRL, before we had a refrigerator, we had a large, old-fashioned wooden icebox. One of my favorite dishes was my mother's "drunken" chicken, which she served at least once a week. Often, after school, I would sneak a peek into the icebox to see if she had left one in there to marinate and chill for dinner. It's a classic Shanghai dish in which a chicken is marinated and then steamed in lots of Shaoxing wine (until the bird is "drunk"), and then served cold as a small dish or first course.

☼ ☼ ☼

A word of warning from Cecilia: don't let the chicken marinate longer than overnight, or it will be too "drunk" to eat!

Chicken broilers or fryers under three pounds work best in this recipe; they're easier to fit in a steamer and will absorb the wine marinade without becoming too boozy. Also, the chicken in this case needs to be chopped, Chinese style, into small pieces, since it's meant to be served as an appetizer.
—L.W.

Serves 6 as an appetizer

1 small (2¹/₂ to 3 pounds) whole chicken. trimmed of extra fat and halved lengthwise

2 teaspoons kosher salt

1¹/₂ cups Shaoxing wine

Thoroughly rinse the chicken under running water and pat it dry with paper towels. Generously rub the chicken inside and out with salt until well coated. Transfer the chicken halves to a medium bowl, pour over the Shaoxing wine and refrigerate for 4 hours.

Fill the bottom of a steamer with water, bring the water to a boil over high heat, and set the bowl with the chicken halves on a steamer tier over the boiling water. Cover and steam the chicken 40 minutes, or until the juices run clear when you cut into the thick part of the thigh. Using tongs, tilt the chicken so that the juices drain back into the cooking bowl, then transfer the chicken to a clean bowl to cool, reserving the liquid. When the chicken has cooled completely, cut each half into four pieces: breast, thigh, wing, and drumstick.

Place the chicken pieces in a large ziplock plastic bag and pour in the reserved cooking liquid. Squeeze out as much air as possible from the bag and put it in the refrigerator to marinate for at least 4 hours, but no longer than 8 hours.

To serve, drain and discard the liquid, and chop the chicken into bite-size pieces. Arrange the chicken on a platter and serve cold.

Grilled Quail

sheng zha an chun

QUAIL IS A COMMON GAME BIRD in most provinces of China. Quail eggs are considered a delicacy, but I had had quail only a few times before living in Shanghai. My husband would order fried whole little birds in one of his favorite Cantonese restaurants there, but I first really fell in love with quail many, many years ago when I had some that Jeremiah Tower put on the barbecue at the Santa Fe Bar and Grill in Berkeley, California. Now, whenever I make quail, I grill them. Simple, but tasty.

✿ ✿ ✿

Many markets sell semi-boneless farm-raised quail with the ribcages removed and leg bones left in. Usually you must order them in advance, although I've often found them in the freezer case.

As an alternative to grilling the quail, you could also broil them or cook them on top of the stove in a ridged grill pan. If quail meat is not overcooked, it is lean, sweet, and tender. It's difficult to give exact cooking times for quail, but you can check doneness by cutting a little into the breast meat, which should be somewhat pink (which, unlike chicken or turkey, is perfectly safe to eat). —L.W.

Serves 2 as an appetizer or first course

2 semi-boneless quail

Pinch of kosher salt

2 thin slices unpeeled fresh ginger

2 tablespoons oyster sauce

Rinse the quail under running water and pat them dry with paper towels. Preheat a grill to medium-high.

Sprinkle a pinch of salt inside the cavity of each quail and rub in well. Stuff each cavity with a slice of ginger. Using a pastry brush, liberally coat the outside surface of each quail with the oyster sauce.

Place the quail, breast-side down, on the preheated grill and cook until golden, 4 to 5 minutes. Flip the quail over with tongs and continue to grill until the skin is glazed and browned and the quail is still a little pink, about 4 minutes.

Transfer to a platter and serve warm or at room temperature.

Tea-Smoked Game Hens

zhang cha zi ji

The process of smoking food has a long culinary history in China, just as it does in the West. Originally, it was a way to preserve food, but later food was smoked strictly for flavor. Nearly every province has its own smoked specialty. Sichuan's Tea-Smoked Duck, with its crispy skin and fragrant meat, is justifiably famous. From the beginning, it was a dish I wanted to serve at The Mandarin; no other restaurant had it on their menu. The problem was that I had no real recipe, only a general knowledge of how it was done. As is true of most of my life, I ran into someone just at the right moment who could help me.

I was attending an art exhibit at Stanford University for a well-known Sichuan artist, Chang Dai-chien (considered China's Picasso), whom I had met briefly during the war, some twenty years earlier. Unbelievably, he recognized me immediately. As we chatted, I remembered that he was also something of a gourmet. I asked him if he'd ever tried to make tea-smoked duck. He hadn't, but one of his students had perfected a home version. The student came to The Mandarin, taught my chef, and from then on Tea-Smoked Duck became one of our signature dishes.

The process of tea-smoking is not difficult to accomplish at home, but because ducks are fatty and large, I decided to substitute Cornish game hens in this recipe.

✿ ✿ ✿

While none of the steps for smoking food Chinese style are difficult, you need to plan at least a day in advance. It's a three-step process: First, the meat (or fish or poultry) is rubbed with spices and allowed to cure overnight in the fridge. Then it's steamed, and finally smoked.

The smoking can be accomplished in a wok or large enameled cast-iron or stainless-steel casserole, or in a stove-top smoker designed just for the purpose. The only must is a good, strong exhaust system over your stove, otherwise this recipe is a certain check to see if your smoke detector is working. Also, if you're using a wok or casserole, it's a good idea to line it with aluminum foil so that the smoke flavor doesn't permanently permeate the cookware.

Dried orange peel is sold in Asian markets, most often labeled as "Dried Tangerine Peel." Whether from a tangerine or orange, in Sichuan Province it's tossed into many dishes to add flavor as well as to lend its supposed medicinal qualities. It's easy, and much less expensive, to dry your own. Using a vegetable peeler, remove the zest and not the white pith from an orange or tangerine (or tangelo). Let dry on a rack overnight and keep in a closed container for up to 3 months. —L.W.

Serves 8 as part of a Chinese meal or
4 as a Western-style entrée

continued

2 game hens (1 to 1¹/₄ pounds each)

1 teaspoon ground Sichuan peppercorns

2 teaspoons kosher salt

¹/₄ teaspoon five-spice powder (page 6)

4 green onions, sliced lengthwise and cut in 2-inch pieces

8 thin slices unpeeled fresh ginger

Smoking Mixture

¹/₂ cup brown sugar

¹/₃ cup white rice

¹/₃ cup loose black tea (any kind you like)

4 pieces dried orange peel, optional

Asian sesame oil, for drizzling

Minced green onions or cilantro sprigs, for garnish

TO BUTTERFLY THE GAME HENS, cut them along their backbones, spread them flat to open them up, and then press lightly to flatten them further. Bend back the wings so they are snugly tucked behind the breasts.

TO MAKE THE RUB, stir together the Sichuan pepper, salt, and five-spice powder. Rub the mixture generously over the game hens so they're well coated inside and out. Put the hens in a ziplock plastic bag and refrigerate overnight.

TO STEAM THE GAME HENS, remove them from the refrigerator. Put the green onions and ginger on a rimmed plate (like a glass pie plate) that will fit in one of your steamer tiers, top with the game hens, and then place the plate on the steamer tier.

Fill the steamer bottom with a generous amount of water, bring to a boil over high heat, and place the tier with the game hens above it. Cover and steam the game hens 15 minutes, then remove the steamer from the heat. Lift off the tier, plate and all, and set it aside to let the game hens cool. Once cooled, the game hens can be covered and refrigerated for up to 2 days. Let the game hens come to room temperature before proceeding with the smoking step.

TO SMOKE THE HENS IN A WOK, line both the wok and lid with aluminum foil. Stir together the smoking mixture, then put it on the foil in the bottom of the wok. Place the hens on a round wire cooling rack (like a cake rack) that will sit a few inches above the bottom of the wok. (Or, you can improvise by arranging bamboo chopsticks in a "tic-tac-toe" pattern in the bottom of the wok for the hens to sit on.) Over high heat, heat the tea mixture until it just begins to smoke. Put in the rack with the hens and, cover with the wok lid, pressing it down so it fits snugly. Decrease the heat to medium and smoke the hens 20 minutes. Remove from the heat and let sit covered for 5 minutes more.

Remove the hens from the wok. If not serving them immediately or letting them cool to room temperature for serving, let them cool completely, then cover and refrigerate for up to 3 days. Reheat the chilled hens, wrapped in foil, in a 350°F oven 10 minutes, or until warmed. If the skin is not crispy you can run them under a broiler.

To serve, put the warm or room-temperature hens on a serving platter and drizzle with sesame oil. Sprinkle with green onions or a few sprigs of cilantro.

Sichuan Crispy Duck

xian su ya

Sichuan Province is famous for its Crispy Duck and rightly so. Whole ducks are marinated, steamed, and then fried whole, so that the duck meat is aromatic, and juicy and the skin crispy and golden. It's a dish also rarely made at home, as frying a whole duck is a greasy mess. I developed this recipe, which uses just boneless duck breasts, and while not authentic it is perfect for the home cook. You still get nearly the same result but with a lot less bother.

✿ ✿ ✿

We used boneless Muscovy duck breasts, which I found frozen at my local gourmet grocer. Good butchers can order them for you, or look online (see Sources, page 240).

This is a very versatile recipe in that it works well in many preparations. It can be a simple dinner with steamed rice and a green vegetable. Or coarsely shred it and serve with steamed buns/pancakes and hoisin sauce, in a way similar to Peking duck. —L.W.

Serves 6 to 8 as a part of a Chinese meal or
4 to 6 as a Western-style entrée

4 boneless duck breasts halves (about 1³/₄ pounds total or a little less than ¹/₂ pound each)

2 green onions, cut into 2-inch pieces, smashed

6 thin slices peeled ginger, each about the size of a quarter, lightly smashed

1 tablespoon kosher salt

2 teaspoons five-spice powder (page 6)

¹/₄ cup Shaoxing wine

3 cups peanut or vegetable oil

Asian sesame oil to garnish

In a medium bowl, combine the duck breasts with the green onions, ginger, salt, five-spice powder, and wine and marinate in the refrigerator for at least 4 hours and preferably overnight.

Place the duck and any remaining liquid in a single layer on a rimmed plate or bowl that will fit inside a steamer tier. Fill the steamer bottom with a generous amount of water, bring the water to a boil, and then place the tier with the duck above it. Cover and steam for 30 minutes. Carefully lift the plate out of the steamer tier and set aside. Discard the juices. Transfer the duck to a baking sheet or plate lined with a double thickness of paper towels and refrigerate, uncovered, to dry completely, at least 4 hours or up to overnight.

Line a plate or small baking sheet with paper towels and have it ready near your cooktop. In a large, flat-bottomed wok or wide, deep saucepan, heat the oil over high heat until it registers 350°F on a deep-fry thermometer. Fry the duck breasts, two at a time, skin side down, for 1¹/₂ to 2 minutes and then turn them over and fry 1¹/₂ to 2 minutes more, until the skin is golden and crispy. Lift them out of the oil with a slotted spoon or tongs and transfer to the paper towel–lined plate to drain. Repeat this process with the remaining duck breasts. Drizzle with a bit of sesame oil.

Chapter 5
Red Envelopes

"REMEMBER THIS MOMENT. This day. This year. It will never happen again."

That was what my father always said to us every New Year's Eve as the large, pendulum clock in the parlor ticked down the minutes to midnight. As I've grown older, his words echo more frequently now, but even when I was a child, the gravity—the seriousness—of his admonition would stay with me for days. It will never happen again. Even from the time I was young, I was able to take his words to heart and understood that once a moment is gone, it is really and truly gone forever. But on New Year's Eve, 1937, when I was sixteen, little did I know just how much my father's words would mean to me in the years to come.

✿　✿　✿

When I woke up on New Year's morning, I was still snug in my dark silk-and-cotton coverlet, which enclosed me like a wrapper around mu-shu pork. It was folded up on the bottom and the sides and then loosely basted so that it formed a packet much like a sleeping bag. My Number Eight sister, Jing, was beside me in the brass bed we had shared since childhood, sound asleep in her own wrapper.

From left: Sisters Number Eight, Seven (Cecilia), Six, Five, Four, and Three, at home, 1940.

Even though I was a teenager and feeling quite adult, I turned into a child again on New Year's morning, because I couldn't wait to find the red envelope that I knew Ah-ba had magically slipped under my pillow as I slept. I wiped the sleep from my eyes, and lying on my back, reached up behind my neck to feel underneath. Ha! There it was. I pulled it out and looked at Jing still breathing out little snorts, assuring me she was asleep. I hated it when she woke before I did and discovered her envelope first.

It was probably the familiar aroma of pine that fully awakened me from my state of semi-sleep. Ah-ba always tied a small flat evergreen sprig for good luck onto the outside of the envelope. In those days, my father folded his own envelopes, which took him a great deal of time considering he made them not only for us, his children, but for all our servants and his nieces and nephews as well. The Chinese believe that giving money, as well as receiving it, creates good luck. I can only imagine the pleasure he must have taken in carefully folding each envelope, upon which he wrote in his beautiful calligraphy a message of hope for the year to come: Xin Nian Kuai Le (Happy New Year) or Gong Xi Fa Cai, which means "wishing you happiness and prosperity." He also gave thought as to how much money each child should receive. He wanted to be fair, but it was a patriarchal society after all. So sons received the most, older daughters more, and younger daughters less. The twins, Ling and Qin, always got equal amounts.

After I had admired my father's handiwork, I played my own little game, shaking the envelope and trying to guess the amount inside. That year I guessed eight silver dollars, based on my memory of last year's envelope (which held six coins) and also what I knew my older sisters had received in years past.

As I ripped open my father's beautifully constructed envelope, eight shiny silver dollars fell onto the mattress. "I'm right!" I said out loud.

At the sound of the coins, Jing woke up with a start and said, "Okay, so you got to yours before I did. You win. Now tell me, how much did you get?"

"Eight dollars!"

"Wow, that's a lot!" Jing opened her envelope to find the same number of coins. As usual. My father always wanted to avoid stirring the pot of sibling envy.

Since monthly or weekly allowances for children were unheard of in Chinese culture, the only money we ever received—which we were free to spend any way we wished—was the money we got at New Year's. Eight dollars was a huge amount, and could go a long, long way. I made a habit of saving a portion of my father's New Year's gift, plus what I received from the other relatives (all of which I kept hidden in an old, square European cookie tin under my bed). Even so, I would still have enough left over to spend (albeit judiciously) throughout the year on items my mother never would have bought us. These were things like makeup (American brands like Max Factor), perfume (French brands like Lanvin), or movies (glamorous Hollywood productions).

As I crawled out of bed, I couldn't wait to put on my new pale-aqua silk cheongsam with the lilac trim. I loved New Year's. Not only did we get those red envelopes and a two-week vacation from school, but best of all, for me, were the new clothes.

If you're the seventh daughter in a family of eight girls, most of your clothes are hand-me-downs. But a new year meant a brand new outfit—from shoes and socks to underwear—for everyone, my parents, my siblings, and the servants. Two full-time tailors were employed for several weeks just to sew all our garments.

The excitement began for me when my Numbers Five, Six, and Eight sisters and I accompanied my mother to the fabric store (the older girls went on a separate trip). From the time we were little, Um-ma let us choose our own material from the hundreds of bolts in every color imaginable (she offered her opinion only if she thought we were leaning in an inappropriately garish direction). We always engaged in a friendly competition to get the prettiest fabrics, and that year I recall my sister Sophie wanted the lilac fabric that I had my eye on first, so I quickly talked her out of it by reminding her that she'd worn a similar color the year before.

Because we were Madame Sun's daughters, we were treated especially well. I remember how, when we were little, we would sit in a line on a bench and sip Coca-Colas from the bottle while waiting to take our turn at the fabric counter. Occasionally, the shopkeeper gave us hot cocoa, which was also nice, but Coca-Cola was an expensive and rare import from America and something that made us feel very important. Between the royal treatment and the special attention we received from our mother, our annual shopping trip was something we looked forward to throughout the year.

✿ ✿ ✿

Of all the many holidays on the Chinese calendar, none is as significant as New Year's. The two-week holiday begins on the first lunar new moon of the year and ends fifteen days later, and centers around celebrations with family, friends, and food. But it's really all about renewal and optimism for the future.

New Year's preparations in the Sun household began early in the fall, when my mother would work with her butcher to choose two very special pigs for slaughter. The legs were cured for ham, and sausages were made from the trimmings. Several weeks before the holiday, she hung ducks and chicken to air-dry, then pickled cabbage and chard. But in the days immediately preceding New Year's, Um-ma, who approached every meal as if she were serving it to the emperor, went from a woman obsessed to a woman possessed. Not only did the pantry need to be stocked for two-weeks' worth of meals because shops and restaurants closed during the two-week holiday, the house had to be spotless to assure us all good luck for the New Year. Instead of dreading the thought of endless preparations, she seemed energized by it. Like an army general leading her troops to battle, Um-ma began by directing the servants in the cleaning of house, personally making sure that every floor tile was polished to a reflective sheen, and every cranny and crevice did not have even a speck of dust.

Once assured that her house was immaculate, she would start shopping for the New Year's Eve banquet, probably the most important task of all. While most of the year she left the job to our Number One cook (the *da-shiu-fu*, or master chef), New Year's Eve was just too important to entrust to anyone else. Transported by rickshaw, with two servants to help her walk, and sometimes her *ya-tou* or one of her daughters at her side to help carry the packages, my plump mother made her way around the winter market, tottering from vendor to vendor in search of Beijing's best meat, fish, fowl, and produce.

From the attention she received, you would have thought she was the only shopper at the market. "Madame Sun. It's so good to see you today. I have some winter bamboo shoots, cut just this morning." First, she smelled a shoot and then squeezed it to see how firm it was.

"Do you have any others? These are too old," she declared.

The fishmonger would be similarly solicitous. "Sun Lao Tai-Tai. Let me help you choose the fish for your wok." Um-ma would point to the fattest fish swimming in the barrel, and the man would scoop it up into a net and hold it out to her for inspection.

"Yes, this one is good. Nice and lively. Do you have time to clean it for me?" she'd ask, already knowing the answer.

"For you, of course. It's my pleasure."

I can't imagine that there was any food to be had in the province, maybe anywhere in all of China, that was better than what graced our New Year's Eve banquet table.

Dressed in an intricately embroidered burgundy silk cheongsam, black hair austerely but elegantly brushed back, and with only her finest pearl earrings and a dark jade dragonfly brooch as accessories, she commandeered the servants, and she and my father graciously greeted everyone as we gathered in the living room.

Sadly though, and I'm sure it was on my mother's mind, not everyone in my immediate family was there. My Numbers One and Two sisters, Ning and Yi, were living with their husbands and children in Yunnan Province. Xiu-Ji, my Number One brother, was an engineer living in Tangshan in Hebei Province with his wife, the temperamental Quan-Quen. Ling, my Number Four sister, Qin's twin, had died of tuberculosis three years before. Ling's picture was displayed in the candlelit altar room with those of other deceased relatives, even our grandparents, as well as one of our youngest sisters, Number Nine daughter, my mother's last child, who died before she was five of meningitis. Even with an uncle and several cousins in attendance, the banquet that year was considerably smaller than usual. For me, it happily meant that for the first time I would not have to sit at one of the extra tables usually brought into the dining room. Finally, my younger sister, Jing, and I were seated at the rosewood dining table with the rest of the family.

The dining room was cast in a romantic scarlet glow from all the red candles and red banners hanging from the ceiling. Quickly, we found our places at the table, set with our best porcelain plates, crystal wineglasses, and Um-ma's treasured ebony chopsticks with the silver tips. My mother briskly clapped her hands, and the servants began to bring in the first courses of our carefully orchestrated dinner.

Um-ma was strictly traditional when it came to the order of service, so our New Year's Eve banquets varied little from year to year. Actually, we probably would have been concerned, maybe even slightly alarmed, if they had, because tradition is, above all, reassuring.

Our banquets invariably began with the arrival of six or eight small, cold, salty dishes and the first of the many glasses of warm wine served throughout the meal, all designed to awaken our appetites, not dull them. In the center of the table were carefully arranged small tasting portions of red-cooked chicken wings, smoked fish, and some of my mother's thinly sliced home-cured ham, along with two or three vegetable dishes, which included tofu in one of its many guises.

My mother, like all good cooks everywhere, allowed herself a little flexibility in terms of the menu, so that she could find out what was freshest at the market. That year there were two dishes we had not seen before, at least not that I could remember. One was a jellied loaf of braised lamb wrapped in pork skin, thinly sliced and served with green chives and a homemade sweet bean sauce. It was delectable. Though I've tried, I've never been able to duplicate it. The other was spicy daikon radish—just the peel—shredded and tossed with a little salt, sugar, and minced green onion.

Individual bowls of steaming hot shark's fin soup were brought in next, and the room immediately fell silent as everyone intently focused on the exquisite delicacy placed before them. Um-ma's version was perfect. The translucent, almost hairlike strands of the fin were floating in an amber meat broth, aromatic with unseen ginger and glistening with just a few tiny beads of fat.

As we were all trying to slurp down the very last drops of broth from our soup bowls, more courses came out of the kitchen. First were shrimp from Tianjin (a city on the coast famous for their seafood), steamed Shanghai style with Shaoxing wine and ginger, and then Three-Shreds, a stir-fry of thinly sliced chicken breasts, abalone, ham, and fresh bamboo shoots.

After the shrimp and Three-Shreds, there were three more dishes: sea cucumbers, which had been laboriously reconstituted over several days from their dried state and then stewed; chicken braised with smoky chestnuts in sandpot casseroles; and water spinach sautéed with long-life noodles. But like turkey or sweet potatoes at Thanksgiving, our Chinese New Year's Eve feast would not have been complete if we didn't have two of my mother's Shanghai specialties—a whole red-cooked pork shoulder, and, finally, steamed whole fish with ginger threads and green onions. *Fish* in Chinese is *yu*, which sounds the same as the word for *abundance*, or "more than enough," and is the perfect way to end a meal—with symbolic leftovers to take into the next year.

The meal concluded quickly in spite of all the many dishes, after no more than a couple of hours. Bowls containing fruit—dried apricots, persimmons, and kumquats, served for their lucky gold color—were passed around. Then we had one last dish, a dessert of sticky rice balls in fermented rice wine. We were sated, relaxed, and happy from all the wine we had during the course of the banquet (New Year's was the one time of the year that we all, even the children, drank wine during dinner). Everyone moved into the parlor where, while we ate, a large table had been set up and covered with red paper marked with numbers, along with teacups of dice and small sacks of coins.

It's a well-known stereotype that Chinese people love to gamble, but my parents were an exception. While most of their friends enjoyed lively weekly mah-jongg parties, my mother and father preferred to spend their evenings quietly reading in the parlor when they weren't going to the opera or out to dinner. But once a year, on New Year's Eve, we got to play games. And Ah-ba. He acted as the dealer, and it always amazed me how much he enjoyed watching us have fun. We'd all collect around the table and place our bets on the numbers. Then Ah-ba would hand someone a teacup of dice, which would be shaken and turned out onto the table, followed by whoops and hollers from the winners and groans from the losers. Even my mother would get into it, enthusiastically shaking her dice and then eagerly watching to see how the dice came up. If someone fell short on coins my father would cheerfully replenish their stack, not wanting anyone to go to bed without some winnings.

As he did every year when the first of the midnight firecrackers began to echo in the city streets, Ah-ba had the children (no matter our age) gather around him, and he would say, "Remember this moment. This day. This year. It will never happen again." Then he'd wish us a "Happy Birthday" as well, since everyone considers themselves a year older on New Year's Day. Um-ma always added, "And now, hopefully, you are all a year wiser."

☆ ☆ ☆

The next morning Jing and I excitedly made our way into in the parlor for the New Year's Day festivities, proudly dressed in our new cheongsams. As expected, the house was immaculate. Chinese tradition dictates that no cleaning or "sweeping" is to be done at the start of the New Year to ensure that nothing new or good is swept out with the old or bad. Since New Year's Day was the one day of the whole year the servants had off, all work had to be finished by midnight. It always amazed me, however, when we came into the parlor in the morning, that it looked as if nothing had ever occurred the night before.

Ah, the night before. Even though I was supposed to be looking to the year ahead, there was something bothering me. While in most respects it seemed like every other New Year's Eve that I could recall, I couldn't shake the feeling that there had been an uneasiness, something whispered, that I had found disquieting. As relatives and friends streamed into the house for a continuation of the festivities, I bowed respectfully, wished everyone Bei Nien, a Chinese expression that can be loosely translated as "Good Luck and Best Wishes," and tried to figure it all out.

Bamboo Brother (my cousin who spent a great deal of time with our family after his mother died), Big Uncle Qui Bou's Number One son, had made the trip from Shanghai where he was working at the Park Hotel. The fact that he had come such a long way just for New Year's made me suspicious, all the more so when I caught him in an animated discussion with my father and uncles in the parlor just before dinner. I was frustrated that I hadn't been able to eavesdrop.

But on New Year's Day, I was able to find a moment to speak to Bamboo Brother alone. He had gone off to the altar room by himself, and I watched as he lit an incense stick. Although he was quite a bit older than I was, the same age as my oldest brother Xiu-Ji, he was much more approachable. I knew he would answer my questions honestly and not treat me like I was just a kid sister to be patronized.

I cleared my throat first so that I wouldn't startle him. "Excuse me, Bamboo Brother, may I ask you a question?"

I got right to the point—before I could lose my nerve—and asked him why he had come all the way from Shanghai. Giving me a big smile, as if it was nothing, he said he simply missed our family. I boldly told him I thought there was more to it than that. I admitted I'd seen him in serious conversation with my father and uncles.

When he replied, there was an immediate change in his expression. Instead of a smile, his mouth grew tight except for a little twitch at the corner.

"I've been corresponding with your brother Xiu-Ji and have talked to our Uncles Ting and Xu" (my paternal aunts' husbands, who were both Nationalist generals). "We all agree that the situation here in Beijing is becoming more dangerous by the day. I've come to urge your father to move your family, at least temporarily, to Shanghai, where I think you'll all be safe."

I felt a tinge of anxiety as I started to put things together. Just a few weeks before, I had spoken to Ah-ba about some disturbing events at school, and he seemed to dismiss my concerns as insignificant.

Six years earlier, in 1931, the Japanese had invaded and occupied Manchuria, the northernmost region of China. Slowly, but steadily, they seemed to be advancing southward. In recent months, the Japanese had begun to set up garrisons around the outskirts of Beijing. I'd noticed that many of the Manchurian students who had enrolled at my high school in previous years had left. Their families, already having endured one occupation, were not going to take any chances and were fleeing farther south. When I asked my father if we might have to leave, too, he told me that the Chinese people had survived hundreds of years of wars and occupations and that life continued.

I had typical contradictory teen-aged feelings. On one hand, I was concerned for our family's welfare, and on the other, thinking about how much fun it would be to move to such a cosmopolitan city. I asked Bamboo Brother, "Do you think Ah-ba will agree to move to Shanghai?"

He hesitated for a long while before replying, as if he was trying to decide how much to divulge. Finally, Bamboo Brother said that my father believed that the Nationalists (Chiang Kai-shek's forces) were going to put up a show of military strength to protect Beijing. Even if the Japanese were to prevail and come into the city, it would only be for a short time. While my father agreed that the Japanese would never try to take Shanghai because of all the foreign concessions there, he felt it wouldn't be worth all the trouble to move the family for what would probably only be a few months.

Bamboo Brother and I looked at each other and realized there was no more to discuss. My father had made his decision.

I said, "Thank you so much for speaking frankly with me. I need to go back now before I'm missed."

Bamboo Brother just nodded, and I went off to join the rest of my family in welcoming our guests.

Perhaps Ah-ba expressed his true concerns with the men in the family, but to me it seemed he cared little for politics and simply wanted to insulate himself and his family from the world outside our home. I didn't understand it at the time, but now I think that maybe he'd lived through too many changes, seen too many wars, and figured that this was just another upheaval we'd weather. Usually, I found Ah-ba's untroubled view of the world reassuring, but at that moment, for the first time in my young life, I doubted my father's judgment and felt true fear.

Six months later, in July of 1937, after an incident at Beijing's Marco Polo Bridge, full war broke out. Generalissimo Chiang Kai-shek, quickly realizing that his forces were about to lose, surrendered control of Beijing to the Japanese and then dispatched his best troops to protect Shanghai and Nanjing (the Nationalist capital of China), leaving us at the mercy of the Japanese troops.

MEATS

What would Chinese civilization have done without the pig? This most maligned of animals has kept whole generations of people alive. Of course, fish and fowl and soybeans, too, have supplied us with protein, but most of all it was the pig that kept us fed throughout periods when nothing else was available. Scholars have found evidence that indicates that as early as 8,000 B.C., wild boars were domesticated in Asia, and for centuries we have used every part of the pig, from snout to tail, to feed us. In Chinese dialects, the words for meat and pork are synonymous, and the Chinese character for *home* depicts a roof with a pig underneath it. In 4000 B.C., the emperor of China, recognizing this important food source, decreed that everyone in the realm had to raise and breed pigs. Now, it's estimated that there is one pig for every three people in China.

In spite of the Chinese love affair with the pig, we do eat meat other than pork. In northern China, which is mostly Muslim, the eating of pig is forbidden. There, lamb, sheep (mutton), and goat are the meats of choice. Beef was popular as well, but since grazing area was limited, draft animals would only be slaughtered after they had become too old to work. Today, beef has become almost ubiquitous, particularly in modern urban areas.

The Chinese approach to meat as part of a meal, however, stands in direct contrast to Western preferences, and to my mind is much healthier. Except at our New Year's banquets, when my mother would often serve a whole red-cooked pork shoulder or a roast suckling pig, meat is usually relegated to a supporting role. In China, you would never see a big steak plopped down on a plate. I remember being pretty shocked the first time I dined at an American steakhouse. "Am I really supposed to eat all this?"

I said when I saw the giant porterhouse. Chinese portions are much smaller and often are cooked in combination with vegetables.

When shopping for pork, your best source is an Asian butcher. Not only can you find cuts like pork belly and shoulder (cuts that are not normally stocked in Western markets), the meat is often fattier and therefore more flavorful (don't worry, you'll be consuming less of it). About thirty years ago or so, because of consumer demand, pig raisers began to breed leaner pigs. Then, when everyone complained about dry meat, they started injected the meat with water solutions to keep them moist. Asian butchers tend to look for producers who raise pigs with less processing. If you're buying ground pork, they will usually have two grades, one leaner than the other.

If you don't have access to an Asian market, look for a butcher that carries organic or all-natural (non-injected) pork. If you're not sure, ask them to look at the packaging from their suppliers. As for beef, I've had pretty good supermarket beef all over the country, but I prefer grass-fed when I can find it. Angus is good too.

Yun-Hui's (My Mother's) Red-Cooked Pork

ma ma's hong shao rou

I'VE HAD DREAMS ABOUT THIS DISH that have been so vivid that I thought I could actually smell the aroma of the meat as it was being carried from the kitchen into the dining room of our family home in Beijing. My mother was from the Shanghai region, famous for its red-cooked dishes—meat or poultry braised in rich, dark, aromatic mixtures of soy, wine, and spices—and her red-cooked pork was famous throughout our circle of family and friends. For New Year's Eve, she served a red-cooked whole pork shoulder. To this day, I think of my mother every time I cook this dish, and sometimes I think that's why I cook it so often.

✿　✿　✿

Unless you live in or near an Asian or Hispanic community, you probably won't be able to find fresh pork belly, although I have been able to special order it from my local butcher and have found mail-order sources on the Internet (see page 240). Pork belly is rich—it's really just a big piece of unsmoked bacon—so small portions are in order. (Five pounds sounds like a lot, but it shrinks at least by half.) You could also substitute pork shoulder, sometimes called pork butt. If there happens to be any pork belly left over, it's wonderful diced and tossed in a stir-fry with green beans or fried rice. As with any kind of braise, it's even better made a day or two ahead. —L.W.

Serves 6 to 8 as part of a Chinese meal or 4 to 6 as a Western-style entrée

5 pounds skin-on pork belly, as lean as possible

1 (24^1/$_2$-ounce) bottle Shaoxing wine

2-inch piece unpeeled fresh ginger, cut into
    6 rounds

1^1/$_2$ cups regular soy sauce

2 chunks rock sugar, or 3 tablespoons granulated
    sugar

2 tablespoons dark soy sauce

Cut the pork into 1^1/$_2$-inch cubes. Put them in a large saucepan or enameled cast-iron casserole, and add water to cover the meat by 1 inch. Bring the liquid to a boil over high heat, decrease the heat to medium-low to maintain a lively simmer, and cook 5 minutes, or until the foaming diminishes. Transfer the pork to a sieve or colander and rinse well with cold water. Discard the cooking liquid.

Rinse out the saucepan and add the pork, wine, ginger, and enough cold water to cover the meat by 2 inches. Bring the liquid to a boil over high heat, decrease the heat to maintain a low simmer, and cook until the pork seems slightly tender when pierced with a fork, about 45 minutes. Add 1 cup of the regular soy sauce; if it doesn't cover the meat, add the remaining ^{1}/$_2$ cup. Continue to cook until the meat is completely fork-tender, about 30 minutes longer.

Gently stir in the rock sugar and dark soy sauce until the sugar dissolves. Simmer 5 minutes more, or until the sauce is slightly thickened and shiny.

Serve in a large decorative bowl, or family style from the casserole.

Mongolian Lamb

cong bao yan rou

LAMB IS NOT THOUGHT OF AS a meat commonly used in Chinese cooking, but there is a large Muslim population in China that does not eat pork. Lamb (and mutton) is quite popular in northern China, where it was first introduced by the Mongols. One of our Beijing cooks made this quick stir-fry for family meals. It's a dish I still turn to when I want an elegant, but simply pre-pared dish for guests. At the restaurant, we served steamed buns alongside the lamb, but at home I usually serve it with rice or stuffed into soft pita breads.

✿ ✿ ✿

Cecilia used to use a leg of lamb for this dish, but if you're only serving a few people, a whole leg is much too big. Butchers have recently been selling just the top round of the leg, which, at about one pound, is perfect for a small gathering. The lamb top round, also called a lamb top or butterball, is one piece of muscle, making it easy to slice. It's also very tender, perfect for quick cooking. —L.W.

Serves 6 to 8 as part of a Chinese meal and 4 to 6 as a Western-style entree

1¼ pounds boneless leg of lamb, preferably in one piece cut from the top round

1 tablespoon soy sauce

1 tablespoon vegetable oil

1 tablespoon oyster sauce

1¼ teaspoon freshly ground white pepper, or more to taste

1 bunch green onions, shredded

1 tablespoon peanut or vegetable oil

Cilantro sprigs, for garnish

So the lamb is easier to slice, freeze it for 30 minutes or so to firm it up. Slice the frozen meat diagonally against the grain ⅛ inch thick, and then cut the slices into 1 inch by 2-inch pieces.

TO MARINATE THE LAMB, stir together the soy sauce, oil, oyster sauce, and pepper in a bowl; taste for seasoning, adding more pepper, if necessary. Add the lamb and stir so that all the pieces are well coated. Stir in half of the shredded green onions. Set the lamb mixture aside to marinate at room temperature for up to 2 hours, or overnight in the refrigerator. Refrigerate the remaining green onions, covered, until you're ready to cook the meat.

Heat a large wok over high heat until a bead of water dances on the surface and then evaporates. Add the oil and swirl to coat the pan. Add the lamb, spreading it out, and let it sear for a minute or so without stirring. Toss in the remaining green onions and stir 2 minutes more, or until the meat's just cooked through.

To serve, turn out onto a platter and garnish with cilantro sprigs.

Lion's Head

yang zhou shi zi tou

IT'S AN OLD AND OFT-REPEATED STORY that this dish—a big, round meatball surrounded by cabbage and noodles—got its name from its resemblance to the shaggy mane of a lion. (The Chinese language is nothing if not descriptive.) However it was named, I love this dish because it's one my mother made a lot. Lion's Head is a Shanghai specialty, although two towns with a friendly rivalry, Wuxi (my parents' hometown) and neighboring Yangchou, also claim to have invented the dish. Yangchou, I have to admit, has recently become something of a food-lover's destination. The food of Shanghai and its region is renowned for deeply flavored, slow-cooked and braised dishes. Although Lion's Head is a rustic and hearty home-cooked dish, I used to serve it at banquets at The Mandarin, particularly to Shanghainese expatriates, who, like me, missed it terribly.

✿ ✿ ✿

Cecilia, the traditionalist, likes to use a cleaver to chop the meat by hand. For simplicity and ease, it's just fine to use ground pork from your butcher. Although she likes pork that is on the fatty side, and that's what we use in a number of recipes, here I like it a little more lean so that fat doesn't leach into the broth. The cabbage cooks down considerably, so add more if you'd like. —L.W.

Serves 6 to 8 as part of a Chinese meal and 4 to 6 as a Western-style entrée

1 large head (about 1¹/₂ pounds) napa cabbage

4 ounces bean-thread (cellophane) noodles

1 pound lean ground pork

¹/₄ cup (about 4 ounces) drained and finely minced canned water chestnuts

1 tablespoon minced green onions, white part only

1 tablespoon peeled, minced unpeeled fresh ginger

3 teaspoons kosher salt

3 tablespoons premium soy sauce

1 tablespoon Shaoxing wine

¹/₂ teaspoon freshly ground white pepper

Peanut or vegetable oil, for frying

1¹/₂ cups Delicious Chicken Broth (page 57)

¹/₂ cup water

Trim off the root end of the cabbage head and reserve. Quarter the leaves lengthwise and then cut them again crosswise into thirds. Set aside.

TO PREPARE THE NOODLES, pour hot water over the bean-thread noodles in a bowl, and let them soak until they are soft, about 15 minutes. Keep the noodles in the water until ready to use, as they tend to dry out quickly.

TO FORM THE MEATBALLS, combine the pork, water chestnuts, green onions, ginger, 2 teaspoons of the salt, 1 tablespoon of the soy sauce, wine, and white pepper in a bowl. Using your hands, gently mix all of the ingredients together until well combined. Don't overmix, or the pork will become gummy. Lightly oil a rimmed baking sheet. Using a ¹/₂-cup measure, loosely form the pork into 4-ounce balls and place them on the prepared baking sheet. Set aside.

Line a plate with paper towels and have it ready near the cooktop. Heat a large nonstick skillet over high heat until a bead of water dances on the surface and then evaporates. Cover the bottom of the skillet with a thin film of the oil and swirl to coat. Arrange the meatballs in a single layer in the bottom of the pan, but do not overcrowd them (depending on the size of your pan, you might need to cook the meatballs in several batches). Decrease the heat to medium and cook the meatballs, turning with tongs to cook evenly, until all sides are well browned, about 6 minutes. Transfer the meatballs to the prepared plate. Repeat this process for as many batches as needed.

Put the reserved root ends of the cabbage in the bottom of a large saucepan. Gently place the meatballs on top, and pour over the chicken broth and the 1/2 cup of water. Bring the pot to a boil over high heat, decrease the heat to medium-low, and simmer the mixture, uncovered, until it has cooked down a bit, about 5 minutes. Add the cut-up cabbage leaves and the remaining 1 teaspoon of salt. Cover the pot with a tight-fitting lid and continue to simmer until the meatballs are cooked through and the cabbage is tender, about 10 minutes more.

Drain the noodles, add to the saucepan with the remaining 2 tablespoons of soy sauce, and stir to combine well. Remove the pan from the heat.

To serve, arrange the meatballs on top of the cabbage and noodles on a platter. Serve immediately.

Sichuan Twice-Cooked Pork

hui guo rou

THE FIRST TIME I HAD THIS SICHUAN DISH was in Chongqing, and I instantly became addicted to it. It's so spicy, so filling, and so good. My Uncle Ting's chef used to make it as a one-pot dish to serve a lot of people, using leftover pork belly to be thrifty. I served it at The Mandarin, but used pork loin because at the time people were afraid of fatty pork. The best way to prepare it is the real Sichuan way, with pork belly, which is now more widely available.

✿　✿　✿

I have to say, this is one of my favorite recipes in the book. Definitely use pork belly. If it makes you nervous doing so, there's a lot of evidence out there now that suggests that pork fat is not bad for you. It may be even good for you, in small quantities, of course, and that's key here: small quantities. (Pieces of pork shoulder, or butt, can be successfully substituted, although I admit that reluctantly.) —L.W.

Serves 6 to 8 as part of a Chinese meal and 4 to 6 as a Western-style entrée

1 1/2 pound piece pork belly, skin-on or off, as lean as possible

2-inch piece unpeeled fresh ginger, lightly smashed

2 tablespoons peanut oil

4 thinly sliced garlic cloves

2 green onions, green part only, halved lengthwise and cut into 2-inch pieces

1 teaspoon black bean sauce

1/4 teaspoon chili oil (page 5)

1/4 teaspoon soy sauce

1 1/2 leeks, white part only, quartered lengthwise and cut crosswise into 2-inch pieces

1 red bell pepper, seeded and cut in 1-inch squares

Put the pork in a medium saucepan and add water to cover it by 1 inch. Bring to a boil over high heat and cook about 2 minutes. Transfer the pork to a sieve or colander and rinse well with cold water. Discard the cooking liquid.

Rinse out the pan and add the pork, ginger, and enough cold water to cover by 1 inch. Return the pan to the burner and simmer over medium-low heat 45 minutes. Remove from the heat and let the pork sit in the liquid for 15 minutes.

Remove the pork from the pan, transfer it to a bowl, and discard the liquid. Refrigerate the pork, covered, until firm and thoroughly chilled. Using a sharp knife, halve the pork crosswise; slice it into thin (about 1/8-inch-thick) pieces.

Heat a large wok over high heat until a bead of water dances on the surface and then evaporates. Add the peanut oil, swirl, and add the sliced pork. Stir constantly 1 minute to coat with oil. Toss in the garlic, green onions, black bean sauce, chili oil, and soy sauce. Stir to combine well and stir-fry 1 minute more. Add the leeks, cook for 1 1/2 minutes, and then toss in the red bell pepper and cook 30 seconds. Transfer the pork mixture to a platter and serve immediately.

Mandarin Oxtails

hong shao niu wei

I THINK IT'S A SHAME THAT OXTAILS are so under-appreciated here in the United States. In China, they're almost a delicacy, since there's only one tail per animal. If cooked slowly, oxtails emerge from their gelatinous braising liquid falling apart, tender, and juicy. And as any Chinese person will tell you, meat cooked on the bone is more flavorful. We often had this dish, another one of my mother's Shanghai specialties, at home in Beijing, and it was her idea to add carrots to make it a one-pot meal with rice.

☆ ☆ ☆

Oxtails don't come from oxen, but from beef cattle. If you like rich, slow-cooked meats and have never tried oxtails, you're in for a treat. I like them cut into 1¹/₂-inch chunks, but even those that are skimpier are delicious. You just have to be willing to pull the meat off with your fingers and then slurp on the bones as the Chinese do.

As with all braised meats, the oxtails benefit from being made ahead. Remove the meat and vegetables from the braising liquid and refrigerate both in separate covered containers. Before serving, you can skim the fat from the liquid. —L.W.

Serves 6 to 8 as part of a Chinese meal and 4 to 6 as a Western-style entrée

2¹/₄ pounds oxtails, cut crosswise into pieces

3-inch piece unpeeled fresh ginger, smashed

3 stalks celery, cut crosswise into 1-inch-thick pieces

¹/₂ cup regular soy sauce

3 tablespoons mushroom soy sauce

2 tablespoons Shaoxing wine

3 carrots (about 1 pound), peeled and cut diagonally into 1-inch-thick pieces

1 tablespoon sugar

Place the oxtails in a large saucepan or Dutch oven and add water to cover the meat by 1 inch. Bring to a boil over high heat and cook about 2 minutes. Transfer the oxtails to a colander and rinse with cold water. Discard the cooking liquid.

Rinse out the pan and add the oxtails, ginger, celery, and enough cold water to cover. Bring the liquid to a boil over high heat, reduce the heat to medium-low to maintain a low simmer, and cook until the meat starts to soften and shrinks from the bone, 2¹/₂ to 3 hours. Add both of the soy sauces, wine, and carrots and bring the liquid back to a boil. Reduce the heat to medium-low to maintain a simmer and cook until the meat and carrots are fork-tender, about 20 minutes. Stir in the sugar. At this point, adjust the liquid by adding additional soy sauce, sugar, or some salt to suit your palate. Remove the pan from the heat.

You can refrigerate the oxtails overnight or up to 3 days ahead at this point. To serve right away, transfer the oxtails and vegetables to a serving platter. Skim off the fat from the sauce and pour the sauce over the oxtails.

Stir-fried Beef with Snow Peas

he lan dou chao niu rou

FOR A LONG TIME I DIDN'T GET IT. What was the deal with snow peas? In the early days of The Mandarin, it seemed everyone thought they were some exotic Chinese vegetable. I'd never even tasted a snow pea until I ate them at a Cantonese restaurant with my future husband when I lived in Sichuan Province during the war. Snow peas are not grown in northern China, only in the southern part of the country, and in fact it's the Cantonese word *shui dou* that translates to "snow pea" in English.

✿ ✿ ✿

To make this dish special, you need extremely fresh snow peas. Look for ones that are smooth, unwrinkled, and slightly translucent, with only teeny-tiny pea bumps in their pods. Don't buy any that have already been stringed and cut on the ends; the processing that's required to do this makes them too old. You can tell if they're fresh if the ends crisply snap off when you bend them.

The freshly ground black pepper added just before serving wasn't something Cecilia would normally add, but was just what this simple dish needed to give it a little oomph. —L.W.

Serves 6 to 8 as part of a Chinese meal and 4 to 6 as a Western-style entrée

1 pound flank steak

3¹/₂ tablespoons peanut oil

1 teaspoon baking soda

2 teaspoons cornstarch

¹/₂ teaspoon freshly ground white pepper

Pinch of kosher salt

1 tablespoon oyster sauce

³/₄ pound (about 4 cups) fresh snow peas, ends snapped and strings removed

Freshly ground black pepper, for finishing

So the flank steak is easier to slice, freeze it for 30 minutes or so to firm it up. Halve the frozen beef lengthwise, then with your knife almost parallel to the cutting surface, slice it diagonally against the grain into thin slices, about ¹/₈ inch thick.

TO MARINATE THE BEEF, toss the slices with 1¹/₂ tablespoons of the peanut oil, baking soda, cornstarch, and white pepper in a medium bowl. Cover the bowl and let the beef marinate in the refrigerator for 1 hour.

Heat a large wok over high heat until a bead of water dances on the surface and then evaporates. Add the remaining 2 tablespoons of oil with a pinch of salt and swirl to coat the pan. Toss in the beef and cook, stirring constantly, 2 to 3 minutes, or until the beef has started to brown. Add the oyster sauce and stir to combine well. Continue to cook 30 seconds more, or until the pieces are still a bit pink. Transfer the beef to a bowl. Set aside.

Return the pan to high heat, add the snow peas, and cook 30 seconds, tossing constantly. Stir in the reserved beef and continue to cook 30 seconds more. Transfer the beef to a serving platter and sprinkle with freshly ground black pepper.

Five-Spice Beef

wu xiang niu rou

IN NORTHERN CHINA, you'll seldom see a cold platter at a banquet that does not include thin slices of spiced beef. I think of it as Chinese pot roast: a tough cut slowly simmered with spices until it becomes meltingly tender. My father used to eat this as part of his *jiu cai* (small wine dishes) before dinner. I remember that my mother would also make sure he had little cubes of the spiced cold meat "jelly" (*dong*), which is like aspic. I love it. This is a great dish for entertaining, because it really is best served cold and needs to be prepared in advance.

✿ ✿ ✿

Beef shin, a small football-shaped piece of muscle from the lower shank, is not a common cut in American markets. I've only been able to find it at Asian butchers. What works here is a solid piece of muscle that's suitable for braising. Beef bottom round would make a good substitute. —L.W.

Serves 8 to 10 as the beginning to a Chinese meal

1¼ pounds beef shin, in one piece, trimmed of fat and cut about halfway through lengthwise

6 whole star anise

2-inch piece peeled fresh ginger, lightly smashed

2 garlic cloves, peeled

4 tablespoons Shaoxing wine

¼ cup plus 2 tablespoons regular soy sauce

1 tablespoon mushroom soy sauce

2 tablespoons sugar

4 teaspoons kosher salt

¼ cup five-spice powder (page 6)

1 cinnamon stick

Dash of Asian sesame oil, for drizzling

Place the beef shin in a saucepan and add enough water to cover the beef by 1 inch. Bring the liquid to a boil over high heat, skimming off fat and foam. Decrease the heat to medium-low to maintain a strong simmer. Add the star anise, ginger, garlic, half of the wine, 2 tablespoons of the regular soy sauce, the mushroom soy sauce, and sugar, and simmer uncovered 15 minutes.

In a small bowl, mix together the remaining wine, regular soy sauce, salt, five-spice, and cinnamon stick. Add the mixture to the beef and continue to simmer, uncovered, until the beef is tender, about 2 hours. Add water until the meat is fully submerged in liquid. Taste the braising liquid and adjust the flavor, adding additional soy sauce, salt, sugar, or five-spice. The liquid should be balanced, but assertive.

When done, transfer the beef to a plate, reserve the braising liquid in a separate container, and cool all to room temperature. The beef can be served or refrigerated for up to 5 days. If refrigerating, store the beef with the reserved cooking liquid.

With a sharp knife slice the beef into very thin slices. To serve, fan the beef on a serving platter and drizzle with sesame oil and a bit of the cooking liquid.

Steamed Rice-Powder Ribs

mi fen zhen pai gu

WHEN MY SISTER AND I ARRIVED IN CHONGQING after our "long walk" from Beijing, starving and down to our last few pennies, we subsisted mainly on Sichuan's justifiably well-known and delicious street food. I clearly remember the first time we were enticed by the spicy aroma wafting from steamers piled high with this classic Sichuan dish: marinated pieces of pork or beef, coated in toasted rice powder and steamed over slices of yams or carrots. I like to use succulent baby-back pork ribs, although pork butt and sliced flank steak are traditional. If you're fond of spicy (hot) foods, add chili paste to the marinade.

✿ ✿ ✿

Although you can purchase toasted rice powder in small packages sometimes labeled as seasoned rice crumb (the ones we bought were 45 grams) from Asian markets, Cecilia likes to make her own. It keeps for months in an airtight container.

You can steam the ribs up to 1 day ahead and keep them covered in the refrigerator. Just before serving, steam them again to heat them through and sprinkle with the onions and pepper. —L.W.

Serves 6 to 8 as part of a Chinese meal and 4 to 6 as a Western-style entrée

1 slab baby-back pork ribs (about 1¼ pounds), trimmed of excess fat, halved lengthwise, and cut in pieces

2 tablespoons soy sauce

1 tablespoon Shaoxing wine

¼ teaspoon freshly ground white pepper

½ teaspoon peeled, finely grated fresh ginger (including any ginger juice)

3 carrots (about 1 pound), cut lengthwise into ¼-inch slabs, or 3 small yams, scrubbed but not peeled, and cut crosswise into ¼-inch-thick rounds

¼ cup toasted rice powder, about 2 (45-gram) packages

2 teaspoons kosher salt

Finely sliced green onions, for garnish

Freshly ground white or black pepper, for finishing

TO MAKE THE MARINADE, toss the ribs with the soy sauce, wine, white pepper, and ginger in a large bowl until well combined. Cover the bowl and let the ribs marinate in the refrigerator for at least 1 hour, or overnight. When the ribs are ready to be cooked, add the rice powder and salt to the mixture and stir to coat the ribs well.

TO STEAM THE RIBS, cover the bottom of a steamer basket with the carrot slices. Arrange the ribs on top of the carrots and place the basket over a saucepan or wok filled with a generous amount of boiling water. Maintain a vigorous boil and steam the ribs for 1 hour, covered, or until very tender.

To serve, transfer the ribs and vegetables to a large serving platter, sprinkle with green onions, and grind over fresh white or black pepper.

Chapter 6
The Too-Long Walk, Part I

EVEN NOW, ALMOST SEVENTY YEARS LATER, there are nights when I lie awake and think about how different our lives would have been if my father had only moved us to Shanghai while he still had the chance. Why didn't he? Maybe he optimistically thought Chiang Kai-shek's Nationalist forces would prevail, or naively believed nothing bad would ever happen to us because our social status granted us some kind of immunity. Everything they loved was in that house, all their possessions as well as their memories and they were at an age where starting over somewhere else would have been more than they could bear, physically and emotionally. Simply packing up, leaving, and hoping the house wouldn't be destroyed in their absence was out of the question. My father never confided in me, of course, his Seventh Daughter, so sadly, I can only guess.

All I know is that our lives changed forever one bitterly cold Beijing afternoon in 1939. About a year and a half after the Japanese took over the city, there was a loud banging at the street entrance gate to our house. Lao Li, our family's oldest, and most loyal, servant, ran down from the main part of the house to open the gate, one of his new duties since the doorman had left. Four Japanese soldiers, dressed in mustard-colored wool uniform jackets, greeted him with their bayonets drawn and pointed

---

Cecilia with sister, Teresa, 1940.

directly at him. Their leader spoke to him roughly in Mandarin, "Move aside, old man, we want to see your master's house." Sensing trouble, Ah-ba had scurried after Lao Li and was nearly knocked over as they swept inside.

My mother and I were both in the parlor reading, but Um-ma's glasses were off and she had begun to snore when the soldiers burst in and startled her awake.

"How many people live in this house, old woman?" he barked at my mother.

As if she had all the time in the world, Um-ma slowly put on her glasses, pulled herself out of the chair to reach her full four-foot, eleven-inch height, and looked directly at the soldier. I was frozen in my seat, terrified.

She cleared her throat and said, "My husband and I are two. We have three daughters still living at home and this is one of them, my daughter Number Seven. Daughters Number Five and Eight are not here this afternoon, because they're visiting friends. We continue to retain a manservant—the one who answered the door—plus two housemaids and a cook. Oh, and a rickshaw boy, who is only here part-time."

Meanwhile, father and Lao Li had arrived. My father quietly moved to my side and put his hand on my shoulder in a silent gesture of comfort.

"Do you have any food such as rice, or any valuables to declare?" growled the soldier, his bayonet pointed toward my mother.

"You may search my house. There is nothing in the pantry that we haven't bought with ration coupons. Anything of value we've sold so we can pay our daughters' school tuitions."

The leader made no reply. He motioned to the other soldiers and they left the parlor to begin their search of our house. For the most part they worked in eerie silence, occasionally knocking over tables or dumping books from shelves. Then, almost as quickly as they had appeared, they vanished, leaving broken lamps, turned-up rugs, ransacked drawers, and opened trunks in their wake. The house was a wreck, but, except for some rice in the pantry, they found nothing to take with them.

The second we heard them leave, my mother began to tremble and my father tenderly put his arms around her. In spite of the palpable fear in the room, I still always enjoyed witnessing any physical affection between them. After a minute or two, when she had recovered her composure, I said, "Um-ma, you were so brave! But where is all your jewelry? Why didn't they take it?"

"Lao Chi, I've been hiding our valuables in the house for years because I knew they, or someone else, would eventually come here looking to steal." And then defiantly she added, "So I decided to let them take our rice from the pantry. I have plenty more hidden under the altar."

I shouldn't have been surprised by my mother's cunning, but I was. She simply never ceased to amaze me. I think my father was amazed as well when she had us follow her to the altar room. There, she pulled up the tablecloth over the altar to reveal a trunk underneath, which had bags and bags of rice hidden under layers of clothes.

"The Japanese are supposed to be superstitious, so I knew they'd never touch the altar," my mother said proudly.

"But, what about your jewelry? And the gold?" I asked.

When she dismissively waved her hand, I knew I had asked one question too many.

"Don't worry. They'll never find it."

☆ ☆ ☆

Life for our family had become more restricted during the occupation—most of our servants had fled to the countryside, there were curfews, and food was becoming more difficult to buy. But, thanks to my mother's clever culinary frugality, our dwindling family was assured of meals, and my father's optimism kept us hopeful for the future.

One afternoon in 1940, it was obvious that our circumstances had changed dramatically. I rode my bike home from an afternoon of marketing to find the gate open and a number of soldiers along with some Japanese civilians in the front of the house where the now-empty servants' quarters stood. My heart almost stopped and I had to get off my bike and catch my breath. I walked my bike back to the main house, where I found both my sisters, Number Five (Qin) and Number Eight (Jing), Old Cook, and Lao Li in the kitchen with my parents. By that time, since the house rules had been relaxed, the kitchen was no longer off-limits.

I had found someone selling spinach and sweet potatoes on my way home, so I handed them to Old Cook. Everyone was quiet, and my mouth had suddenly gone dry.

Ah-ba said, "I'm glad you're here now, Number Seven daughter, so you can hear what has happened." I listened as best I could since the blood was pounding in my ears. My father explained to us in a low voice that the Japanese soldiers, on their most recent inspection, had declared our house too big for one family and were going to take it over. Um-ma, I could tell, was distraught—she had a habit of wringing her hands when she was upset. But, she was able to add that we all would have to very careful about everything we said or did or even what we ate. We would be watched, not just occasionally and in public, but constantly and in our own home.

My initial panic turned to anger at the thought of sharing our home with strangers. Enemy strangers, no less. Several Japanese civilian families made themselves comfortable in what had formerly been our servants' quarters, their children playing in the gardens. We were confined to the dining room, kitchen, and two bedrooms. Lao Li and Old Cook had to sleep in the storeroom. Qin, Jing, and I shared our bedroom with the two maids who had stayed on. My parents had the other bedroom. We felt fortunate compared to many other families, who had lost their homes entirely, but it was not easy for any of us, my mother in particular, who had to watch as her house was essentially destroyed. Within months, her once immaculate floors were scratched, and the furniture was stained and broken. My father could not keep up with the damage done to his once carefully tended gardens.

Our situation continued to worsen over the next year. At the university, I noticed that students and teachers began disappearing. On my way home from school one day, I saw soldiers removing furniture from Chu Jia-Ning's house. She and her family were neighbors of ours, and she was a friend of my Number Five sister, Qin (who like me had been given an English name at school, Teresa).

Soon many of my classmates who remained spoke clandestinely about leaving Beijing and making their way to Chongqing, where Chiang Kai-shek had moved the Nationalist government headquarters after the fall of Nanjing, his previous capital. The thought appealed to me. I had begun to hate the Japanese for what they had done to our lives, but more than that, I was well aware that it was getting harder and harder for Um-ma to creatively stretch our food rations. We had long since run out of her secret stashes of rice, and I was spending more time traveling farther distances on my bicycle to find food for us. For a couple of months I began to scheme how to get away, just as I had when I made up my mind to get a bicycle.

First, I talked Teresa into going with me. She was key because I knew my parents would never let me go alone (nor did I dare to). But Teresa was not a hard sell. She was also well aware of the burden placed upon our parents. Together we mapped out a plan. Our basic argument—that the household expenses would be eased with two fewer mouths to feed—was embarrassing for my parents, as they never would have admitted we were a burden. So we needed to give them one other reason for going that they could accept. We added that we might be able to go to Yunnan Province to see our

Numbers One and Two sisters, as well as our brother Zhen-Ji, who was teaching somewhere in that region. Teresa and I knew our parents were concerned because there had been no communication from any of them for quite a while.

When we broached the subject with my parents, my mother started to cry. But, surprisingly, she listened and really seemed to hear what Teresa and I said. For once she didn't just react automatically. Ah-ba, conversely, wasn't as receptive at first to our idea.

"I'm not so sure this is a good idea, Number Seven. You are two young women who know little of the world outside of Beijing."

"I know, Ah-ba, but we know many students, male and female, who are going and so we will find others to travel with. Also, our Uncle Ting is working in Chongqing in Sichuan Province, and he will take care of us once we get there."

He seemed to really think about what I said for quite a few moments, which made me pretty nervous. Then, my mother started wringing her hands, not a good sign.

Surprisingly, he turned to my mother and said, "The baby birds' feathers are getting dry. It's time for them to find their way in the world."

I've always wondered if he agreed to let us go because he didn't fully realize the danger we were putting ourselves in, or if our situation at home had become so desperate that he was actually relieved that there would be two fewer mouths to feed. I choose to believe the former, because at the time, I was elated. Naively, I thought it would be an adventure.

✿ ✿ ✿

Once Um-ma accepted that we were going to Chongqing, she set about with her typical zeal to make sure she prepared us well for our journey.

Almost feverishly, she began to gather clothes from storage that could be layered, garments that we could shed as the weather improved. It was also important for us to have outer, very warm cheongsams (traditional Chinese dresses), which she needed to have custom made, because not only did they have to protect us from the cold, their other major function was to hide the gold we would need to carry. My father knew that in the various provinces we would be traveling through to get to Sichuan, the Japanese had issued different paper currencies. The only common money in China was gold, which we could exchange in each province for paper money when we arrived. So, Um-ma designed ingenious cheongsams that were quilted dark cotton on the outside, like something a peasant would wear, with removable fur linings. Around the inside waist, hidden under the curly sheepskin, were one-ounce gold pieces, each stitched in such a way that with a few snips of thread they could be removed individually.

Um-ma packed everything for us in two large leather suitcases: several changes of clothes, soaps, hairbrushes, medicinal herbs, plus extra socks and pairs of shoes that she had specially sewn with comfortable padding, good for walking over rough terrain. Impractically, though, my mother also insisted we each take along a dressy outfit, including silk hose. When she was done, and each bag was only half full, I asked, "Um-ma, couldn't we just take two smaller cases, or at least put everything in one?"

"I also want you take some clothes to your sisters—they may be short of money to buy anything nice—and I have a few presents for Uncle Ting and his family."

Quickly, she had crammed both suitcases full of clothes, as well as several small vases, tea cups, silk handkerchiefs, and a few small brooches. If we'd had any food to spare, I'm sure she would have packed it, too.

✿ ✿ ✿

In January, 1942, under the cover of early-morning darkness, two hooded rickshaws, one for Teresa and one for me, pulled up to the entrance gate. While Um-ma had worried that hired rickshaws were riddled with fleas, Ah-ba argued successfully that our family rickshaws might attract too much attention. "Yun-Hui, you've gone to great lengths to disguise them as peasants, and now you want to send them to the train station in rickshaws that announce their true status?"

Ah-ba, Teresa, and I were already outside waiting on the icy street. We quickly loaded the heavy leather suitcases into the rickshaws and we hugged Ah-ba good-bye. We had already said good-bye to Um-ma, who wept the whole time she was trying to get us to eat some *congee*. She claimed she was concerned that it might be a long while before we had anything more to eat than the *bao* and dried meat she had packed for us. I suspected, though, that feeding us was the only way she knew how to express her love.

Thanks to the waning moonlight, I could make out a glint of moisture in Ah-ba's eyes. "Be well, daughters. Um-ma and I will be waiting to hear of your safe arrival in Chongqing. Send word as soon as you can. Oh, and don't talk to strangers."

I thought to myself that everyone we would meet would be a stranger.

We climbed into the rickshaws. Ah-ba sweetly tucked the quilted cotton blankets around each of us. I could see my breath as I tried to sound brave, and chattered, "Don't worry, Ah-ba. We'll look out for each other and promise to be very careful."

VEGETABLES

Like most Buddhists, my mother would cleanse her body by not eating meat twice a month, on the new moon and the full moon, as well as the entire month of the sixth lunar moon. It was healthful, and practical, since this fell during the summer, when there was a large variety of vegetables.

I love vegetables and always have, but as a child, I thought my mother odd for her vegetarian regime. Meat wasn't forbidden to us, because even during her "month of vegetables," as we called it, she still allowed it to be served at our dinners. When I arrived in Sichuan Province after the war, the first thing I thought of as we descended the steep hillsides into a basin carved out by the Yangtze River was how much my mother would have loved the view of the lush green and fertile agricultural valleys. At the sight of the abundance before her, she probably would have been thinking about how she would use that bounty in our dinner that night.

Sometimes after a busy day, I look forward to coming home to a simple stir-fry of spinach or bok choy and a few cabbage and mushroom wontons alongside a bowl of rice. It's a deeply satisfying meal that is welcome after a few days of dining indulgence.

I prepare vegetables in so many ways it was difficult for me to narrow down my recipes for this chapter. Besides that, much of what I do when I cook vegetables is so simple it's almost embarrassing. But the recipes I've included here are favorites.

Sautéed Mixed Mushrooms

chao si zheng mou gu

I ADORE MUSHROOMS OF ALL KINDS, but when I was growing up most of the mushrooms we ate were dried, which have their own special flavor. A mushroom's earthy flavor is intensified when it's dried, so I still like good-quality dried shiitakes. Today, at least in urban areas, we're fortunate to have almost year-round access to freshly gathered wild mushrooms, which make a wonderfully delicious and quick stir-fry.

✿ ✿ ✿

One variety we include here is the king-oyster mushroom, which resembles a fresh porcini because of its bulbous stem and small cap.

When sautéing mushrooms for any recipe, the key is to not crowd the pan. Cook them in small batches and use as high a heat as possible so they brown without steaming. Also, many cooks make the mistake of stirring them. Don't move them around too much in the pan; let the mushrooms sit for a minute or so to get some color. —L.W.

Serves 6 to 8 as part of a Chinese meal or 4 to 6 as a Western-style side dish

1 tablespoon Asian sesame oil

1 tablespoon premium soy sauce

2 tablespoons oyster sauce

1/4 cup plus 1 tablespoon Shaoxing wine

1/2 cup plus 2 tablespoons peanut oil

1/2 pound fresh king-oyster mushrooms, sliced 1/8 inch thick

1/2 pound fresh shiitake mushrooms, stems discarded and caps quartered

1/2 pound fresh cremini mushrooms, stems removed and caps halved

1/2 pound oyster mushrooms, halved or quartered

4 garlic cloves, thinly sliced

TO MAKE THE SAUCE, whisk together the sesame oil, soy sauce, oyster sauce, and 1 tablespoon of the wine in a small bowl. Set aside.

Heat a large wok or nonstick skillet over high heat until a bead of water dances on the surface and then evaporates. Add 2 tablespoons of the peanut oil and swirl, then add the king-oyster mushrooms and sauté, stirring and tossing every few seconds, until they have released their liquid and begin to brown. Transfer to a large bowl. Using the same pan and 2 tablespoons of peanut oil per batch, repeat the cooking process with the rest of the mushrooms, cooking each kind separately and transferring them all to the same bowl once cooked.

While the pan is still hot, immediately add the remaining 2 tablespoons of peanut oil and heat on high until shimmering. Add the garlic and cook 15 seconds, or until soft and golden, but not brown. Add the reserved mushrooms and their accumulated juices back into the pan with remaining 1/4 cup of the wine. Cook about 20 seconds, allowing the wine to evaporate slightly. Pour in the reserved sauce and toss well to combine. Immediately remove the pan from the heat. If the sauce is too thick, add a bit of water. Turn out onto a platter and serve immediately.

Asparagus with Gingko Nuts and Wolfberries

bai guo gou ji chao lu sun

UNTIL RECENTLY, ASPARAGUS HAS ALWAYS been an expensive delicacy in China and was usually saved for banquets and special occasions. When I first came to California, I was delighted to find that asparagus, particularly in the spring, was plentiful and inexpensive, allowing me to frequently indulge in one of my favorite vegetables. This is a recipe my mother would have loved for its balance of flavor and color as well as its nutritional value—the Chinese believe gingko nuts are good for the lungs, and wolfberries for the eyes.

✿ ✿ ✿

Wolfberries resemble small dried cranberries or cherries, but are not as tart or sweet as either. If they look more brown-red than red-red, pass them up because they're too old. Fresh shelled gingko nuts and pitted dried wolfberries are both sold in Asian markets, the gingko nuts in vacuum packages in the produce section, and the wolfberries in cellophane packages usually with the dried fruit and vegetables. Unfortunately, there's really no substitute for wolfberries.

Roll-cutting is a technique that I think is unique to Chinese cooking and very clever. Long vegetables are cut in a way to expose more surface area so they absorb more flavor during cooking. To roll-cut a vegetable, diagonally slice off a piece from the root end. Give it a quarter turn and make another diagonal cut into the length specified in the recipe. Continue until the whole spear has been cut into odd-shaped triangles. —L.W.

Serves 4 to 6 as part of a Chinese meal or 2 to 4 as a Western-style side dish

1¹/₂ pounds medium asparagus

2 tablespoons pitted dried wolfberries

1 (3¹/₂-ounce) package shelled fresh gingko nuts

2 tablespoons peanut oil

1 teaspoon kosher salt

¹/₄ teaspoon sugar

¹/₂ teaspoon Asian sesame oil, for drizzling

Snap off the tough ends of the asparagus and roll-cut into 1¹/₂-inch pieces.

Put the wolfberries in a small bowl, cover with warm water, and let them sit until softened, about 5 minutes. Drain and set aside.

Put the gingko nuts in a bowl, cover with boiling water, and let them sit for 3 minutes. Drain, then dry the gingko nuts and set aside.

Heat a large wok over high heat until a bead of water dances on the surface and then evaporates. Add the oil and swirl, then add the asparagus along with the salt and cook, stirring continuously, 2 minutes. Add the gingko nuts and cook 15 seconds, then add the wolfberries and cook 1 minute more; taste the asparagus for tenderness. Add the sugar and cook until the asparagus is crisp-tender. Remove from the heat.

Transfer to a platter or bowl. Drizzle with the sesame oil and serve.

Eggplant in Garlic Sauce

da suan ban qie zi

EGGPLANT IS ACTUALLY NATIVE TO ASIA, although most Westerners (particularly Italians) think it is native to the Mediterranean. There are hundreds of varieties, but when I first came to America I was astonished that the only eggplant I could find was in either in San Francisco's North Beach, the Italian community, or in Japantown, where they sold the variety I was more familiar with—the long, slender, thin-skinned kind. This dish is one I've served since the early days on Polk Street. At first, my customers had difficulty with the idea that eggplant could be served cold. Most eggplant recipes at the time were fried and served hot (dripping in oil, I might add). But this spicy version quickly won them over.

To serve the eggplant, I like to line the pieces up on a platter, drizzle with the dressing, and let my guests turn pieces in the extra dressing on the bottom of the platter before transferring them to their plates. You could also first toss the eggplant in a bowl with some of the dressing and then arrange the eggplant on a platter and pour over the remaining dressing (which is how it's written here).

☼ ☼ ☼

It's important to use Asian eggplant in this dish, either the long, thin, lilac-colored variety or the smaller purple-black ones. Both kinds have tender skin, are less bitter, and have fewer seeds than the globe eggplant Westerners are more familiar with. —L.W.

Serves 4 to 6 as part of a Chinese meal or 2 to 4 as a Western-style side dish

3 large Asian eggplants (about 1 pound)

3 tablespoons premium soy sauce

1^1/$_2$ teaspoons chili oil (page 5)

1 tablespoon Chinkiang black vinegar or good-quality balsamic vinegar

1 tablespoon minced fresh ginger

1^1/$_2$ tablespoons minced garlic

1 green onion, white and green parts thinly sliced

Trim the eggplants. Cut them lengthwise in quarters and then again crosswise in 2- to 3-inch pieces.

Fill the bottom of a steamer with water, bring the water to a boil over high heat, and set the eggplant pieces on a steamer tier (they don't need to be put on a plate first) over the boiling water. Cover and steam 4 minutes, or until soft when pressed with a chopstick. Set aside to cool to room temperature.

TO MAKE THE DRESSING, whisk the soy sauce, chili oil, vinegar, ginger, and garlic in a small bowl until combined.

To serve, toss the room-temperature eggplant in half of the dressing and arrange it on a platter. Pour over the remaining dressing. Garnish with green onion.

Mapo Dofu

cheng du ma po dou fu

AS WITH MANY FAMOUS CHINESE DISHES, this one has a story, and like the others, it's been told by so many people over so many years that you have to question its truth. Legend has it that Mapo Dofu is named for an old pock-marked Sichuan woman, Madame Chen, who owned a restaurant where people came from far and near to sample her special tofu (in Mandarin, *dofu*) in meat sauce. When I lived in Sichuan, where I tasted Mapo Dofu for the first time, it was a dish served just about everywhere—at restaurants as well as at home—because it's cheap, nutritious, and filling if accompanied by rice. It's also really tasty, so really, does the story even matter?

✿ ✿ ✿

Tofu is made by a number of producers. Find a brand you like; just make sure it's the silken type for this recipe. Cecilia and I like Azumaya brand, which is consistent in quality and available throughout the country.

The quality of chili oil here is just as important as the quality of the tofu. The best chili oil is the kind you make yourself, but if you have to use the commercial stuff, make sure it's fresh and made with real sesame oil. —L.W.

Serves 4 to 6 as part of a Chinese meal or
2 to 4 as a Western-style side dish

1 teaspoon black bean sauce

1 teaspoon Shaoxing wine

1 tablespoon soy sauce

4 teaspoons minced garlic

2 tablespoons peanut oil

1/4 pound ground pork shoulder (pork butt)

1/4 cup (about 1 ounce) minced *zha cai*

16 ounces silken tofu, water drained off and cut into 1 by 2-inch cubes

1 teaspoon chili oil (page 5)

Pinch of ground Sichuan peppercorns or white pepper

1 tablespoon minced green onion, plus a little extra for garnish

TO MAKE THE SAUCE, whisk together the black bean sauce, wine, soy sauce, and 1 teaspoon of the garlic in a small bowl. Set aside.

Heat a large wok over high heat until a bead of water dances on the surface and then evaporates. Add the oil and swirl to coat the pan. Add the pork and stir constantly, breaking the meat apart with a spoon. Toss in the remaining 3 teaspoons garlic with the *zha cai*, and continue to cook until just a trace of pink remains in the pork, about 2 minutes. Using a spoon, very gently add the tofu to the pan. Quickly stir in the reserved sauce, then the chili oil, and top with Sichuan pepper and 1 tablespoon of the green onion. Immediately remove from the heat.

To serve, transfer to a serving platter and garnish with the remaining minced green onion.

Shanghainese Winter Bamboo Shoots

shanghai you men sun

I CAN'T EVEN DESCRIBE TO SOMEONE who has never tasted fresh bamboo shoots the difference from those that are canned. It's like trying to describe the difference between a canned pea and a sweet pea freshly picked from the garden. And just like most American urban housewives in the early 1960s who could only get canned peas, the only bamboo shoots available to me when I owned The Mandarin were the ones in cans. Then, about two years ago, I began to see fresh bamboo shoots in Asian markets. Bamboo shoots have a short season, in which the best—the sweetest ones—are grown during winter. Olivia Wu, a wonderful food writer for the *San Francisco Chronicle* who is originally from Shanghai, became teary-eyed over a platter of sautéed winter bamboo shoots when she came to my house for dinner. "These are just like my mother's, and I haven't tasted anything like this in a long time. I must be a little homesick."

✿　✿　✿

See Long-Life Noodle Soup (page 63) for information on buying and preparing fresh bamboo shoots. —L.W.

Serves 4 to 6 as part of a Chinese meal and 2 to 4 as a Western-style side dish

2 tablespoons peanut or vegetable oil

2 cups (about 8 ounces) fresh winter bamboo shoots, trimmed and cut into 1/4 by 1/4 by 2-inch pieces

1 teaspoon peeled, minced fresh ginger

2 tablespoons Shaoxing wine

2 tablespoons premium soy sauce

1 teaspoon sugar

Pinch of kosher salt

Heat a large wok over high heat until a bead of water dances on the surface and then evaporates. Add the oil and swirl to coat the pan. Add the bamboo shoots, spreading them out in a single layer. Reduce the heat to medium-high, and turn the bamboo shoots after 2 minutes, again spreading them out in a single layer. Cook 2 minutes more.

Toss in the ginger, stir to combine with the bamboo shoots, then add the wine and cook until the liquid is reduced by half. Stir in the soy sauce and sugar and continue to cook until the sauce is glossy and coats the bamboo shoots.

Spread the bamboo shoots on a plate to cool, then cover and refrigerate until well chilled. Arrange on a platter and serve cold.

Hot-and-Sour Cabbage

snan la bai cai

IF YOU COME TO MY HOUSE tomorrow and look in my refrigerator you'll be sure to find this Hot-and-Sour Cabbage. My mother made a version that was more sour than hot to help us get through the cold Beijing winters. Later on, during the Japanese occupation, cabbage, both dried and pickled as in this recipe, helped keep us fed. Then, when I lived in Sichuan, I discovered preserved cabbage that was similar to what my mother made, but bathed in chili oil. At The Mandarin we used to serve Hot-and-Sour Cabbage as a small dish or starter. It pairs nicely with Champagne.

✿ ✿ ✿

This is a great use for older cabbage because the tougher leaves stand up quite well and stay crunchy. On that same note, Cecilia doesn't like to shred the cabbage too finely so that it retains some texture after sitting.

Unless you're working on a commercial stove, you need to prepare this recipe in at least two batches, as we've done here. If your burners don't put out a lot of heat or you only have small-to-medium skillets, divide the recipe into thirds or even fourths for cooking. —L.W.

Makes about 4 cups

1 large head napa cabbage (about 2 pounds)

2 tablespoons kosher salt

$1/3$ cups peanut or vegetable oil

12 to 15 dried red chile peppers

$1/2$ cup white vinegar

$1/2$ cup sugar

$1/4$ cup chili oil (page 5)

Halve the cabbage lengthwise, put each half cut-side down, and halve each piece again lengthwise. Cut the quarters crosswise in thirds so you have 12 pieces. Cut each piece again crosswise into shreds a little wider than $1/4$ inch. Put the cabbage into a large colander and sprinkle with 1 tablespoon of the salt. Let sit 30 minutes.

While the cabbage rests, stir together the vinegar and sugar in a small bowl and set aside near the cooktop.

Heat half of the oil in a large wok or skillet over high heat until it just begins to shimmer. Add the remaining 1 tablespoon of salt and toss in half of the chiles, stirring about 10 seconds. Add half of the cabbage, tossing and stirring for about 1 minute, or until the cabbage has just begun to wilt and is combined with the hot oil. Stir in half of the vinegar mixture and half of the chili oil and cook for 30 seconds. The whole process should take no longer than 2 minutes. Turn the cabbage out into a large bowl. Return the pan to the heat. Repeat the cooking process with the remaining cabbage and add it to the bowl with the first batch of cabbage.

Put the cabbage into 1 large or several smaller containers that will hold the cabbage snugly and keep it submerged in the liquid. Refrigerate for up to 2 weeks and let come to room temperature before serving.

Spinach in Sesame-Seed Paste

zhi ma ziang ban bo cai

WHEN WE ESCAPED TO JAPAN IN 1949, I thought we were going to starve to death. The country was still devastated from the war, and foodstuffs were in meager supply and strictly rationed. Not only that, I thought raw food was repulsive—everything that had touched my lips to that point had been preserved or cooked. At the time I barely even knew how to make tea. All that changed, though, when we hired a Chinese cook I could talk to. Together, she and I would go to the market, buy some fish and vegetables, and then return home to make a few simple, comfortingly familiar Chinese dishes. Eventually, and on a full belly, I began to try more Japanese food, beginning with the cooked things. One of the first things I tasted was Horenso no Goma-A (Spinach with Sesame Dressing), which, to this day, I still love to order in Japanese restaurants, to go along with my sashimi, of course. This is my Chinese version of that dish.

☼ ☼ ☼

Since there are so few flavors in this dish, it's of utmost importance that the spinach is fresh. Also, there's nothing worse than biting into this lovely dish and tasting even a speck of grit. Make sure your spinach is well washed in several changes of water. Although you can use bags of prewashed spinach, sometimes the loose kind is fresher. —L.W.

Serves 6 as part of a Chinese meal or 4 as a Western-style first course or side dish

1 tablespoon sesame seed paste

1 tablespoon Asian sesame oil

1 teaspoon sugar

2 teaspoons rice vinegar

1 1/2 tablespoons premium or regular soy sauce

2 large bunches very fresh spinach, stemmed and well washed

1 tablespoon toasted sesame seed for garnish

FOR THE DRESSING, whisk together the sesame seed paste, sesame oil, sugar, vinegar, and soy sauce until the sugar is dissolved. Set aside.

Fill a large bowl with ice water and have it ready near the cooktop.

Bring a large pot of generously salted water to a boil over high heat, and drop in the spinach. As soon as the spinach wilts (2 to 3 seconds), quickly scoop it out using a wire skimmer and drop into the bowl of ice water.

Drain the spinach in a colander and squeeze it dry by hand or with a potato ricer to remove as much liquid as possible.

Put the spinach in the bowl with the sesame-soy mixture and stir so that all the leaves are well coated. Serve at room temperature, garnished with a sprinkling of toasted sesame seed.

Three-Shredded Salad

leng ban san si

I HAVE A FRIEND NAMED BILL WHO, along with his wife Linda, owns an authentic and critically acclaimed Sichuan restaurant called South Legend in Milpitas, California. He is a very dedicated and knowledgeable young man who takes pride in the cuisine of his native province and is also a very talented cook. During a multi-course dinner at his restaurant, he served us this pretty and refreshing salad—a welcome respite from all the spicy dishes—which was light and crisp and had just enough acid in the dressing to balance out all the other flavors of the menu.

✿　✿　✿

For the prettiest presentation, the vegetables should be cut with a mandoline. I know a number of accomplished cooks who get nervous at the thought of using a mandoline, so here are some suggestions: Use the largest vegetables you can find, then cut on the outside of the food, rotating the vegetable as you cut so all you're left with is the core or a section that just includes the seeds. Rather than use the guard, which can be awkward, protect your fingers with a mitt or towel when holding the vegetable. One other suggestion: Several manufacturers make peelers that create julienne pieces. These tools are quite nifty, particularly if you have a pile of carrots to cut. —L.W.

Serves 4 to 6 as part of a Chinese meal and 4 to 6 as a Western-style side dish

2 tablespoons premium soy sauce

2 tablespoons Chinkiang black vinegar or balsamic vinegar

2 tablespoons rice vinegar

1 1/2 tablespoons Asian sesame oil

1 1/4 teaspoons sugar

2 cups peeled and julienned carrots

2 cups peeled and julienned daikon radish

2 cups peeled and julienned cucumber

TO MAKE THE DRESSING, whisk together the soy sauce, vinegars, sesame oil, and sugar in a small bowl and set aside.

For a special presentation, arrange the vegetables in three separate piles on a platter and drizzle a little of the dressing over each pile, then toss the vegetables together tableside. Alternatively, if serving family style, simply toss the vegetables and dressing in a bowl until well combined.

Chapter 7
The Too-Long Walk, Part II

AS I LISTENED TO THE ICE-HARDENED snow crunching under the wheels of the rickshaw, I was afraid, but I was in control of my own destiny.

I felt a shiver of fear when I realized Teresa and I were amongst just a handful of female Chinese civilians in a train station full of Japanese soldiers, but the blue-and-white cotton peasant scarves and dark cheongsams helped us blend in. No one noticed us. A porter loaded our large suitcases into the back of the train, and we made our way through several crowded, smoky cars to find our first-class seats, the ones Ah-ba had purchased for us. They were together, that was the good part. But the seats were made of wood and the small cushions did little to make them more comfortable. We counted our blessings, when we realized that anyone not in "first class" was standing.

I don't remember much of the two-day train ride from Beijing to Xuzhou. Teresa and I were exhausted from preparing for the trip and the emotional good-byes. We slept most of the way, waking up only occasionally to buy some tea on the train to sip with the *bao* and snacks Um-ma had packed for us.

Train travel ended abruptly in Xuzhou, a town about 400 miles from Beijing. Departing the train, groggy and disoriented, we discovered that in spite of being at the

Cecilia with Qi Ze Lin wearing her cheongsam from The Long Walk, 1944.

junction of four provinces, Henan, Anhui, Jiangsu, and Shandong, wartime rail service had been disrupted so that there were no trains traveling west toward Chinese-occupied territory. Our only option, short of returning to Beijing, was to walk. Even though we were discouraged and very scared, we chose to just keep moving.

"My God," I still ask myself, "what were we thinking?" We were two very sheltered young women—I was twenty-two and Teresa twenty-eight—who had traveled no farther in their lives than just a few hours from Beijing. The only answer I have—and believe me that I've thought a lot about it—is fairly simple. We were astoundingly naive and blinded by youthful invincibility. We carried no maps, nor had even really looked at a map of China at school, so we didn't fully appreciate how far we had to travel to get to Chongqing. We somehow trusted that we would find people to guide us, and none of us had any concept of the havoc wreaked by the war on our country.

At the busy rail station in Xuzhon, we found someone we could pay to carry our bags. The wiry little man took out a rope, cinched our two suitcases together, strapped them onto his back, then amazingly walked several miles south with us until we reached a small village. From there we were able to find someone with a cart to accompany us to another small village. And so we went for days, slowly working our way west, village to village, hiring someone in each place with a cart or a wagon.

My sister and I ended up walking for about two weeks, then crossed into Henan Province, finally arriving in Shangqui, a small village where we stayed the night at a little inn. The next morning, we hired a man to pull a cart with our bags. Not far from town, two Japanese soldiers on horseback stopped us.

I had been forced to learn some Japanese at school after the occupation of Beijing, but I didn't need to know their language to understand the men wanted our bags. Bayonets speak louder than words. The man pulling our cart stood mute and shaking. While one of the soldiers strapped our suitcases onto his horse, the other soldier pointed his bayonet at us. Just as quickly as they had appeared, they took off, but not before the realization hit me that they had our bags. Absurdly, I took off after them, screaming the only Japanese curse I knew, which I thought meant something like "you sonofa turtle egg." Whatever I said though, must have meant something bad, because the soldier immediately stopped his horse, dismounted, and came toward me, screaming in Japanese and poking me with his bayonet. Teresa was terrified and came running toward us, grabbed me by the sleeve, and screamed, "What are you doing? Are you trying to get us both killed?" She jerked me away and, just like a slap in the face, I was shocked back to reality. I was so blinded by anger that I hadn't realized the dangerous position I had put us both in. The soldiers took off with our bags and probably laughed at the two young women, one of whom seemed a little crazy.

Suddenly, we were left with literally nothing but the clothes on our backs (and of course the gold pieces hidden inside). All the things my mother had so carefully packed were gone forever.

Unable to let the incident go, and determined to get our luggage, I made Teresa walk with me back to the inn. I was still angry as I spoke to the innkeeper and told him what had happened.

"I feel very bad for you. You are nice girls, but I have to tell you that I think your bags attracted the attention of someone working here," he said, "who is paid to tip off the Japanese soldiers to travelers of 'means'." His tone was apologetic and his eyes betrayed his fear as they darted across the room.

"Who was it? What is his name?" I asked. "Maybe if I, too, pay him some money he can get our bags back."

"It was the Korean, Qing Mu, but if you give him even a little money it will make him wonder if you're carrying more. I think you're better off without those bags."

Clearly I understood his meaning and asked meekly if he would put us up one more night.

❄ ❄ ❄

We left Shangqui and walked for about a week—this time without the burden of having to hire someone to help carry our luggage. We met some fellow students also headed toward Chongqing. They told us of a place they had heard about near Kaifeng where we could pay someone to help us across the border into the Neutral Zone, a two- or three-mile-wide "no-man's land" between Nationalist China and Japanese occupied territory. "Finally!" we thought. "Free China. We're almost there."

When we arrived at Kaifeng, our excitement quickly turned to horror when we found a huge mud-filled trench that stretched for miles and miles in either direction. It was at least ten feet wide and probably fifteen feet deep, dug by the Chinese to prevent the Japanese tanks from advancing into the Neutral Zone and on into Nationalist territory. The townspeople were very helpful, and discreetly directed us to a man who, for a fee, of course, could arrange to pull us over the trench with a rope. We had no alternative other than walking several more days out of our way to avoid the ominous trench, so we agreed to first pay what would have probably been the equivalent of ten U.S. dollars on one side and another ten on the other side. At the time, it seemed to me a fairly stiff price, but considering the alternative, Teresa and I decided it was worth it.

We were instructed to meet at a designated time near the trench, and watched as a young man hung on and like a gymnast pulled himself across, while two or three men stood on either side holding the rope taut. Teresa looked ashen. Just as I was going to ask for our money back, one of the men barked, "Tie her up." Teresa was quickly cinched to the rope and pulled across to the other side, where two of the men lifted her up onto the ground. I was next, and just kept my eyes shut so I wouldn't have look at the murky stew below. A few strong arms lifted me onto the other side, and it was over. I paid the men their money and we were on our way. There we were joined by a few more students who had also crossed the trench into no-man's-land. Everyone, it seemed, knew to head southeast toward Jieshou to get to Free China.

✿ ✿ ✿

For several more weeks, we walked. And walked. In each village, we would find townspeople who were eager to offer us food or somewhere to bed for the night, a few times even for free because they felt sorry for us.

The weather began to change. Earlier, we had to gather straw to strap onto our shoes so we could get across the half-frozen mud. Now, the mud quickly turned into caked earth as it started to warm up.

We were still wearing the heavy fur-lined cheongsams that held our now-dwindling gold pieces, terrified that if we removed them they would be stolen. So we were sweating, hadn't had a bath, brushed our teeth, or combed our hair, and were flea-ridden. I actually laughed when I thought about how Um-ma didn't even want us to ride in the hired rickshaw, worried that it contained fleas. What would she think if she saw us now, our bodies almost black with fleas that we futilely tried to kill with our fingers? We reached Jieshou at the end of May after traveling for almost four months from the time we left Beijing.

Teresa and I straggled into Jieshou. Our first impression was that it was like every other town and village we had been through, although a little bigger. But then we saw a larger-than-life poster—actually a billboard—of Generalissimo in his regal black cape with Madame Chiang Kai-shek by his side. The caption read "Welcome to

Free China." Tears rolled down my cheeks as weeks of unexpressed fear, anger, confusion, and exhaustion hit me all at once. My sister and I embraced and held on to each other for a long time, sobbing uncontrollably. "We made it, we made it," was the only unspoken thought that came to my mind. I wished I could tell Ah-ba.

✲ ✲ ✲

We arrived with a group of other young people at a makeshift tented student center, where we were able to sign in, take a quick tub bath, and get a cot and a hot meal—simple noodles in broth, my favorite under any circumstances. We'd been there less than twenty-four hours, talking to other students and planning the next part of our journey on to Chongqing, when two uniformed men came up to us and asked if we were the Sun sisters and pointed to our registration. "Yes, we are," I replied a little hesitantly. One of them handed me a sealed envelope. Inside was a note that read, "Sun Yun and Sun Qin, welcome to free China. Please let these officers accompany you to my house." It was signed "Qi Ze Lin."

Qi Ze Lin was an older classmate of mine in high school. I was excited, but my very next thought was that there was no way we could meet her looking the way we did. In spite of our baths, we hadn't cleaned up very well. Our faces were peeling from all the exposure to sun, wind, and dust. We were still squishing fleas with our fingers.

"No, sir, you will have to give her our regrets. We're just not in the condition to meet anyone now."

They bowed, but returned about an hour later.

"Madame Xu has asked us to respectfully tell you she will not take 'no' for an answer. Please come with us." Teresa and I looked at each other in resignation.

✲ ✲ ✲

Qi Ze Lin's Manchu lineage showed in her regal height. She was at least six years older than I, but we had been in the same class for many years. Qi Ze Lin began first grade when she was twelve years old because she had been tutored at home, an old-fashioned practice that some upper-class families continued to follow for their daughters. Some of my classmates made fun of her, not only because she was older and very tall, but because she was very deliberate in her studies, which made them think she was slow. I befriended her, and we stayed close until we parted ways in high school. Teresa and I quickly found out that Qi Ze Lin had married a Kuomintang general several years her senior, General Xu, the man in charge of patrolling the borders along the neutral zone. She had seen our names on the student register and immediately contacted us.

The minute I saw her, I forgot about how horrible I must have looked, and she certainly didn't seem to care. First she hugged me, and then Teresa. If she was concerned about fleas, she didn't let on. She did, however, immediately offer us a bath. And with it a rinse of gasoline to kill the fleas and whatever else had been infesting our hair. While someone took our clothes to be laundered (after we first removed our gold pieces), Qi Ze Lin gave us clean cotton cheongsams.

Qi Ze Lin had invited a few military couples over. After a deliciously simple dinner of stir-fried pork and cabbage with rice, we were unexpectedly treated to an impromptu mini opera when the general and two of the other men broke into song. It took us by surprise to see these serious men singing both male and female parts, and it made us giggle. Teresa and I had something to smile about for the first time in months. After retiring for the evening, we slept in real beds with sheets that were soft and smelled like the fresh air in which they had been hung to dry.

We stayed with Qi Ze Ling for more than a week. While we were there, we were introduced to another high-ranking Kuomintang officer, General Chao, an army engineer in charge of the Yellow River. He was a distinguished older gentleman who listened intently as Teresa and I told him the story of how we had traveled from Beijing on the train to Xuzhou, were robbed, crossed into the Neutral Zone, then walked for weeks before finally arriving in Jieshou. He kept shaking his head in amazement.

"All we want to do is find our way to Chongqing, where our uncle General Ting lives," I told him. "Can you help us?"

"I can't take you directly to Chongqing from here, but if you first go to my home in Xian in Shaanxi Province, my wife can take care of you for a while and help you both get your strength back. Then, I'm sure I can find you some transport from there to Chongqing."

Of course, I had no concept of how far out of the way Xian was, and was disappointed he couldn't get us directly to the current war capital, Chongqing, in Sichuan, but recognized we could no longer make this trip alone and needed to accept help wherever we could find it. I spoke for both of us when I said, "Thank you very much. We would love to take you up on the offer."

The General mapped out our route to Xian. Though we would have to spend more time walking, he said that if we stayed on the roads, we'd also be sure to find some Nationalist soldiers on the way who could give us rides.

I was glad that Um-ma was not there to see our fur-lined, flea-infested cheongsams being burned, although I had no desire to ever see them again. Qi Ze Lin gave us some new clothes for the next part of our journey, a small bag to carry some toiletries, tin cups, and chopsticks, as well as some Chinese currency (which I tried to repay her many years later, to no avail). We didn't have to use our gold pieces, since we were now in Free China and could use paper money.

✿ ✿ ✿

We left the very next day for Xian. I had thought that since we were traveling through Chinese territory, we would be safe. I was wrong. No more than two days into our trip, the army truck we were riding in stopped abruptly and the driver screamed at us to get out and run. Panicked, everyone jumped out and ran every which way. Teresa and I took off into a tall cornfield. We could hear the drone of airplanes become louder and then suddenly, a very loud pop-pop-pop-pop-pop. Dirt clods flew up around us. Instinctively, I quickly lay down between the corn rows and covered my head.

I heard Teresa calling me for several minutes, but every time I opened my mouth to call back, my teeth were chattering so badly that no words would come out. Finally I mewed, "Teresa, I'm here, I'm okay." One of the soldiers found me, helped me up, and then together we found my sister.

The three of us walked back to the truck. The young soldier, probably as shaken as we were, protectively put his arms around our shoulders. We almost stumbled over the bloodied and grotesque bodies of two soldiers from our truck lying on the side of the road; until that moment, I really had had no idea just how lucky we had been.

I had assumed that once we crossed the border into Chinese territory we were safe, that our enemies were behind us, and that we'd never see them again. How incredibly wrong I'd been. The Japanese were behind us geographically, yes, but were constantly nipping at our heels as their air force pushed farther and farther into China.

Greatly relieved, but still terrified, we experienced only one more air strafe on our trip to Xian. It didn't scare us as much as the first one had, probably because, for the entire rest of our trip, Teresa and I dove for cover the very second we heard the whirr of an airplane engine.

✧ ✧ ✧

Two days from Xian, we picked up a ride with some soldiers in a Jeep. They delivered us safely to Madame Chao's doorstep, where we spent the next two weeks being fed and doted upon. The General and his wife were childless, and for the short time we were there, the plump sweet woman made it her life's work to spoil us. And fatten us up. Meal upon meal, we were urged to eat.

Xian, the capital of Shaanxi Province in north central China, is famous for its many kinds of handmade noodles. Luckily for us, Madame Chao had a wonderful cook. I watched in fascination as he would perch a mound of dough on his shoulder and then, with his razor-sharp cleaver, shave off small pieces into a pot of boiling water. Sometimes he would spin and twirl the dough in front of our eyes like a magician, creating silky strands of thin noodles. For another one of his special noodle dishes, he would pull off pieces of dough and pinch them into little dimpled shapes called "cats' ears," which he served with sweet potatoes. In addition to noodles, we also had tofu and lots of mutton, which is common throughout Shaanxi because of its large Muslim population, which does not eat pork. One dish in particular, a kind of spicy mutton stew into which we dipped yeasty flat bread, is something I still remember. Mutton is something I've never liked, but whatever that Xian cook did with it was delicious.

At one point during our stay, General Chao came home, and while he was there tried to convince us to stay on, even going so far as to say he would adopt us.

"With all due respect, General, we have parents in Beijing."

"I understand," he said. "My wife and I will be your godparents, then."

For most of our journey to Chongqing, General Chao had made sure we had someone to ride with. It was a good thing, too, because to get to Sichuan Province basin from Shaanxi Province, you need to go south over the Qin Ling mountain range. General Chao had warned us to save our strength as we traveled over the mountains and wait until we could find a truck or Jeep, which we did, but I had little concept of a mountain. Up we went, bumping along on roads that were sometimes barely wide enough for even one vehicle. The worst times were when we'd have to get out and help push the vehicle to get it over a rocky or steep slope.

The mountain villages were desolate, and the people depressingly poor. I remember that at one point Teresa and I were hungry, so we stopped at a small place that had a few scrawny hens in front. Teresa loved eggs; it seemed she asked for them wherever we went. A man approached us and, predictably, Teresa asked him if we might buy some eggs. Curiously, he had a large, very-scary looking balloonlike growth around the front of his neck, something we'd seen on a number of other people on the mountain.

"We just sold one of the two eggs the hens laid this week. I can sell you the other for a silver dollar."

"That's more than we can afford. Do you have any noodles? Or broth? We could pay you for that," I said.

"All I have is some flour." He shrugged his shoulders and said, "You don't need to pay me."

He went away and within a few minutes came back with something I can only describe as a sandy white soup.

"What is this?" I asked.

"Flour and water. I'm sorry, it's all I can give you."

Teresa said to him as he walked away, "Can't we at least have some salt to season it?" The man just ignored us.

It's amazing what you'll eat when you're hungry. Much later I learned about the connection between iodine deficiencies and the large growths on their necks—goiters—and was embarrassed that we had asked the humble man for salt.

✿ ✿ ✿

We made our way out of the mountains from Shaanxi into Sichuan Province, where the vistas were breathtaking. I'd never seen scenery so beautiful. At the lower elevations, there were lush, terraced green hills, forests of pine and cypress, and morning blankets of valley fog. In the heat of the day, the fog would burn off to reveal farms full of corn, soybeans, and rice, and orchards with green-leafed nut and fruit trees.

Gradually, the farms were replaced by houses, the houses replaced by factories, and quickly we realized we were in the city of Chongqing, war capital of Chiang Kai-shek's Nationalist Party. I don't know what I was expecting, but the city was gray, smoky, and poor—nothing like Beijing. It was almost July and the weather had gone from comfortably warm to blazing hot and humid within what seemed like a day, but Teresa and I didn't care about either the weather or what the city looked like. We had each other, we were safe, and we had reached Free China.

NOODLES, DUMPLINGS, AND RICE

While many people may be under the impression that China is a nation solely of rice eaters, the country is actually divided into two populations: people north of the Yangtze River, who primarily eat wheat products (noodles, breads, and so forth), and those south of the Yangtze, who mainly eat rice. I grew up eating both, schizophrenically sometimes even at the same meal. My parents were from Shanghai, rice eaters who moved to Beijing, the land of wheat and grain products (millet and sorghum). My mother employed two cooks: one from the north, who made his own *jiao zi* skins, as well as a cook from her home area of Wuxi near Shanghai, who could steam rice to perfection.

These recipes reflect the dual nature of my love for both rice and noodles. A typical day for me begins with a bowl of *congee*, a rice porridge. Later in the morning, I'll also make a pot of rice in my little electric rice cooker so I can have it for dinner. If I'm home for lunch, I'll add a few wontons or soup noodles to the chicken broth I usually have simmering on the stove. At dinner, I can serve it alongside a quick stir-fry, or if it's cold use it to make fried rice with vegetables. Often I will boil some fresh noodles and serve them with my own Chinese version of bolognese sauce (zha ziang mian), which I like to make in quantity and keep in the refrigerator.

The array of fresh noodles in Asian markets can be confusing, even for me. If you don't have an Asian market, there are some nationally distributed brands of fresh pasta sold in the refrigerator case that are quite good and come in angel hair and linguine widths. Some supermarkets also carry fresh Asian noodles. Dried pasta has never cooked up quite right for me, so I hesitate to recommend it.

Fried Rice, My Way

dou ya cai dan chao fan

MY MOTHER, WHO HATED WASTE of any kind, would admonish us to eat everything we were served by saying, "Each grain of rice represents one worker's drop of sweat." Fried rice is a thrifty cook's resourceful way of using leftover rice. Also, in China fried rice is eaten primarily as a snack, never as part of a traditional meal. The variations for fried rice are endless, but one thing it should never become is a jumble of too many old or odd ingredients from your refrigerator. The best fried rice for my palate is light and never greasy, and has only three or four freshly prepared ingredients. It's also not darkened with soy sauce, but seasoned with only a sprinkle of salt.

This recipe is fluffy and snowy white, with just a little bit of color from broccolini stems, ham, and green onions.

✿ ✿ ✿

It's important to use cold rice so that the grains stay separate when stir-fried. Any long-grain rice, including basmati and jasmine, will work, but short-grain rice is too clumpy. If you're preparing rice from scratch instead of using leftovers, spread the warm rice out on a baking sheet to cool more quickly.
—L.W.

Serves 2 to 4 as a snack or light lunch,
6 to 8 as part of a Chinese meal

2 cups cooked long-grain white rice, cold

3 tablespoons peanut oil

4 large egg whites, lightly beaten

1/2 cup broccolini stems, cut into 1/4-inch dice

1/4 cup minced green onions

1/3 cup Virginia ham, cut into 1/4-inch dice

Freshly ground white pepper, for finishing

Wet your hands with cold water and rub the rice to separate the grains; set aside.

Heat a nonstick skillet over medium-high heat. Add 1 tablespoon of the oil and swirl to coat the pan. Add the egg whites, swirl to make sure they're spread evenly in the pan, and cook, stirring constantly, until lightly scrambled. Transfer the eggs to a plate and set aside.

Return the pan to the stove and heat on high until a bead of water dances on the surface and then evaporates. Add the remaining 2 tablespoons of oil and swirl, then toss in the broccolini dice and cook until tender, about 2 minutes. Add the green onions, stir constantly for about 30 seconds, and then add the ham and toss to combine well. Add the rice and, using a wooden spoon or chopsticks, break the rice apart and stir to completely warm it through. Toss in the cooked egg whites, break them up as you are stirring, and cook for a few seconds more.

Remove from the heat, turn the rice onto a platter, and sprinkle with pepper. Serve warm.

California Congee with Condiments

xi fan he xiao cai

I HAVE A GREAT AFFECTION FOR *CONGEE*. It was the last meal my mother cooked for us when my sister Teresa and I set out on a cold January morning for what turned out to be a very long journey to Free China in Sichuan Province. For me, *congee* is warm and nourishing Chinese comfort food. It's basically bland rice cooked to a porridgelike consistency, then served with a number of spicy and or flavorful condiments to liven it up. In some regions, *congee* is cooked with sugar and salt, but our family preferred it made with just rice and water. At New Year's, my mother would prepare huge pots of *congee* to feed the poor at the gates of our home.

✿　✿　✿

Be sure to use Japanese short-grain white rice (not sticky rice) and cold water. It's the condiments that make congee *special, so choose any or all from this list (they're all available at Asian markets.) Or be creative like one of Cecilia's friends, who adores her* congee *garnished with a dollop of sour cream and caviar. —L.W.*

Serves 4

1 cup Japanese short-grain white rice

8 cups cold water

Condiments

Fermented or fresh cold-pressed tofu

Pickled vegetables (like *zha cai*—pickled mustard tuber—or greens)

Dried fish

Thousand-year eggs

Dry-shredded pork

Dried shrimp with celery

Salty duck eggs

Cold five-spice beef

Deep-fried peanuts

Leftover tea eggs

A sprinkle of kosher salt or any specialty salt, like fleur de sel

In a large saucepan, cover the rice with a generous amount of cold water. Swish the rice around in the water to rinse the grains of their starch. Drain off the liquid, and repeat this process until the rice is thoroughly washed and the water remains clear, about twice more.

In the same saucepan, cover the washed rice with the 8 cups of cold water and bring to a boil over high heat. Decrease the heat to medium to maintain a simmer. Stirring frequently, cook the rice, uncovered, until it thickens to a porridgelike consistency and the grains are very tender, but still separate, about 30 minutes.

Ladle the hot *congee* into individual bowls and allow your guests to garnish as they please with the prepared condiments. Serve immediately.

Very Thick Hot-and-Sour Noodles

beijin da lu mian

WHEN I HAD THIS DISH AT THE Xian home of my "godfather," General Chao, I remember thinking, "This is like hot-and-sour soup only with noodles." He was the man who took care of us when my sister and I were trying to make our way to Free China, and his wife, who didn't have any children, kept trying to fatten us up. I don't know if it was because we were hungry and scared, but to this day, when I make this soup-noodle dish, I feel nourished and as if all is right with the world.

✧ ✧ ✧

Cecilia suggests adding shrimp or crab to make this a more elegant dish, plus chard or spinach shreds for color, in which case I think Double Delicious Chicken Broth (page 58) is in order. Look for fresh bamboo shoots while you're at it, and guests will swoon over this basically humble dish. —L.W.

Serves 8

$1/3$ cup dried tree-ear mushrooms

$1/3$ cup dried lily buds

5 ounces lean pork loin

1 teaspoon cornstarch

4 cups Double Delicious Chicken Broth (page 58) or Delicious Chicken Broth (page 57) or canned low-sodium chicken broth

2 tablespoons peanut or vegetable oil

1 tablespoon Shaoxing wine

$1/2$ cup (about $2^1/2$ ounces) drained canned bamboo shoots, cut into 2-inch julienne pieces, rinsed with cold water

1 teaspoon peeled, minced fresh ginger

1 tablespoon soy sauce

2 green onions, white and light green parts only, halved lengthwise and thinly julienned

$1/2$ pound fresh $1/8$-inch-wide Chinese noodles

2 eggs, lightly beaten

Freshly ground white pepper, for finishing

Splash of Chinkiang black vinegar or balsamic vinegar (optional), for finishing

In separate bowls, generously cover both the dried lily buds and tree ears with very hot tap water and soak until soft, about 30 minutes. Once softened, drain them both, making sure you rinse the wood ears well to remove any grit or sand. Remove and discard the tough stems from the tree ears and tear the caps into small pieces. Squeeze the excess water out of the lily buds, remove and discard their tough ends, and then halve the rest crosswise.

So the pork is easier to slice, freeze it for 30 minutes or so to firm it up. Slice the frozen meat diagonally against the grain $1/8$ inch thick and then julienne into strips. In a small bowl, toss the pork with the cornstarch and set aside.

Just before you're ready to cook the pork, bring a large pot of water to a boil over high heat. In a separate saucepan, bring the chicken broth to a boil over high heat and then lower the heat to maintain a simmer.

TO COOK THE SAUCE, heat a large wok over high heat until a bead of water dances on the surface and then evaporates. Add the oil and swirl to coat the pan. Add the pork, and toss to coat in the hot oil. Stirring frequently, cook until just a bit of pink remains and it begins to brown, about 2 minutes. Pour in the wine. Add the bamboo shoots, ginger, and soy sauce, and toss to combine, then add the lily buds and wood ears. Cook, stirring constantly, until the entire mixture is well combined, about 30 seconds more. Toss in the green onions and remove the pan from the heat.

TO COOK THE NOODLES, remove them from their package and fluff the strands to separate. Add the noodles to the pot of boiling water and cook until they are tender, but retain a little "bite," about 2 minutes. Drain the noodles well and then turn them out into a large serving bowl.

Slowly pour the beaten egg into the hot broth, stirring gently, until wisps of egg are visible. Turn off the heat and pour the broth over the noodles in the serving bowl. Top with the pork mixture and toss to combine the noodles and pork well. Grind or sprinkle with white pepper, add a splash of vinegar, and serve.

Green-Onion Oil-Tossed Noodles

shanghai cong yu ban mian

IN SHANGHAI, THESE SIMPLE but flavorful noodles are very popular in restaurants, in homes, and from street vendors. My mother, who came from a town near Shanghai called Wuxi, often made them at home for us. They're super simple and very tasty. I also like the green-onion oil drizzled over rice or baked potatoes. The dried shrimp, which is an ingredient that Chinese love but that I realize is an acquired taste, can be left out if you'd rather. The noodles are still delicious without them.

✿ ✿ ✿

The flavor of this dish depends on the freshness and quality of the green onions. Be sure to buy onions with a firm texture and vibrant green stalks. Any onions with wilted greens should be avoided.

Dried shrimp come in packages in the refrigerator section of Asian markets and are sold according to size. Check the color of the shrimp in the package—they should be pink-orange, never gray. They keep in a sealed bag in the refrigerator for 3 months or can be frozen for up to 6 months. —L.W.

Serves 4

1/2 ounce extra-large dried shrimp (optional)

3 tablespoons peanut oil

Pinch of kosher salt

2 bunches green onions, thinly sliced lengthwise on the bias into very thin, 2-inch-long strips (about 4 cups)

1/3 cup soy sauce

1 pound fresh 1/8-inch-wide Chinese noodles

Put the shrimp in a bowl, cover with hot water, and soak for 30 minutes, or until softened. Drain the shrimp over a small bowl, reserving the soaking liquid separately, and set both aside.

TO COOK THE SAUCE, heat a large wok over high heat until a bead of water dances on the surface and then evaporates. Add the oil and a healthy pinch of salt and swirl, then toss in the green onions and cook until they have just started to wilt and turn bright green, about 20 seconds. Add the shrimp and 2 tablespoons of the reserved soaking liquid and toss to combine with the green onions. Pour in the soy sauce, bring the liquid to a boil, stir to thoroughly coat, and continue to cook 30 seconds more. Transfer the mixture to a bowl and set it aside to cool to room temperature.

TO COOK THE NOODLES, bring a large pot of salted water to a boil over high heat. Remove the noodles from their package and fluff the strands to separate. Have a colander ready by the sink for draining. Add the noodles to the boiling water and cook until they are tender, about 2 minutes. Drain the noodles and rinse them under cold water. Drain them again and remove as much water as possible. Transfer the noodles to a large serving bowl. Top the noodles with the green-onion mixture. This dish is best served at room temperature.

Zha Ziang Mian

beijin zha ziang mian

THE FIRST TIME I HAD SPAGHETTI bolognese in Rome, prepared the authentic way with very little tomato and mainly meat, I thought, "Just like *zha ziang mian*!" The two dishes are similar, and legend has it that after spending time in China, Marco Polo took this dish back to Italy. *Zha ziang mian*, a staple dish in most every home in northern China, can be hard to get right. Each of the ingredients needs to be in perfect proportion to the other.

✿ ✿ ✿

You need to have pork that is coarsely ground for this dish, like what you might buy for chili, or the pork can become mushy and hard to break apart. The sauce reheats well, and the recipe makes about 2¹/₂ cups of sauce so, just as I do when I make bolognese, I like to double or triple the recipe and freeze extra for later.

You can also serve this dish cold or at room temperature. Rinse the noodles after cooking with cold water and drain them well to prevent them from sticking together. —L.W.

Serves 4

2 tablespoons bean sauce

2 tablespoons hoisin sauce

2 tablespoons soy sauce

3 tablespoons peanut oil

1 teaspoon minced garlic

¹/₂ pound coarsely ground pork shoulder (pork butt)

1 tablespoon Shaoxing wine

1 teaspoon peeled, minced fresh ginger

1 tablespoon minced green onions

¹/₂ pound fresh ¹/₈-inch-wide Chinese noodles

¹/₂ English cucumber, partially peeled, cut into 2-inch-long julienne pieces (about ¹/₂ cup)

TO MAKE THE SAUCE, whisk together the bean, hoisin, and soy sauces in a small bowl.

Just before you cook the pork, bring a large pot of water to a boil over high heat (for the noodles).

TO COOK THE PORK, heat a large wok over high heat until a bead of water dances on the surface and then evaporates. Add the oil and swirl to coat the pan. Toss the garlic in the hot oil and cook until it's fragrant and slightly golden, about 10 seconds. Add the pork and, using a wooden spoon or chopsticks, stir constantly to break the meat apart. Cook the pork until just a bit of pink remains and it begins to brown, about 2 minutes. Add the wine and ginger and continue to stir a few seconds more. Pour in the reserved sauce, bring the liquid to a boil, and stir to thoroughly coat the pork. Add the green onions and toss to combine well. Remove the pan from the heat.

TO COOK THE NOODLES, fluff the strands to separate them. Add them to the boiling water and cook until they are tender, about 2 minutes. Immediately dump them into the colander. Shake the colander to drain the noodles well and then turn them out into a large serving bowl. Pour the sauce over the noodles and garnish with the cucumber and serve immediately, tossing the noodles with the sauce at the table.

Cantonese Home-Style Rice with Cured Meats

quang dong la wei fan

THIS SIMPLE CANTONESE one-pot dish of rice cooked with cured meats is a great one to make after a long day at work when you want something filling, but are too tired to cook or even go to the grocery store. If you use a rice cooker, it does all the work for you, and the ingredients can be kept on hand in your pantry and refrigerator.

☼　☼　☼

We used two kinds of cured meat, lop chong sausage and la rou, a piece of cooked, cured pork cut from the shoulder or leg. Both are sold in Asian markets in vacuum-sealed packages in the refrigerator section. lop chong is cured, but not cooked, so it must be steamed before eating. For this dish, you could use sausage or any kind of cured meats you like.

We've written this recipe to be made in a rice cooker. If you don't already own a rice cooker, I highly recommend adding one to your kitchen pantry. Alternatively, you can use a medium saucepan on your cooktop, and add the meat when the water comes to a boil. —L.W.

Serves 6 to 8 as part of a Chinese meal and 4 to 6 as a Western-style entrée

1 cup Japanese short-grain rice

1/2 cup long-grain rice

1 1/2 cups cold water

3 1/2 ounces cured pork (*la rou*), sliced crosswise into 1-inch pieces

3 1/2 ounces (2 pieces) Chinese sausage (*lop chong*)

Add both kinds of rice and the water to the bowl of your rice cooker. When the water starts to boil, put the meat on top of the rice, cover, and continue to cook following the manufacturer's instructions. The rice should be tender, but not mushy, and the pork heated through.

Remove the cured meat from the pot and cut diagonally into 1/2-inch pieces. Transfer the rice and meat to a serving bowl and eat while still warm.

Chapter 8
A Fortunate Cookie

IN AMERICA, PEOPLE TEND TO look at astrology and fortune telling as forms of entertainment, but in China, we take it very seriously. Psychics and astrologers are consulted by people from all walks of life who seek advice for everything from business investments to major life decisions, like whom to marry or when to have children.

I'm the rare Chinese person who has always possessed a certain skepticism when it comes to seeing into the future. For some reason, and contrary to most everyone I knew, I absolutely believed when I was young that my future was in my own hands, and that if I worked hard enough and persevered through tough times, I could affect my own fate. There was a time though, when I faced an unknown future, that I wanted answers. Now, however, as I look back at my life, I'm amazed at all the good fortune that's come my way. Whenever I've been in trouble or danger, someone always came to my rescue, so I certainly can't deny that I've been blessed with more than my share of good luck.

My Number Five sister, Qin, and I arrived in Chongqing in late June of 1942, after an arduous journey that took us through seven of China's provinces and across hundreds of miles, the majority of them on foot. However, as relieved and happy as we were to have finally made it safely, our problems were far from over. The Japanese were bombing the city with frightening regularity, forcing us even on our first day to seek

Wedding photo, Cecilia and Chiang Liang, Chongqing, China, 1945.

shelter. We'd lost the weight we had gained back under kind Madame Chao's nurturing (and nourishing) regimen in Xian, and were starving again. And finally, I was worried that we would not be able to pay for more than a few days of lodging. Our money was running low, and we had no idea where our uncle General Ting and his family lived. None of the soldiers we met along the way from Xian, or even General Chao (the man who helped us get to Chongqing and became our godfather), had ever heard of him.

But, in spite of all our concerns, we were almost delirious with excitement to finally be in Chongqing. We were in the city where Chiang Kai-shek, the chairman of the Nationalist government, had set up his war capital. More than that, we were two young women who had a whole new world ahead of us to explore.

We located a room for rent, and after checking first to make sure the room was clean (and the single cot free of fleas), we dropped our bags and immediately set to resolve our next most pressing concern: finding something to quiet our growling stomachs. If there was any place to do that cheaply, it was Sichuan Province, home to some of the most delicious snack food, *xiao chi* ("little eats"), in all of China. As soon as we stepped out to find the nearest market, the aroma of warm, yeasty bread beckoned us from an alleyway. We nearly bumped into a vendor selling *bao zi*, meat-filled buns, which we hastily paid for and even more hastily devoured. A few blocks farther, we found another vendor selling noodles topped with a tongue-numbing chile-meat sauce—my first taste of the famous Sichuan *dan dan mian*.

Our hunger temporarily sated, we were energized and eager to explore the city, which was lively with vendors of all kinds hawking their wares. Chongqing was nothing like Beijing. The city appeared to have sprung out of nowhere, with no urban organizing principles. The buildings were dusty gray and seemed almost thrown together. The "streets," if you could call them that, were mostly unpaved and unnamed. We saw no cars or trucks, just rickshaws, bicycles, and carts. In contrast to Beijing, which had lost its vitality during the long years of Japanese occupation, the people of Chongqing seemed optimistic and united in a patriotic fervor that Qin and I found exhilarating. Everywhere we turned, there were posters of the Generalissimo and Madame Chiang Kai-shek, as well as banners proclaiming "The Final Victory Is Ours!" When we were in Jieshou, General Chao had quizzed us about why we wanted to go to Chongqing. I blurted out that I thought I might want to join the army.

"Really, why is that?" he asked, when I said that I wanted to enlist.

"I hate the Japanese and I want to help my country."

The General didn't really know us at the time, but at least knew enough to say, "Miss Sun, I appreciate your ambitions. But you're from a good family. You're educated, and I know your parents did not raise their daughter to join the army. Trust me when I say that when you get to Chongqing you'll be able to find other ways to contribute to your country."

✿ ✿ ✿

For two days after our arrival, we asked nearly everyone we came in contact with if they had ever heard of General Ting, an older man from Beijing who was probably living with his five grown daughters. No one had any leads, but one person suggested that we put an ad in the newspaper, which we promptly did. "Sun Qin and Sun Yun, Numbers Five and Seven daughters of Sun Long Guang, looking for General Ting and family from Beijing." We gave the phone number of our rooming house.

We were afraid that a call would come for us while we were both out, so we decided that one of us would go for food while the other would stay in the room. A couple of days later we got the call we'd been waiting for. It was from our cousin, General Ting's Number Two daughter, Ting Wei-Rou, who said she would come to get us that afternoon. We tried as best we could to describe the location of our rooming house, and at our designated time went outside to look for her. We waited and waited and started to get nervous, when a woman we didn't recognize approached us.

"Number Five Sun sister? Number Seven?" she said.

"Yes," I replied. "Are you here to take us to meet our cousin?"

"I am your cousin, silly. Ting's Number Two daughter!"

Suddenly, I was embarrassed. Although she was still pretty and wore her hair up as she always had in a stylish chignon anchored with an ebony barrette, she was much older than I remembered.

"I barely recognized you," she said cheerfully.

✿ ✿ ✿

Our Uncle Ting Jin had married my father's younger, Number Two, sister. Everyone addressed him as General Ting out of fond respect, because although he wasn't officially a military officer, he had worked first as a civil engineer, and then in aeronautics for the Nationalists (the Kuomintang). He and his family of five girls and one son had lived in a big, comfortable home near ours in Beijing, and I had many happy memories of holidays and special occasions spent with them. General Ting and my father were good friends, and he frequently came over to play chess or discuss politics. Fiercely loyal to Chiang Kai-shek, Ting and his family followed when the Nationalist capital was moved first from Beijing to Nanjing, and then to Chongqing.

Unlike my father or even his older brother, Sun Qui Bou (whom we all called Big Uncle), General Ting was very traditional in many respects. I always found him to be cordial, but rather patronizing, even slightly intimidating. I heard from my sisters that for years, General Ting had longed for a son, and when my aunt became pregnant again after bearing five healthy daughters, he told her that if she had another girl, he would take a concubine, or several, until he got a son. They went on to say that my aunt went to the temple every day of her pregnancy to pray for a boy. She consulted astrologers who all told her something different. Some said she would have a boy, some said a girl. One even said she'd have twins—a girl and a boy. Finally, the moment of truth arrived when she went into labor. It was a difficult birth, taking three days, but to everyone's relief and joy, my aunt gave birth to a healthy son. But just before his one-month birthday, as preparations were being made to celebrate with red eggs and a baby-naming, my aunt, who never really recovered from the ordeal of his birth, died. Within a year General Ting had remarried—to the nurse he had hired to take care of my aunt.

✿   ✿   ✿

As it turned out, the General and his daughters lived not far from our rooming house in what appeared to be a dilapidated office building. I shouldn't have been disappointed, considering how all our circumstances had changed, but I was, particularly because I recalled how lovely and tastefully decorated their house in Beijing had been.

We climbed some rickety stairs to the second floor and entered a small, three-room apartment where we were immediately and warmly greeted by my uncle's wife. The rooms were tidy, but crowded with cots, quilts, tables, chairs, books, and an assortment of children's toys. As my cousin Wei-Rou had explained on the way over, she and three of her sisters, their husbands and children, and Number One brother, all lived under the same roof, but not with them. My uncle had set up an office on the first floor where, although officially retired, he continued to do some part-time administrative work for the Nationalist government.

Within moments of our arrival, General Ting walked in. Although he seemed to have shrunken somewhat and added a few more wrinkles, he still commanded the room and we were overjoyed to see him. He was pleased to see us, too.

"Number Five and Number Seven Sun daughters! Come and sit, let's have some tea. And some snacks. You look like you haven't eaten for days. I want you to tell me how you got to Chongqing."

Over tea, and then dinner, Qin and I told him the story of our long journey from Beijing, and how fortunate we were to meet so many people who wanted to help us: Qi Ze Lin and her husband, General Xu, and then, of course, General and Madame Chao. When we had finished, General Ting insisted we leave the rooming house and come to live with them. It was a very generous offer, considering their circumstances.

"We may be cramped, but I will not have my nieces living amongst strangers."

"Thank you, Uncle. We're very grateful for your kind offer, but we'll only being staying a short while because we want to go to Yunnan to be with our Numbers One and Two sisters and brother Zhen-Ji."

He let out a little sigh of exasperation and said, "I strongly advise against it. First, you girls are not in good enough physical shape to make the difficult trip to Yunnan. Second, you've already told me you've run out of money. Third, and maybe most importantly, you have no idea how primitive the province is and how dangerous the tribal people are who live there. It would not be safe for you."

Yunnan had become nothing more than a motivator to keep us going. If I was to be truly honest, I needed to admit our long walk was over. I was tired. Qin—ever uncomplaining Qin—was tired, too. It wasn't a difficult decision. The very next morning we moved in with our Uncle Ting, his wife, our five cousins, and their children. We stayed for almost three years.

✿　✿　✿

It didn't take me long to find a job. At General Ting's suggestion, I applied at the American Embassy as a Mandarin language teacher and was immediately hired by the OSS (the forerunner to the CIA), as was Qin. Soon after, I also got another part-time job teaching at the Russian Embassy. The work gave me a sense of pride that came from more than earning money for the first time in my life or the feeling that I was contributing in some small measure to the war effort. I think it was also that I loved the

Mandarin language and enjoyed immersing myself in it after traveling through so many provinces with dialects that we didn't understand.

Each evening after work, I went home to General Ting's. His wife looked after us as if we were her own daughters, inquiring about our day, and asking if there was anything we needed. It felt good to be part of a family again, and dinnertime was especially fun, with everyone squeezed around the tables (two tables barely held us all.) The General and his wife had a really good Sichuan cook. Although his dishes were simple, usually a stew or hot pot of some kind along with one or two vegetables, I really looked forward to the meals he prepared. I'd become addicted to his fiery orange chili oil.

✿   ✿   ✿

About a month after our arrival in Chongqing, I passed a man on the street who, seconds later, called my name. I turned around and recognized him as Chiang Liang, a professor at Fu-Jen, the Catholic university I had been attending in Beijing.

"Yes, I'm Sun Yun. You remember me from Fu-Jen?"

"Of course I do, although it took me a few moments." I knew he was being polite because I had only regained some of the weight I'd lost and still looked quite thin. "What a happy surprise to run into you here in Chongqing. May I take you to tea so you can tell me what you're doing so far from home?"

"Thank you, but, no, I'm on my way to work. I have a job teaching at the American Embassy."

"Where are you living? Is there anything you need? At least let me take you out another time."

I explained that my sister Qin and I were living with our Uncle Ting, gave him the phone number, and he gave me his business card in exchange.

"It was good to see you, Miss Sun. I'll be in touch."

I didn't think much of the meeting at the time, other than that it was nice to run into someone who remembered me from Beijing, so I was surprised a few days later when he called and then came to visit us at my uncle's.

We learned that Chiang Liang had left his post teaching economics two years previously to work for Wa-Fu Tobacco Company in Chongqing. He was an exceptionally well-educated and sophisticated man. I remember all of us being quite charmed by him, including General Ting, with whom he discussed politics at length.

After a wonderful evening of lively conversation, I was pretty thrilled when Chiang Liang turned to General Ting and asked permission to take his nieces to dinner the following night. I assumed that because he was fourteen years older than I was, Chiang Liang was more interested in Qin, my older sister, and included me to be polite, but I didn't care. I was excited just at the thought of going out to dinner.

❊ ❊ ❊

Qin and I panicked when we realized we had nothing to wear. Luckily, our cousins came to our rescue and lent us dresses, shoes, and stockings. We may have looked a little thrown together, but at least we were appropriate.

The following night, Chiang Liang arrived right on time to pick us up and said, "You know, I'm originally from Canton, and there's a small, but very good Cantonese restaurant here in Chongqing I thought you girls might enjoy." (Of course, only later did we find out that it was the only Cantonese restaurant in Chongqing.) I didn't want to let on that I had never had Cantonese food, so I said, "That's great! We love Cantonese food!" Qin rolled her eyes at me, but at least she didn't say anything.

The meal began with thinly sliced barbecued pork, and went on to a stir-fry of beef with fresh snow peas, followed by wild river fish steamed with ginger and green onions. We finished the meal with a delicate soup of fresh corn with egg whites.

Maybe it was the thrill of dining out a restaurant, or that we were young and impressionable and everything was so new. Maybe it was that the food was fresh (Sichuan is known for its abundance of year-round crops), well prepared, and absolutely delicious. For whatever reason, and in spite of the fact that it's been almost sixty-four years and thousands of meals since, I can still taste everything we had that night.

❊ ❊ ❊

Qin and I had several more dinner dates with Chiang Liang. Then, one night, he suggested that the three of us go to the Hall of Victory for Western-style "big band" dancing. By that time, we had started borrowing clothes from another of our cousins, Xu-Fang, who had also married a general, and was living in Chongqing. Her wardrobe was quite stylish, mainly American and European clothes. She would let us know what she would be wearing on her nights out with her husband, and then Qin and I would get to choose from some of her other outfits. We argued incessantly over her alligator shoes and purse.

Dancing became a regular after-dinner event, and it seemed that everyone who was anyone in the capital sooner or later ended up at the Hall of Victory. Chiang Liang seemed to know them all and started introducing us, so that slowly we began to make friends and develop a social life in Chongqing.

Two of the people he didn't have to introduce us to were Generalissimo Chiang Kai-shek's Number One son, Chiang Jing-Guo, who often came over to play chess with our Uncle Ting, and Jing-Guo's half brother (Number Two son), Chiang Wei-Guo. The five of us became fast friends. A sixth friend was soon added to the group: Chiang Kai-shek's nephew Pei-Fung.

Perhaps because I was so naive or more probably because the changes were subtle and took place over a year, I didn't realized what was happening. One evening when we all went out, it finally dawned on me that three of the men, Wei-Guo, Pei-Fung, and Chiang Liang, were flirting with me. I had known for a while that Chiang Liang was interested. Qin had started staying home on some of the nights we were all supposed to go to dinner. Finally I asked her about it and she said, "It's obvious to almost everyone that Chiang Liang is courting you, not me. That's okay, though," she smiled. "I knew it a long time ago and I don't mind."

Wei-Guo was very handsome and quite the playboy, which in my book made him hard to take seriously as a suitor. He was well aware of his good looks and knew that in his uniform (he was in an army tank division), women found him irresistible. He also had a mother who made me really nervous.

Madame Yao was Chiang Kai-shek's second wife and the first of his two mistresses. She was also Wei-Guo's adoptive—and doting—mother.

At any rate, the mother-in-law of Xu-Fang's sister happened to be good friends with Madame Yao. One afternoon, my cousin called and asked me to accompany her to tea at her mother-in-law's house. I didn't think much of it, but when we arrived and I discovered Madame Yao was there as well, I became a little suspicious. Madame Yao proceeded to ask me lots of questions about my parents, where they were from, what my father did, what my brothers did, where we went to school, and on and on. "You have a very lucky face," she said, which translated meant that I might make a good match for her son.

My suspicions were confirmed several days later when Madame Yao sent word asking me for my *ba zi*, which in China is something like a cross between a birth certificate and an astrological chart. I didn't have one. And even if I did, I probably would not have let her read it, because instinctively I knew a marriage to Wei-Guo would be no fun at all. Any woman he married would end up confined like a bird in a gilded cage.

Of the three men, I was probably most attracted to Pei-Fung, Chiang Kai-shek's sister's son. Though not as good looking as either of his cousins Wei-Guo or Jing-Guo, he was bright, educated, and sweet. He was an air force pilot who trained in the United States. I discovered that we had a connection which endeared him to me even more: he had become friends with my brother Zhen-Ji when they went through flight school together. Not long after arriving in Chongqing, Qin and I learned from Uncle Ting that Zhen-Ji was not teaching in Yunnan, but had joined the Nationalist Air Force. In fact, my brother was frequently in Chongqing and would join us on our evenings out.

☼　☼　☼

Over the next several months I started to seriously date both Chiang Liang and Pei-Fung and really started to worry that soon I was going to have to choose between the two men. I was torn because I had feelings for both of them, and the worst part was that I was unable to ask my parents for advice. I did talk to my sister, of course, and Uncle Ting. His choice for me was completely predictable. He thought I should marry Pei-Fung. Although he didn't say so, I knew he would have loved to have his niece become a member of Chiang Kai-shek's family.

All of this was weighing on my mind one morning as I was on the way to my cousin Xu-Fang's house to return some shoes I had borrowed. Their home was at the top of a very steep Chongqing hill, which could be reached by ascending a famous public stairway. At the foot of the steps, I passed an old man with a sign advertising that he was a fortune teller. Most cities in China are crawling with sidewalk "seers," and I had never paid any attention to them, much less considered paying for a consultation. This time was no different, but as I started up the stairs I heard him say, "Do you want to know which man you should marry?" I stopped abruptly.

At that moment, I didn't care if I was being conned. I had to hear what he would say.

Slowly and methodically he first felt my head, then the contours of my face, and finally the bones in my hands.

"You're trying to choose between the military man and the businessman."

I was dumbfounded.

"You've already decided against the ladies' man."

I couldn't believe my ears.

"If you decide to marry the military man you will become a young widow. If you marry the businessman you will live in prosperity."

The very next week, when Chiang Liang asked me to marry him, I accepted.

Several years later, when I was living in Shang-hai, I learned that Pei-Fung was on a plane that disappeared and was never found.

Letters from Pei-Fung.

STREET FOOD

As children growing up in Beijing, my nine siblings and I were forbidden by my mother to eat street food, as she feared we would be poisoned or at the very least become ill from food prepared in less than sanitary conditions. Although we thought her rule ridiculously unfair when all our friends were buying food from vendors—delicious-smelling buns, breads, noodles, and dumplings—I have to admit she may have been right, because it was rare that any of us got sick.

That's not to say she'd never buy food from a little café, or the vendors at the opera who sold savory and sweet snacks. She just had to know the owners personally or had scrutinized how they prepared their food. The best tea eggs I've ever eaten were the ones we would get at the opera. Every New Year's there was one old man who would pedal by our house and sell us red bean cakes he had warming over steamers on the back of his rickshaw. Once, when I was in college, riding home on my bicycle and hungry after a long day with nothing to eat, I succumbed to temptation and bought some *jiao zi* from a vendor not too far from our house. Guiltily, I downed them quickly, and my hunger sated, I had to admit they were tasty, but definitely not as good as the dumplings our cook made at home.

It wasn't until my sister Qin and I arrived—broke and almost starving—in Chongqing, in Sichuan Province, after our long trip from Beijing, that I truly began to appreciate the diverse and delicious range of street food snacks. In fact, Sichuan is home to the best street food in all of China. Eating such delectable and filling dishes like the famous *dan dan mian*, stuffed glutinous rice balls, and all kinds of tofu dishes like *mapo dofu*, Qin and I thrived. It was also all we could afford.

Sadly, the years of Communist oppression have taken their toll on street vendors all over the country, discouraging individual ambition and enterprise. Recently however, street snack sellers have begun to reappear, riding on the wave of renewed tourism.

Dan Dan Mian

dan dan mian

I BECAME QUITE ADDICTED TO THIS famous Sichuan street snack during the time I lived in Chongqing and would rush to the street upon hearing the peddlers cry "*Dan dan mian! Dan dan mian!*" *Dan* is the name of the bamboo shoulder pole from which wood buckets were suspended carrying the noodles (*mian*) on one end and a cooking vessel on the other.

☆ ☆ ☆

Authentically, the sauce for the noodles contains zha cai, which is sometimes called Sichuan preserved vegetable, pickled mustard tuber, or Sichuan pickled mustard. This salted cured vegetable adds rich flavor to all kinds of dishes.

The correct width of the wheat noodles for this dish is 1/16 inch, not the wider 1/8-inch-thick linguine-type noodles that are used in Zha Ziang Mian (page xxx). These days, many supermarkets carry fresh refrigerated Asian noodles, but fresh angel hair pasta can substitute. —L.W.

Serves 6 to 8 as part of a Chinese meal and 4 to 6 as a lunch, snack, or side dish

2 tablespoons peanut oil

2 tablespoons peeled, minced fresh ginger

2 tablespoons minced garlic

$^1/_4$ cup finely chopped green onions

$^1/_2$ pound ground pork

$^1/_4$ cup (about 1 ounce) chopped *zha cai*

2 tablespoons Shaoxing wine

3 cups hot Delicious Chicken Broth (page 57)

2 tablespoons plus 1 teaspoon soy sauce

2 teaspoons chili oil (page 5)

$^1/_4$ teaspoon Chinkiang black vinegar or good-quality balsamic vinegar

1 pound fresh extra-thin ($^1/_{16}$-inch) Chinese noodles

2 cups cold water

$1^1/_2$ pounds spinach, blanched 5 seconds and drained, for garnish

$^1/_3$ cup chopped unsalted roasted cashew nuts or peanuts, for garnish

$^1/_2$ teaspoon toasted ground Sichuan peppercorns

TO MAKE THE SAUCE, heat a large wok over high heat until a bead of water dances on the surface and then evaporates. Add the peanut oil and swirl to coat the pan. Add the ginger, garlic, and green onions and cook, stirring, just until fragrant. Add the pork and the preserved vegetable and stir until the meat loses its raw color, about 1 minute. Add the wine and cook for a few seconds to evaporate the alcohol and then add $^1/_2$ cup of the chicken broth, soy sauce, chili oil, and vinegar. Bring the liquid to a boil and remove from the heat.

TO COOK THE NOODLES, bring a large saucepan of water to a boil. Remove the noodles from their package and fluff the strands to separate. Add the noodles to the boiling water. Let the pot come back up to a boil, then add the 2 cups cold water. Bring to the boil again and immediately drain the noodles. Shake the colander to drain the noodles well and then, divide the noodles between individual serving bowls.

To serve, top each serving of noodles with some spicy pork mixture and ladle over a bit of the remaining hot chicken broth. Place some of the blanched spinach on one side of the noodles and sprinkle with the chopped nuts and a little ground Sichuan peppercorns. Serve immediately.

Red Bean Cakes

hong dou cheng gao

WHEN I WAS A GIRL, vendors with steamers set over braziers on the back of their rickshaws used to ride through the alleys and streets of Beijing selling warm sweet bean cakes. Bean cakes are a very traditional, very common street food, particularly around New Year's.

☆ ☆ ☆

Chinese red beans are sold in bags in Asian markets. Usually they're just labeled dried red beans. Japanese azuki beans can be substituted. The bean cake can be kept wrapped and refrigerated for 1 week, or frozen. —L.W.

Serves 12

10 ounces (about 1¹/₃ cups) dried Chinese dried red beans or azuki beans

1¹/₂ cups sugar, plus additional for dipping

16 ounces (about 4 cups) rice flour

Peanut or vegetable oil, for frying

TO COOK THE BEANS, put them in a large saucepan, cover with water by 3 inches, and bring to a boil over high heat. Decrease the heat to medium-low to maintain a lively simmer, and continue to cook until the beans are tender, about 1 hour and 15 minutes. If need be, add more water during cooking, as the beans should be generously covered with water for the duration.

Add the 1¹/₂ cups sugar and bring the pot back to a boil. Turn off the heat and let the beans soak in the liquid until completely cooled. Using a colander or a sieve, drain the beans and reserve the cooking liquid.

TO MAKE THE BEAN CAKE, put the rice flour in a large bowl. Add 3 cups of the cooled beans and

1¹/₂ cups of the cooking liquid and gently knead to incorporate fully. The chunky batter should be moist and come together easily (it will be quite sticky, but should not have excess liquid). Use a bit more cooking liquid or a dash of flour to compensate accordingly.

Spray an 8-inch cake pan with nonstick cooking spray and pour in the batter. Fill the bottom of a steamer with water, and bring the water to a boil over high heat. Put the pan in a steamer tier and place the tier over boiling water, cover the steamer, and cook until the cake is firm, about 1 hour. Let the bean cake cool in the pan. The cake can be covered and refrigerated in the pan for up to 3 days, or frozen for up to 1 month.

To serve, turn the cake onto a cutting surface. Cut the cake in half to create 2 half-moons and then cut each half-moon into ¹/₂-inch slices. Heat a large nonstick skillet over high heat until a bead of water dances on the surface and then evaporates. Cover the bottom of the skillet with a thin film of peanut oil and swirl to coat well. Arrange the cake slices in a single layer and fry in the hot oil until the outsides are crispy, about 1 minute per side. Depending on the size of your pan, you might need to fry the slices in several batches. For a sweeter version, you can dip both sides of the cake slices in sugar before frying in the hot oil. In either case, serve hot.

Beijing Wontons in Rich Broth

beijin wonton tang

IN CHINESE-AMERICAN RESTAURANTS, particularly ones that are Cantonese, wontons are most often seen in elaborate soups or fried as appetizers. But all over China, and in Beijing where I grew up, they're usually prepared much more simply, either steamed and served with a dipping sauce, or in little bowls with just a bit of broth, which is the way I like them. If you like spicy foods, serve them drizzled with chili oil. Wontons freeze beautifully. Double the recipe so you can cook them on a moment's notice when you have unexpected guests or want to make a spur-of-the-moment soup.

✿   ✿   ✿

Wonton wrappers come in different thicknesses, with a varying number of skins to a package. There's enough filling in this recipe to make about 48 wontons. Any extra skins can be kept well wrapped in the fridge or freezer. I like to cut them into ¼-inch strips and fry them to use in salads. —L.W.

Makes about 48 wontons

5 ounces ground pork shoulder (pork butt)

1 teaspoon peeled, minced fresh ginger

1 teaspoon minced green onion

1 teaspoon kosher salt

2 tablespoons Asian sesame oil

1 tablespoon Shaoxing wine

1½ tablespoons soy sauce

Flour, for dusting

2 large eggs, lightly beaten

1 package (about 12 ounces) wonton wrappers

Delicious Chicken Broth (page 57)

Thinly sliced green onions, for garnish

TO MAKE THE FILLING, combine the pork, ginger, green onion, salt, sesame oil, wine, and soy sauce in a bowl until well combined. Using your hands, gently mix together all of the ingredients just until combined. You want the filling to be a little loose.

TO ASSEMBLE THE WONTONS, lightly dust a rimmed baking sheet with flour and set it aside. Open the package of wontons and cover with a lightly dampened towel so the skins don't dry out. For each wonton, hold a wrapper in one hand so it looks like a diamond rather than a square and place 1 teaspoon of the filling in the center. Dip a finger in the water and run it along the perimeter of the diamond, then fold the wrapper up so the bottom point meets the top point, forming a triangle. Press the edges closed and using your finger again, dab a little egg on the two opposite side points of the long edge of the triangle. Bring the two points together so they overlap, and press to seal. Place the wonton on the floured baking sheet and repeat with the remaining wrappers. At this point, the wontons should be cooked within an hour.

For 4 servings, bring 3 to 4 quarts of water or chicken broth to a boil in a large saucepan over high heat. Carefully drop in 8 to 12 wontons, decrease the heat to medium-low to maintain a lively simmer, and cook until they float to the top, about 2 minutes.

To serve, place 2 or 3 wontons in the bottom of 4 small soup bowls, ladle a ½ cup or so of the broth over the wontons, and garnish with a sprinkle of sliced green onions.

Tea Eggs

cha ye dan

THESE BEAUTIFUL MARBLEIZED EGGS are the ultimate snack food. They're nutritious, can be served warm or cold, are portable, and best of all, are easy to make. But not only are they perfect for a picnic, they're quite elegant on a platter at a buffet. When I was a girl, they were sold on every Beijing street corner by vendors, but I thought some of the best ones were sold as snacks at the opera house. Today, I still make them at home to have in the morning with my congee. When my son, Philip, and daughter, May, come to visit with their families, they always seem reassured to find tea eggs in the refrigerator waiting for them.

✿ ✿ ✿

It's not necessary to use expensive black tea leaves, or even loose black tea—Cecilia prefers Lipton's tea bags—but whatever kind of tea you use, make sure it's fresh and doesn't smell musty.

I save eggs that have been in my fridge and are close to their pull date for hard-boiling because I find "old" eggs much easier to peel.

You want to keep the shells on the eggs after they've been cracked, but if a few shells fall off it won't affect the flavor of the eggs, just their appearance. Be very, very gentle when tapping the shells with the spoon. Cecilia's way of cracking the shells is much more efficient, but then, she's been doing this recipe forever. I found that I had more control if I lifted an egg out of the water with a slotted spoon and then tapped it gently all over with a teaspoon. —L.W.

Makes 10 eggs

10 large eggs

4 black-tea bags

1 tablespoon kosher salt

¼ cup soy sauce

Put the eggs in a large saucepan with enough cold water to cover them by 2 inches and bring to a boil over high heat.

Reduce the heat to medium, add the tea bags and salt, and cook 15 minutes. Using a metal spoon with a long handle, make fine cracks in the shell of each egg by gently tapping the surface several times, trying to keep the shells intact.

Pour in the soy sauce and reduce the heat to medium-low. Cover the pan and continue to cook for about 1 hour and 15 minutes. Remove the pan from the heat, leave covered, and let the eggs soak in the liquid for about an hour, or until they are darkly colored. You can test them for color by carefully removing one of the eggs from the pan and peeling off a bit of the eggshell. If they're too light, let them sit longer, testing them after 30 minutes. Using a slotted spoon, remove the eggs to a plate and discard the liquid.

They can be peeled and served at this point, or refrigerated in a covered container in their shells for up to 4 days.

Green-Onion Pancakes

cong you bing

ONIONS IN ALL THEIR VARIETIES are grown everywhere in China, and green onions in particular are often found in even the smallest of backyards. A clever use for an abundant green-onion crop, these pancakes are common throughout northern and central China, sold as snacks by street vendors and also made at home. There are many versions, some thick and breadlike, others thin and chewy, and, my favorite, flaky and crisp. This recipe is similar to those made by our old cook in Beijing. Typically, we had them for our after-school snacks, or for lunch with soup. For a recent cocktail party, I made some, cut them in wedges, and topped them with smoked fish.

☼ ☼ ☼

The recipe uses two doughs, one made with boiling water, the other with cold water, and then both are briefly kneaded together in a food processor. (The dough can also be made by hand using a spoon or fork to stir the boiling water with the flour). According to the late Barbara Tropp, non-yeasted boiling water doughs are slightly chewy but delicate. Non-yeasted doughs made with cold water are a little heartier, have more bite, and stand up to frying. By combining the two doughs you get the characteristic delicate but chewy and crispy texture that distinguishes green-onion pancakes.

Many recipes for green-onion pancakes use a lot of oil, but Cecilia uses only a minimal amount so the pancakes are light and relatively un-greasy.

The idea of rolling the dough several times into logs and then a snail shape is to create as many layers of dough as possible so the pancakes are flaky. When Cecilia rolls the dough into the snail shape, she does it in such a way that the center of the coil is higher, so that when it's rolled flat again there are even more layers. —L.W.

Makes 6 (6-inch) pancakes

3 cups all-purpose flour, plus additional for dusting

1 teaspoon kosher salt, plus additional for sprinkling

1 cup boiling water

1/3 to 1/2 cup cold water

2 tablespoons Asian sesame oil

1/3 cup minced green onion

2 to 3 cups peanut or vegetable oil, for frying

TO MAKE THE DOUGH, put the flour and 1 teaspoon of the salt in a food processor fitted with a metal blade and pulse a few times to combine well. With the food processor running, carefully pour the boiling water through the feed tube in a slow stream and process until the dough starts to pull away from the sides of the bowl, about 10 seconds. Pour 1/3 cup of the cold water through the feed tube and process until the dough comes together in a ball, about 15 seconds more. If the dough is dry, add a bit more water, or if it is sticky, add a bit more flour, and continue to process a few seconds longer.

On a lightly floured surface, knead the dough for a few minutes until it is smooth, elastic, and no longer sticky. Add a bit more flour as needed to reduce stickiness. Shape the dough into a ball and transfer to a lightly oiled bowl, cover with plastic wrap, and let it rest for 30 minutes.

TO SHAPE THE PANCAKES, knead the dough again on a lightly floured surface until it is very smooth, 1 to 2 minutes. Roll the dough into a 2-inch-diameter log and divide it into 6 equal pieces. Flatten each piece into a disk. For each disk, roll into a 9-inch round, about $1/8$ inch thick. Brush the top with sesame oil and evenly sprinkle with 2 tablespoons of the green onions and a pinch of salt. Roll two opposites sides of the round in so they meet in the middle, then lightly press them together. Tightly coil the dough into a snail shape, press to flatten it slightly, and then roll it out again into a 5- to 6-inch disk, about $1/4$ to $1/3$ inch thick. Repeat this process with each piece of dough.

Have a plate or cutting board ready by the cooktop. To cook the pancakes, heat a large wok over high heat until a bead of water dances on the surface and then evaporates. Cover the bottom of the skillet with a thin film of peanut oil and swirl to coat well. Add 1 pancake and fry it in the hot oil until the bottom is golden brown, 2 to 3 minutes. Carefully turn the pancake over and fry until the bottom is golden brown, 2 to 3 minutes more. Transfer the pancake to the plate and keep it covered and warm while you fry the remaining pancakes.

To serve, cut each pancake into wedges with a sharp knife, transfer to a serving platter, and serve hot.

Chapter 9
Shanghaied to Tokyo

"COME LOOK, SUN YUN," Chiang Liang called to me. "Come up here. You've got to see this!"

In spite of my seasickness I crawled out of the bunk to find out what had my husband so excited.

For a few seconds after I got on deck, I thought the sun had set, it was so dark. Then I realized we were traveling through a deep gorge. The emerald green walls on either side of the boat were so close that we could almost reach out and touch them, and so tall that when we looked up all that was visible was a bright jagged slash of sunlight.

It was October of 1945, two months after VJ (Victory over Japan) Day, and we were traveling from Chongqing up the Yangtze River through the famous Three Gorges on our way to a new life in Shanghai. It was the maiden voyage of a commercial cruise boat owned by a friend of Chiang Liang from Shanghai. Along with his friend were his friend's parents and my sister Qin.

✿ ✿ ✿

Cecilia and Chiang Liang at Nara National Park, Kyoto, Japan, 1952.

Chiang Liang and I had been married in May of that year in Chongqing. For the ceremony and catered reception, Chiang Liang had rented the Hall of Victory ballroom where we'd spent many nights dancing to big bands. We were joined by about a hundred people, mostly our friends and business associates of Chiang Liang's. A few of my family members who were living in Chongqing were there: my sister Qin, of course, my brother Zhen-Ji, who was in the air force and based in the war capital, and both my uncles, Generals Ting and Xu, with their daughters and their families. Neither Chiang Liang's parents nor mine were there, nor the rest of my siblings. In fact, my parents didn't even know I'd been engaged, much less married, until much later. Long-distance communication—telephone, telegraph, and mail—had never been reliable in the first place. With the country still divided by war, such service was virtually nonexistent.

In the days leading up to the wedding, I became depressed thinking about how different mine was going to be from those of my older sisters.

Most difficult for me to deal with emotionally was that I missed my mother. I kept remembering how involved she had been with every detail of my sisters' weddings, from designing their wedding gowns to consulting with the chefs on the menus for the banquets. In my fantasies, I knew what she would be saying:

"This dress needs to be fitted better around my Number Seven daughter's waist to show off her lovely figure." Or, "My daughter Sun Yun has a discriminating palate, just like mine, and she will recognize if the shark's fin for the soup is of inferior quality." The truth was that I had to rent a wedding dress and I hated it. It made me look fat, even though I probably weighed less than a hundred pounds. And I hadn't even been included in the conversations with the chef for the reception menu. Chiang Liang took care of everything. (In fairness, I need to point out, however, that this was in perfect keeping with Chinese tradition. It's the groom's family that pays for the wedding.)

Despite my doubts, I somehow managed to have a pretty good time at my wedding. When I crawled into bed that night, dizzy after one too many *gan bei* toasts (*gan bei* means "dry cup," and one is expected to empty their drink in one gulp), my last thought before I fell asleep was that my father would probably be proud of his new son-in-law, and my mother would have deemed the shark's fin soup delicious, though I'm sure, not hot enough.

✿　✿　✿

Within days of the Japanese surrender to the Allies on August 15, 1945, Chiang Liang announced that he wanted to move to Shanghai where he could manage his family's many residential properties (and still maintain his job on the Board of the Wa-Fu Tobacco Company). I was pretty excited. I had harbored a secret dream of going to Shanghai ever since I was eight years old, when my much older cousin (Uncle Xu's Number One son), a surgeon in Shanghai, brought his new wife to Beijing to meet the family. Rosalind made an indelible impression on me when she wafted in on the scent of French perfume, dressed in chic European clothes, batting her false eyelashes. She was the epitome of glamour. With visions of a new and exciting life, not to mention a new wardrobe, dancing in my head, I simply said to my new husband, "When do we leave?" Chiang Liang had only recently bought us a beautiful three-bedroom home in Chongqing, and I couldn't believe that within seconds I was already thinking about how I was going to pack it up.

"What about Qin?" I asked. At Chiang Liang's insistence, she had left General Ting's and was living with us.

"Of course, she should continue to live with us in Shanghai," he replied. My husband was generous to a fault.

✿ ✿ ✿

The scenic trip up the Yangtze from Chongqing to Shanghai covered 1,500 miles and took us two weeks, with a lot of stops along the river to pick up supplies and food. Usually, I was too seasick to come to the table to dine with everyone. Often, Chiang Liang would bring me some clear chicken broth with noodles, or a piece of freshly caught and steamed river fish with a little rice.

As our boat maneuvered through the busy Shanghai harbor on the Huangpu River (which meets the Yangtze), Chiang Liang again called to me to come up from our cabin to see the view. To this day I can vividly recall the thrill I felt as the city's skyline came into focus through the summer haze. The beautiful high-rise buildings, in European architectural styles I'd never seen before, lined a one-mile stretch along the river embankment called the Bund. In my imagination, I could not have created a more beautiful city.

✿ ✿ ✿

I fell in love with the pretty, European-style two-story house that Chiang Liang bought on Bubbling Well Road, a prestigious street in the French Concession. I discovered, to my delight, that within walking distance were antiques shops, bakeries, salons, chic boutiques (where I was sure I would run into Rosalind), and fine French, German, and Russian restaurants.

I couldn't wait to explore Shanghai. The very next morning after our arrival, I grabbed my sister and said, "Come on, let's see the city." Chiang Liang had told me that Wing On department store on Nanjing Road was something we'd love, so I decided that it must be our first stop. It was the first department store we'd ever seen, and we couldn't believe our eyes when we saw so much merchandise gathered from all over the world, all under one roof.

We knew about elevators from all the Hollywood movies we used to go see, but we'd never ridden in one and enjoyed stopping at every floor on our way up. On our way down, I started to feel the same queasiness I felt on board the boat. As the white-gloved elevator operator called out "first floor," I murmured to Qin that I didn't feel well and passed out. I woke up to sharp smells and the worried faces of strangers. That afternoon I found out it wasn't the rocking of the ship that made me feel ill, I was pregnant.

Our daughter, May, was born in June, 1946, after a very difficult three-day labor. Fortunately for us, Shanghai, has some of the very best medical care available in post-war China. We were also lucky that Dr. Sun at the French Concession hospital was enticed by some of the gold pieces Chiang Liang always kept for emergencies.

✿　✿　✿

I truly enjoyed my time in Chongqing—I met my husband there and had developed a close circle of friends—but I began to enjoy my life in Shanghai even more. After all, China had won the war with Japan. I was married to a successful businessman and the mother of a healthy, adorable daughter, and amazingly, I was now living a comfortable life in the most exciting, sophisticated, and cosmopolitan city in Asia. In addition, my Number Six sister, Sun, was working at the Park Hotel, where my favorite cousin, Bamboo Brother, was general manager. Immediately I would have connections to more family.

One of the first things I made sure to do right after we moved to Shanghai was to write to my parents in Beijing to tell them I had been married and was pregnant. Mail service, at least between major cities, was slowly being restored. I received a surprisingly quick reply from my father expressing his and my mother's good wishes for a healthy baby and saying that they would look forward to meeting my husband soon.

Upon our arrival in Shanghai, Chiang Liang was immediately occupied with his many business deals, so he left the management of the household up to me. To be given so much responsibility seemed a pretty scary thing at first. What did I know about running anything? As I thought about it a little further however, I told myself, "Well, Sun Yun, you've had the best model in the world for how to be a good housewife. Do exactly what you think your mother would advise."

So, that's what I did. Not literally, though. Mail service was still painfully slow and I was unable to talk to her directly, but in my mind I would ask my mother questions and then listen to her advice.

Cecilia and husband, Chiang Liang, Shanghai, 1957.

It was obvious that my first task was to find a nanny for May; next, to find a housekeeper. Then I hired a chef, a wonderful young woman who had grown up in Shanghai and was well versed in the dishes of the region. And, because I remember Um-ma saying that "all good dishes begin with good ingredients," I accompanied my chef as she shopped the markets of Shanghai. It was when we were looking for fish that my mother's voice grew the loudest.

Um-ma was from Shanghai, which was known throughout China for its spectacular seafood. The markets were full of all kinds of fish and shellfish, like the hairy crabs that were a delicacy. Every year, my mother would order the sweet crabs by the dozens and dozens, having them shipped from Shanghai to Beijing where they would arrive live, packed in straw-filled crates. For two days, we feasted on them.

I remember how excited I was the first time my cook and I returned home with a handsome carp in our bag. Just as my mother had instructed me, I had chosen the liveliest one in the tank. He fought ferociously as the fishmonger tried to capture him in the net. The cook suggested that she steam the fish. I told her to heat some oil with ginger and green onions and pour it over the carp just before it was served. That night, as Chiang Liang and I sat down to dinner, I kept silent as he put a piece of the fish in his mouth. I could tell he was savoring the flavor. After a few seconds he looked at me and said, "Sun Yun, this is the best fish I've had since we've moved to Shanghai. Our cook did this?"

With a little help from me, I thought, but mainly from my mother.

✿ ✿ ✿

Around the time my daughter was born, Chiang Kai-shek moved the Nationalist capital from Chongqing back (for the second time) to Nanjing, which is close to Shanghai. When his sons, Jing-Guo and Wei-Guo, as well as his nephew Pei-Fung and their wives, also relocated to Shanghai, Chiang Liang and I were happily reunited with our best friends from Chongqing. Suddenly our calendar became filled with evenings out, either entertaining Chiang Liang's business associates, or dinners and dancing with Wei-Guo and Pei-Fung. Although both men had been my suitors before I decided to marry Chiang Liang, we all remained good friends.

The exotic, glamorous, decadent, and neon-lit nightlife that Shanghai became famous for in the 1920s and 1930s went into hibernation during the war with Japan, but, in the late 1940s, it woke up, raring to go. There were restaurants from all over the world, elegant bars, supper clubs, ballrooms, jazz lounges (Shanghai was the jazz capital of Asia), cabarets, and exclusive, members-only clubs that catered to rich and well-connected Asians, Americans, and Europeans.

Chiang Liang had money to spend, and there was nothing he loved more than going out with friends for a night on the town, dressed in his custom-tailored suits, and driving his new Pontiac convertible. For a while I, too, loved that almost every night we had plans for the evening and looked forward to getting dressed and going out. I had even started to become confident enough in my entertaining skills that we began to have our friends over for dinner. But sometimes I just longed for us to spend a quiet night at home with our daughter. I enjoyed the nightlife in the beginning, but more and more often during those first months after her birth, I would find myself making excuses not to come. After two or three months of months of more frequent excuses, Chiang Liang finally said to me one night, "Sun Yun, I do not want to be married to a nanny. Your responsibility is to be with me, your husband." I was indignant but didn't express my feelings. Instead, what came out of my mouth were the words I knew my mother would have uttered, "Yes, Chiang Liang. You're right. I'm very sorry."

✿ ✿ ✿

In late January of 1947, my husband received word from his mother that his grand-mother in Beijing was ill and wanted to see him. May was only seven months old and I was nervous to fly with her, so Chiang Liang and I decided to go ourselves, leaving our daughter with the nanny. I sent my parents a letter letting them know that I would be coming to Beijing with my husband.

In February, we booked an Air China flight from Shanghai to Beijing. We had a long wait at the airport. The weather was horrendous. It was another first for me, my first airplane trip, and I was feeling pretty nervous, especially so when we heard that a flight before ours had crashed. I turned an apprehensive eye to Chiang Liang and he was reassuring, "Don't worry, we'll be fine." We were, but I was a jittery mess for hours after we landed. The ride was so turbulent, and I was so anxious about the thought of seeing my parents for the first time in five years—with a husband by my side.

✿ ✿ ✿

It was funny to me. On one hand, it seemed like a lifetime since I had left Beijing. On the other hand, it seemed like yesterday. From the taxi, it appeared as if nothing had changed. However, when we pulled up to the house, I noticed that the red gate was faded and peeling. My heart sank. Even when the Japanese moved in and occupied the house, I remembered how my father still wanted to make sure the gate was meticulously maintained.

Then, I was startled to see that, curiously, in addition to the old brass knockers, there was a bell at the gate. We rang it and waited for one of the servants to open the door. I must have been wearing an expression of dread, because Chiang Liang, without exchanging any words, tried to calm my anxiety by holding my hand. I took a deep breath and felt a momentary calm. I heard footsteps and then the door creaked open to reveal my father's smiling face.

"Number Seven Daughter, it's good to see you."

That was a shock. Not what he said of course, or that he looked so much older than I remembered him, but that my father opened the door himself.

Respectfully, Chiang Liang bowed as I introduced him, and then I had my second shock. My father began to pick up our suitcases to carry them into the house. I started to say, "Ah-ba, what are you doing? Where is Lao Li?" But my husband, anticipating my reaction, grabbed me by the shoulder to quiet me, and said to my father, "Ah-ba, please. Allow me to bring these in." My father simply nodded, and then we followed him to the main living quarters.

As we walked through the courtyards and past the buildings in the front where our servants had lived before the occupation, everything was at once familiar, yet uncomfortably strange. I don't know what I had really expected, because the house was in disrepair when I left. I should have taken the faded red gate as my first clue that all was very different.

The house seemed darker and colder than usual. We walked through the parlor, following a light that was emanating from the living room. It was a glow from a brazier in the center of the room. No wonder it was cold; the doors were open. I could barely keep from gasping. A ghostly figure was standing in the shadows. It was my mother. I swear her smile illuminated the room, but I also remember thinking I was glad for the darkness, so she wouldn't be able to see the tears coursing down my cheeks. Chinese decorum still needed to prevail.

"Um-ma, I want you to meet my husband, Chiang Liang."

✿　✿　✿

There was a lot to talk about that evening, so we were up into the wee hours of the night. I needed to tell my parents about our journey to Chongqing. They told me about their experiences under the Japanese occupation after Qin and I left. Um-ma wanted to hear all about our wedding. Though her face betrayed her sadness that she couldn't have been there, if there was anything to be learned from our dark years of occupation, we both realized that there are just some things over which we simply have no control.

The subject on all of our minds, however, was the all-out civil war that had just resumed between the Nationalists and the Communists, and which, I think, accounted for the fact that Beijing still hadn't recovered from the occupation. Shanghai had been relatively protected because of its international concessions; the Japanese even had many of their own civilians living there. But the rest of the country had been decimated, barely starting to recover when civil war broke out. Only two weeks before, the American General George Marshall had been recalled after his efforts to maintain a truce between them failed. Soviet Russia had been aiding the Communists in a takeover of Manchuria. After years of war and occupation, the mood in the country was angry.

The one bright spot that evening was that I remember going to bed comforted by the thought that my parents really seemed to like my husband, and he them. The next day, Chiang Liang and I visited his mother and grandmother (though she was so ill I was not allowed to see her). I returned to my parents' house, while he stayed with his mother.

For the next few days, I made myself as useful as I could. My parents still had one servant, but not our old faithful Lao Li, who had sent his nephew as his replacement when he became too ill to work. The nephew did some very basic housecleaning, laundry, and a little cooking, but my father had to do the shopping and maintenance of the buildings and yards. There were so many things that needed to be done, I almost didn't know where to begin. I dusted every crevice, mopped and polished the slate floors, scrubbed wash basins, and washed quilt covers. A couple of times I went shopping, stocking up on rice and preserved vegetables, and even bought two ducks that, with my mother's instructions, I hung to air-dry. Um-ma, my perfectionist mother, was strangely quiet while I went about my tasks, partially, I think, from embarrassment at the sad state of affairs in her once immaculate household, but also because she couldn't believe that I was capable of such hard work.

At one point, the day before we left, she said to me, "Lao Chi, where did you learn to clean so well? I thought you had servants in Shanghai."

"Yes, Um-ma, I have a housekeeper. But as you yourself told us many times when we were growing up, 'You need to learn how to do things properly, because you'll either need to instruct your staff or have to do it yourself someday.' I paid close attention to how you wanted things done, and always ask myself, 'How would my mother want me to do this?'"

"You say this to yourself?"

"Yes, Um-ma."

She grabbed both my hands and enclosed them in hers. Winking at me, she said, "Well, then you've had a very good teacher, and you've also been a very good student."

The next day, as Chiang Liang and I got into a taxi to take us back to the airport, I began to sob as I realized with absolute clarity that my parents were never going to move to Shanghai, and we would never live in Beijing. I had always imagined that somehow, some day, our family would be together for holidays and celebrations. We'd all laugh when, as if on cue, my mother would exclaim, "We're one big happy family!"

✿ ✿ ✿

In the two years since our trip to Beijing, the country had endured nonstop, full-scale civil war. The Nationalists moved south after capturing Manchuria and the northern provinces, and we were on the verge of complete takeover by Mao Zedong's Communists. It was clear that the Nationalists were losing. In January, 1949, the Communists took control of Beijing, and we hadn't had any word from my parents or Chiang Liang's mother for months. Again. It was amazing to think that it happened so quickly, but the truth was that while Chiang Kai-shek's forces were fighting the Japanese, the Communists had been waging a shrewdly successful campaign to capture the hearts and indoctrinate the minds of the rural Chinese people.

Soon after the surrender of the Japanese, Chiang Kai-shek moved the government back to Nanjing, and a year or so later, appointed his elder son, our friend Chiang Jing-Guo, special administrator. The support that the Nationalists had retained in the cities had eroded because of rampant inflation, and also to the perception that many government and military officials were lining their pockets with the gold and silver we exchanged for what turned out to be worthless paper money.

✿ ✿ ✿

Sometime around four or five in the morning in mid-April, there was a knock at our door. It was so soft that it was barely audible. I heard it because I had been up with our fourteen-month-old son, Philip, who was getting over a cold, and hadn't fallen back to sleep. The housekeeper was answering the door just as I was padding my groggy way out of the bedroom. Chiang Liang was still asleep.

"Don't worry," I said to the housekeeper. "Go back to bed. I'll get it."

I opened the door to find Chiang Jing-Guo. His serious expression alarmed me.

"Sun Yun, I'm sorry to disturb you at this hour, but you and Chiang Liang are my good friends. I feel it's my obligation to warn you that you're no longer safe in Shanghai. You need to make arrangements to leave as soon as possible."

"Come in, Jing-Guo. Let me wake up Chiang Liang and we'll talk. I'm sure everything is going to be all right." I wasn't really quite processing what he was telling me.

"No, I'm sorry, but I have no time. I beg you, Sun Yun. Just do as I say."

Because of his personal relationship with Wei-Guo and Jing-Guo, as well as his friendship with many government officials, Chiang Liang had known for some time that it
looked like the Nationalists were going to lose the war, and had been preparing for
us to leave. On their advice, we bought two houses in Taiwan. Just a couple of weeks
before Jing-Guo's appearance at our door, we had packed up Chiang Liang's rare-book
collection—part of which he had inherited from his father—in order to ship it ahead
to Taiwan for safety. Along with the books, we also sent another of his most valued
possessions, his blue Pontiac convertible. The ship, overloaded with the possessions of
people fleeing the country, just as we were, sank in Shanghai Harbor almost as soon as
it was unmoored from the dock.

Chiang Liang was almost inconsolable when we got the dreadful news, but there
wasn't really much time for him to dwell on what he'd lost. The following day the
Communists took control of the Nationalist capital, Nanjing. We knew it was just a
matter of time before they would reach Shanghai.

Chiang Liang began to make departure plans for us. While talking to friends
in government, trying to get us either boat or air passage out of China to Taiwan, he
was offered a diplomatic position in Tokyo by the director of the Nationalist Chinese
Mission (forerunner to the embassy).

"Tokyo?" I almost screamed at him. "No way. I can't live there. As far as I'm
concerned, they're still our enemies. Have you forgotten what they did to our country?"

"Of course I haven't forgotten, Sun Yun, but you can't continue to hold all of
a country's people responsible for the acts of its leaders. I've spent time in Japan, and
I guarantee that you'll find the Japanese people to be good overall." Chiang Liang's
grandmother had lived in Japan for a time, as had his father. I'd even forgotten that he
could speak a little Japanese.

"Besides," he said with a sly smile. "Tokyo is still an international city, and Taipei
is just a small town. I know you'll be bored if we go to Taiwan." He always knew how
to get to me. I hated being bored.

On April 28, Chiang Liang brought home airplane tickets for our flight to Tokyo.
I had been truly frightened that our need to leave Shanghai was so urgent. In a state
of disbelief, I spent the day almost paralyzed, just trying to figure out what to pack
for May and Philip. The day before, Chiang Liang and I had hastily packed, or more

accurately, figured out what could be concealed, the valuables that could be most easily transported. There was jewelry, of course, some of which was from my mother (pieces she had hidden from the Japanese and given me when we were in Beijing), and precious artwork, which we cut out of their frames and rolled up to fit in our suitcases. Looking around our house, I became depressed thinking about all the precious things we would not be able to take with us.

I was in one of the bedrooms when he came in with the tickets. "I don't know what to bring for May and Philip, Chiang Liang. They have so many toys they're attached to. And so many beautiful clothes I hate to leave behind." I was trying to hold back my tears and appear strong, but I could feel it was a losing battle.

"I need to tell you something, Sun Yun. I could only get three tickets to Tokyo. And the flight we're on tomorrow is going to be the last flight out of Shanghai."

"What do you mean, only three tickets? We're four with May and Philip, and Qin makes five."

"You're not understanding what I'm saying to you. I have only three tickets. That's it. Believe me when I tell you we're even lucky to have that many. You and I and one of the children, probably May, will go to Tokyo. Then I can get tickets to send Qin and Philip to Taiwan. From there it should be easier to get them to Tokyo."

I could no longer hold back the tears. They came in a torrent. "But why not take Philip? He's just a baby."

"For that very reason. He will be too young to remember, but May is almost three years old and will wonder where we are."

✿ ✿ ✿

Just after dawn on April 29, Chiang Liang and I, with our daughter, May, climbed into a taxi that would take us to Hong Qiao Airport. Qin was in the bedroom sleeping with Philip. We had said our goodbyes the night before, so I didn't wake her.

Shanghai was bathed in a warm pink glow that made the scenes on the streets all the more surreal. There were sandbags piled on the sidewalks. The windows of many of the stylish shops and cafes were boarded up. Every once in a while, a burst of distant gunfire would startle me and cause me to hold May tighter. Most of the roads were eerily quiet, with very little traffic, and no people to be seen until we got farther out of the city. Slowly, our taxi was joined by ever-increasing numbers of cars, trucks, bicycles, and people on foot, all going in the same direction we were, away from Shanghai. By the time we got close to the airport, the taxi could barely move, so Chiang Liang paid the driver and we got out and walked. I carried May, and he carried the two suitcases we were allowed to bring, crammed full of what were now our meager—and only—possessions.

At the airport we made our way to a crowded room, where before we could enter, a pilot checked our tickets. After a short wait, when it seemed all the designated passengers had arrived we followed the pilot out to our plane through a throng of people, barricaded and kept at bay by armed Nationalist troops, the first soldiers we had seen since we left the house.

Standing in line at the base of the stairs by the plane, we waited while the pilot once again checked our tickets before we were allowed to board. However, just as he was almost to us, a man broke through the barricade and ran up to him, holding out a small silk bundle. "Take this, all my gold, for a seat on your plane!" he pleaded. Suddenly, three or four more people surged toward the plane from the crowd, all offering gold and jewelry to the pilot. At that moment, I was terrified that the plane would be swarmed and we'd be lost in the crowd, but the troops eventually pushed the people back and the pilot decided to simply let the rest of us through.

My heart was pounding so hard that I thought it would burst through my chest. Chiang Liang's hands were shaking and May was crying, but at least we were safely in our seats when we heard the start of the engines.

✿　✿　✿

Chiang Liang had been right. We were very fortunate indeed to have escaped Shanghai when we did. I was grateful that the three of us were on our way to Tokyo, but my thoughts all during the flight kept returning to Philip and Qin. The night before, I had rocked Philip to sleep and continued to hold him for a long time afterward. In the morning, I hugged my sister and tried to reassure her.

Within three days of our departure, to my prayerful relief, Chiang Liang was able to get Qin and Philip on a ship to Taipei. Shanghai fell to the Communists three weeks later, on May 25, 1949.

✿　✿　✿

Hostilities continued between the Communists and Chiang Kai-shek's defeated Nationalists, who fled to Taiwan. The disorganized post-war bureaucracy in Taiwan created further chaos. So it was more than a year and a half before Chiang Liang was able to get Philip and Qin visas and bring them back to Tokyo.

Fortunately, by the time I was reunited with Philip, I had finally adjusted to my new life in Tokyo, but it hadn't been easy. After my initial relief at having barely escaped China had worn off, I became depressed and rarely ventured outside of the Chinese Mission for several months after our arrival.

I had ignorantly imagined that Tokyo would be like Shanghai in its beauty and sophistication. I had never even considered that it had been brutally destroyed by the war and still hadn't recovered. The Japanese people scared me. Everywhere I went, when I looked into the eyes of a Japanese man, all I could see was the soldier who pointed his bayonet at my mother in our living room, or the one who robbed us on our trip to Chongqing. Added to all that, Chiang Liang was working long hours and I was alone. I had none of the staff I'd become accustomed to in Shanghai. Suddenly, I had to care for a young child without a nanny, and prepare meals without a chef. (I'm embarrassed now when I think of how spoiled I had been.) I couldn't speak the language, and when I went to the food markets, there was little that I recognized and no one to ask for help. There were many times when May would cry for her nanny, and I would cry along with her.

About four months after our arrival in Tokyo, with May in tow, I was on my way back one afternoon from buying some fish for dinner—fish was in no short supply and was the one thing I knew how to choose and cook. I stopped to observe a fire raging in a building not far from the Chinese Mission. It was a frightening scene, I stood, transfixed, along with a small crowd of onlookers, watching as firefighters were passing huge buckets of sand and water hand-to-hand to extinguish the flames. What amazed me, and I continued to think about for days, was that all the firefighters were women. There wasn't a man among them.

Everywhere I went after that, I began to be aware of women directing traffic, climbing telephone poles to repair the wires, digging ditches, and framing houses. In post-war Tokyo, where women outnumbered men ten to one, they not only kept the city running, but were rebuilding it. Suddenly, I knew I needed to pull myself together and stop feeling so frightened and sorry for myself. If these women could be strong, so could I.

The change was gradual, but slowly I started to get out more and make friends outside the Chinese Mission. I lost my fear of the Japanese people and came to admire their gracious nature and beautiful culture. Our family was reunited. May adored and doted on Philip—she always seemed to have hold of his hand—and he adjusted quickly. While we never again lived as well as we had in Shanghai, eventually we hired a cook—a Japanese woman who spoke Mandarin—and I began to take over chauffeur duties in Chiang Liang's big, black Buick Roadmaster.

I missed my family and constantly worried about my parents in Beijing, but I was finally at peace and happy with my life—except for one thing. I was homesick for Chinese food. It seemed that every time a group of Chinese expatriates gathered together, the subject invariably turned to how much we missed the food of our homeland. In fall, 1951, along with a small group of Chinese friends, I opened a restaurant called The Forbidden City. It was a huge success from the very beginning. What surprised us was that it became popular not just with the Chinese community in Tokyo, but with the Japanese as well. At last, we had a place to go where we could get dishes like *jiao zi*, shark's fin soup, and Peking duck.

Not long after we opened The Forbidden City, Chiang Liang and I attended a party in honor of the emperor at his palace. It was the first time since we had moved to Tokyo that we been invited to such an event. I was thrilled and had bought a beautiful gold brocade cheongsam for the occasion.

It was a glittering affair, and many of the guests were important government officials. At the dinner table, I was talking with General Chu, an old friend of my father's, along with several other guests, when a waiter presented us with a beautiful, but what appeared to be an empty, Imari porcelain platter. I looked at the General and whispered in Mandarin, "What is this? Why is he showing us a platter?" The General smiled and said the sushi was sliced so thinly that you could see through to the pattern on the plate. The waiter offered me a set of chopsticks and I picked up a piece of raw fish I couldn't see. In the three years I'd lived in Japan, I'd been able to avoid eating raw fish. The Chinese like their fish fresh, but cooked. Just the very thought of it made me want to gag. But with the General and several guests looking on, I dipped the invisible fish into a small bowl of soy and, as if I'd feasted on sushi every day of my life, took it into my mouth. I smiled and swallowed. I delicately wiped my lips with my napkin and said to the waiter, "Perfect. Your chef is a master."

It really was delicious, and I realized I'd adapted to my new life in Japan.

FISH AND SHELLFISH

Going to the market with my mother to buy a fish was an experience. Most of the time, one of our cooks performed the task, but every so often she would have one of us accompany her, just so she could teach her daughters how it was done. What that meant was we would go from market to market, and at each place, it was the same routine. The fishmonger would scoop a live fish into a net and hold it up for her inspection. If the fish was not thrashing about, if its gills were not red enough, or if there were holes or tears in its flesh, she would shake her head "no" and we were off to the next place. Only after she thought we had learned our lesson would she finally select the one, the only, the most perfect fish to grace our table. Then immediately we had to rush home to get our "catch" to the kitchen. All good Chinese cooks are fanatical about finding not only freshly caught fish, but cooking them as quickly as possible to assure that their flavor and goodness is captured in the wok.

My mother was from Wuxi, a town near the great port of Shanghai, a region known for its diverse and divine dishes from the sea. The centuries-old Chinese love affair with swimming creatures, however, is not limited to just the coastal areas. Even in the large landlocked interior, people have been fishing the thousands of lakes, rivers, streams, ponds, and swamps for not only finned fish, but all kinds of shrimp, crab, eels, and frogs. Preserved and dried seafood is also available where fresh is not.

In addition to the obvious nutritional role seafood plays in the Chinese diet, there is a great deal of symbolic importance the Chinese place on fish, which almost borders on reverence. The word for fish is *yu*, which, with only a slight change in inflection, sounds the same as the word for abundance. Whole fish are served at banquets throughout every region in China, and symbolize luck, unity, and fertility. At New Year's Eve banquets, whole fish is the last course to be served, representing the notion that there is always a surplus, a little something extra, to carry us forth into the new year.

As I discovered when I moved to San Francisco back in the early sixties, finding fresh seafood is not easy. Although the situation has changed and fresh fish can be found in good markets even away from the coasts, Asian markets have the widest variety of fresh seafood, and you can use the same criteria for judging fish as my mother did. Most importantly, live fish should be lively. If you're buying cleaned whole fish, they should be displayed on ice. Check the gills to make sure they're deep red and moist. Eyes should be clear, bright, and not sunken.

In American markets, particularly away from the urban coastal areas, where the majority of fish are sold as fillets and often have been shipped frozen and then defrosted, it's not so easy to detect freshness. My first rule is to find a fishmonger you trust so that you can ask when the fish was brought in or if it was frozen (although I generally don't buy frozen fish, I know that sometimes frozen fish are better than fresh that have been kept too long on boats or on ice in the store). If you're buying fillets, make sure they're not sitting in a pool of water and that they are glistening with moisture. Finally, ask to smell them. Old fish is "fishy" smelling. If you're buying shrimp, which is the exception to my rule since most shrimp is frozen, sniff them to detect any ammonia or off-odors.

Sesame Shrimp

sheng zha zhi ma xia

COCKTAIL PARTIES WERE A REGULAR OCCURRENCE at The Mandarin in Beverly Hills, and these shrimp, along with our Pork Riblets in Sweet-and-Sour Sauce, were perennial best sellers. I had one chef who did nothing but fry shrimp, sometimes for hours. In fact, guests loved the shrimp so much that we eventually put them on the menu.

✧ ✧ ✧

One of the nice things about this recipe, other than the fact that the shrimp are incredibly delicious, is that you can easily prepare them almost entirely ahead of time and do the final frying at the last minute. The recipe can be doubled or tripled, which is a good thing since they seem to disappear rapidly. If you prefer, use Sweet-and-Sour Sauce (page xxx) instead of the dipping sauce recipe given here.
—*L.W.*

Serves 6 to 8

1 pound medium shrimp, shelled and deveined, with tails attached

2 teaspoons kosher salt

1 1/2 cups all-purpose flour

2 to 3 cups white sesame seed

1 teaspoon Asian sesame oil

2 tablespoons Shaoxing wine

2 large eggs

1/2 cup cornstarch

1 teaspoon baking soda

1/2 cup peanut oil, plus additional for deep-frying

1 cup water

Dipping Sauce

1/4 cup Dijon mustard

2 tablespoons honey

2 tablespoons peanut oil

2 tablespoons soy sauce

TO MAKE THE SAUCE, whisk together the mustard, honey, oil, and soy sauce until well combined. Set aside until ready to serve.

In a bowl, gently mix the shrimp with the salt to coat well. Cover with cold water, slosh around a few times, drain the shrimp well, and then transfer to a cutting board. Using a paring knife, carefully cut lengthwise down the back of each shrimp almost completely through, leaving it attached at the tail.

Put 1 cup of the flour in a shallow bowl and put the sesame seed in a separate bowl. Set both aside.

In a third bowl, whisk together the sesame oil, wine, eggs, cornstarch, baking soda, the remaining 1/2 cup of flour, 1/2 cup of the peanut oil, and the 1 cup of water until well combined. Set aside.

Line a rimmed baking sheet with paper towels and have ready, along with all three bowls (flour mixture, egg batter, sesame seed), near the cooktop. Fill a

continued

wok no more than one-third full with the peanut oil and heat the oil over high heat until it registers 360°F on a deep-fry thermometer. Work with a batch of 4 or 5 shrimp at a time. For each shrimp, hold it by the tail and dip first in the flour, then the batter, then the sesame seed. Carefully lower the coated shrimp into the hot oil and cook until all the shrimp are golden, about 1 minute. Transfer to the prepared baking sheet to drain. Fry the remaining shrimp in batches. Just before you are ready to serve, put the shrimp back in the hot oil and cook until they are crispy and deep brown, about 1 minute more. (They can be fried in larger batches during the second frying.) Carefully scoop the shrimp out of the hot oil onto clean paper towels and serve while still hot, with the sauce on the side.

Steamed Black Bass with Ginger and Green Onions

qing zheng hei ban yu

AT THE CONCLUSION OF EVERY NEW YEAR'S EVE banquet we always looked forward to the arrival of the fish. No matter how it was prepared—steamed or fried—it was served whole, with its head and tail intact, representing a good beginning and good ending to the year. (My uncles and father used to fight over the fish cheeks and tails.) This preparation is typically Cantonese (who have mastered the art of steam-cooked foods) and I love it for its ease and simplicity. I often will steam a small whole fish just for myself at home and to make cooking even easier, I use the microwave.

✿　✿　✿

We recommend using small whole fish, about 1½ pounds, because unless you have a large steamer (or a fish poacher), any fish larger than that is difficult to work with. If you want to microwave the fish, as Cecilia sometime likes to do, put it in a covered baking dish for 3 minutes. —L.W.

Serves 4 to 6 as part of a Chinese meal or
2 to 4 as a Western-style entrée

1 small, very fresh whole black bass, striped bass, rock cod, or snapper (about 1 to 1½ pounds), cleaned, and scaled, with head and tail left on

6 large paper-thin slices peeled fresh ginger

2 tablespoons Shaoxing wine

2 tablespoons peanut oil

3 tablespoons premium soy sauce

1 tablespoon oyster sauce

2-inch piece fresh ginger, peeled and cut in julienne pieces, for garnish

2 green onions, white parts only, thinly sliced lengthwise and cut crosswise into 2-inch strips

¼ cup fresh cilantro leaves, for garnish

TO PREPARE THE FISH, with a sharp knife held at an angle, make 3 slashes about 1 to 1½ inches apart in the flesh of both sides of the fish, almost to the bone. Stuff each slash with 1 slice of ginger. Place the fish on a rimmed plate that fits inside a steamer. (If the fish is too long, you can curl it up.) Drizzle 1 tablespoon of the wine over the fish.

Fill a steamer bottom with about 2 inches of water and bring to a boil over high heat. Place the plate with the fish in a steamer tier and set over the boiling water. Cover and steam 5 minutes.

While the fish is steaming, bring the peanut oil to a boil in a small saucepan over medium heat. Keep the oil hot until ready to use.

TO MAKE THE SAUCE, whisk together the remaining tablespoon of wine, soy sauce, and oyster sauce in a small bowl. Set aside.

When the fish is cooked, carefully lift the plate out of the steamer tier and transfer the fish to a platter. Garnish with the ginger, green onions, and cilantro. Drizzle the sauce over the top and around of the fish. Pour over the hot oil and serve.

Clams in Black Bean Sauce

dou chi chao xian

THIS DISH FROM CANTON (now called Guangzhou) is a classic pairing of seafood with salty, pungent black beans, garlic, and ginger. My long-time friend Jim Nassikas and his wife, Helen, frequently call me to come over and make it for them, they love it so much. Jim is retired now, but was president of the Stanford Court Hotel in San Francisco, and was one of the first people to recognize that, for a long time, hotel restaurants were never very good and made sure the restaurant at his hotel would be different. He turned Fournou's Ovens into one of the best dining destinations in the city. I've learned a lot about the restaurant business from him and, in turn, I think he's learned a lot about Chinese food from me.

✿ ✿ ✿

Make sure you have all your ingredients prepped; the dish is cooked in a flash. You can also substitute other shellfish like mussels or clams, or even shucked oysters if you poach them first for about 1 minute. —L.W.

Serves 6 to 8 as part of a Chinese meal and 4 to 6 as a Western-style entrée

1¼ pounds small Manila clams

¼ cup fermented black beans

3 tablespoons Shaoxing wine

2 tablespoons soy sauce

1½ tablespoons oyster sauce

2 tablespoons vegetable oil

Pinch of kosher salt

3 chopped garlic cloves

1 tablespoon peeled, minced fresh ginger

¼ teaspoon freshly ground white pepper, for finishing

¼ cup thinly sliced green onions, green part only, for garnish

Swish the clams in a large bowl of cold water to clean them. Drain well and set aside.

In a small bowl, generously cover the black beans with cold water and soak until soft, about 10 minutes. Drain the beans, rinsing off any excess salt, and squeeze until dry. Set aside.

TO MAKE THE SAUCE, whisk together the wine, soy sauce, and oyster sauce in a small bowl and set aside.

Heat a large wok over high heat until a bead of water dances on the surface and then evaporates. Add the oil and a pinch of salt and swirl to coat the pan. Add the garlic, ginger, and reserved black beans, and stir constantly to coat in the oil for 30 seconds. Toss in the clams and cook 30 seconds. Pour in the sauce and cook, stirring and tossing constantly, until the clams open, 1 to 2 minutes. Sprinkle with the white pepper and green onions and quickly remove from the heat.

Turn the clams out onto a serving platter and serve immediately.

Chapter 10
Saying Goodbye

EVER SINCE MY HUSBAND AND I AND DAUGHTER, May, left China on the last plane out of Shanghai after the Communist takeover in 1949, I had dreamt of someday returning to China to visit my parents. It turned out to be an almost-impossible dream.

After our hairbreadth escape, we had flown to Tokyo, the three of us, where Chiang Liang had gotten a job at the Nationalist Chinese Mission (forerunner to the embassy). Eventually, we were reunited in Japan with our young son, Philip, who had been cared for by my sister Qin, in Taiwan (which was where she decided to remain), but the Communists had sealed off the mainland so that no one could enter or leave. Our lives went on for more than ten years without any word from my family.

Then I moved to San Francisco from Tokyo in 1960 and opened The Mandarin, and our lives changed yet again. Philip and May came to live with me. My restaurant grew and prospered, and in 1968 I moved The Mandarin to bigger quarters at Ghirardelli Square. All the while, I kept hoping that the political situation would change in China. It did, but not for the better. During the Cultural Revolution, which was officially from 1966 to 1969, Mao kept the country isolated while he terrorized its

Cecilia's father, at doorway of Beijing home, China, late 1930s.

citizens. The repression continued until Mao's death in 1976, but after Nixon's historic visit to China in 1972, communication opened up a little bit.

I wrote to my family in China frequently, never receiving a reply. But, in 1972, I finally received a letter from my father. I screamed out loud when I saw it in my mailbox, and cried as I read it, but it was obvious that his letter had been censored. I got a second letter from him in 1973, and I noticed that he began by heaping praise on Chairman Mao before he proceeded to ask when I might be able to get a visa to return home. Not long after my father's last letter, I received one from my nephew, my older brother's Number One son, co-addressed to my Numbers Five and Six sisters (Qin and Sun), who were also living in the United States, saying that our ninety-three-year-old father was seriously ill and would like us to come to see him. That letter was immediately followed by a telegram (a more reliable and speedy way to send brief information) from my Number Eight sister, Jing, who still lived in Beijing, imploring me to come home.

The early seventies were a difficult time for me. Not only was I worried about my parents and thwarted in my pursuit of a visa to visit China, in 1972 I began a dispute with the San Francisco Culinary Workers' Union which in an effort to recruit Chinese restaurant workers chose the highly visible The Mandarin to picket. (The irony was that unlike many of the restaurant owners in Chinatown, I made sure our employees were well paid, and had full benefits, but the union's tactics turned ugly. My tires were slashed and my life and my children's lives had been threatened. Seven long and expensive years later, in 1979, we were able to demonstrate libel and won our court battle with the union.)

Luckily, my father's condition improved and he was out of immediate danger, but in spite of my problems with the union, I continued to pursue my quest for a visa, knowing that time was growing short for one last visit to Beijing.

In early 1975, I seized the opportunity to speak to an old friend, Van Long, who called to say he would be coming to The Mandarin on one of his many visits to San Francisco. Van was very well connected, both in China and in the United States. When I first came here in the early 1960s, Van and I had been introduced to each other in New York by another friend of mine, Yvonne, who was the widow of Madame Chiang Kai-shek's favorite nephew. Van's father had been the governor of Yunnan Province, and Van owned a Chinese restaurant in Washington, D.C., that was very popular with many of the political powerbrokers. On several occasions,

Van had called me at The Mandarin to make reservations for one of his regular customers, Henry Kissinger, who with his wife, Nancy, was a big fan of Chinese food. I was aware that Van possessed a Chinese visa because, in addition to his restaurant enterprise, he had been making regular trips to mainland China for his sideline business of importing hard-to-get ingredients like thousand-year eggs, jellyfish, and *mao-tai*, the Chinese firewater made from sorghum that got Nixon tipsy during his visit to China in 1972.

Finally, over after-dinner drinks at The Mandarin, I asked Van how to get a visa to China, explaining that I'd been

Cecilia with her father during her last visit with him in Beijing, China, 1975.

trying for years to visit my family. Now my ninety-five-year-old father was ill, and I was getting desperate. I pulled out and carefully unfolded the aging telegram I had received from my sister Jing in 1972, as if to offer proof.

"Well, I do have some connections, Cecilia," said Van. "Can you come to D.C.? You can stay with me. It just so happens that in a few days, the head administrator of the Chinese Liaison Office in Ottawa, Canada, Huang Hua, is coming to Washington to look into setting up an embassy there. I'll speak to Henry Kissinger and see if he can arrange a meeting. Bring along your passport and extra photos. I'll make sure Huang Hua has some forms there for you to fill out."

"I already asked Ottawa to send me forms years ago and never got them," I said.

"This is different Cecilia, this will be from the top."

Less than a week later, Van called me and I flew to Washington, D.C., to meet with Huang Hua, and I got my long-sought visa. Unfortunately, Van's connections were good only to a point, and my sisters could not be included. I took comfort, however, in knowing that, for the first time in thirty years at least, one of us would be able to return to our homeland to visit our parents.

✿ ✿ ✿

My thirty-day visa stipulated that I must use it within ten days of receipt, which meant that I had only a few days to prepare for my journey. I became frantic, thinking about all the things I wanted to bring to my parents, sisters, and brother, as well as my nieces and nephews, many of whom I'd never met. I ended stuffing my suitcases with things like clothes, sweaters, sundries, watches, and even a couple of transistor radios (which were confiscated at Chinese customs)—so many items that I knew were impossible or difficult to for them to get—that my luggage was 200 pounds overweight when I checked in for my flight.

✿ ✿ ✿

On what was shaping up to be a stifling hot morning in July, 1975, almost three decades since I left my homeland, the Japan Airlines plane circled Beijing. I peered through the window over the landscape below, eagerly searching for familiar landmarks like the golden roofs of the Forbidden City. Was it raining? Images blurred and I realized I was crying.

Waiting for me at the gate were my Numbers One, Two, and Eight sisters, who had aged so much I scarcely recognized them, along with a man I definitely did not recognize. He introduced himself as my "escort," and I was so exhausted by my journey and overwhelmed with emotion that my first thought was, "How nice of Huang Hua and Dr. Kissinger to arrange this for me!" As it turned out, he was actually an agent sent by the government to be my watchdog. Before I barely even had time to embrace my sisters, he ushered me away to a waiting car and checked me into the Beijing Overseas Chinese Hotel, where every nonresident Chinese visitor was required to stay.

Even though I was still in an emotional time-travel warp, I immediately noticed that there was a hole in the door to my hotel room, obviously where a lock had once been. The room itself was depressingly gray with grime. There was one small rough and stained towel in the bathroom, and bars on the small window. I felt like I was in prison. Little did I know, I might as well have been.

At dawn the next morning, the door to my (unlocked) room flew open and the attendant yelled, "Hot water!"

"I didn't ask for hot water," I sleepily replied, even though he was already yelling, "Hot water!" in the room next door. This went on every morning during my stay, a not-too-subtle reminder to all the "guests" of the hotel that we were being watched.

After my rude, early-morning wake-up call that first morning, I waited eagerly for my so-called escort to arrive to take me to my parents' apartment. Instead, he handed me my day's itinerary, which consisted of a tour of some Communist-run factories and communes. All I could do was grit my teeth in frustration and go along. Everywhere we went, he would remark about the progress of the country under Mao. All I kept thinking was how drab, how depressed, and how poor the country looked. Not only that, it seemed that everyone kept to themselves. No one smiled or even interacted. It seemed to me that everyone was afraid.

Finally, on my third day on Chinese soil, the escort took me to see my parents. I was not so naive as to think they would be living in circumstances that reflected the cultured and graceful lives they had once led, but the shock I felt upon seeing the squalor of the Beijing neighborhood and the crumbling courtyard home they shared with fifteen other families left me shaking and speechless. I could hardly catch my breath as I was led down a narrow, muddy alley, past the courtyard's foul-smelling communal latrine, to a dark, windowless room, barely bigger than my walk-in closet at home. When my eyes adjusted to the darkness, I could make out a small hibachi on the dirt floor, a wash basin, and a bamboo cot set against a newspaper-lined wall, upon which lay my withered father.

Slowly he turned his head toward me and whispered, "Number Seven daughter."

Awkwardly, and completely at a loss for words (I was afraid of the emotions that might come rushing forth if I started talking), all I could think to do was to pull out the bottle of gold foil-wrapped cognac I'd brought with me from the States.

"Thank you for coming such a long way to see me and for the cognac. It's been too long since I've had any," he said with a sly little smile. I couldn't help but blurt out the question nagging me since I first entered the room: "Where is Um-ma?"

"It's a long story, Lao Chi, sit down here with me."

My heart began to ache, and I felt a little dizzy, so I sat on the floor next to his cot. Our heads were so close together that I could feel his breath hot on my cheek.

"I'm glad you're here now, so I can tell you myself that your mother died five years ago," he whispered.

Suddenly the room seemed stifling hot, but I said, "Tell me about everything that has happened to you and our family. Thirty years is a long time, so I will come here every day and we can talk as long as you can bear it."

"If you pour me some little cognac, I might talk longer," he said. Although his body was failing, at least his mind—and his humor—was still intact.

✿   ✿   ✿

He ended up talking for many days. We developed a small ritual: I would bring him some treats from the concession where visitors were able to purchase things unavailable to Chinese residents, who were strictly regulated with ration coupons. It was called the Friendly Store (a name I thought somewhat ironic). There, I could buy tea, sugar, small preserved fish, buns, butter, and sometimes fresh fruit. My father ate very little, but the gesture of me bringing him food was comforting, and we grew more relaxed with each other. He also had reached a point where he no longer feared putting me or anyone else in our family in jeopardy by speaking candidly about all the hardships they had endured over the last decade. It helped that I kept bribing my escort with cigarettes so that he would let us have some private moments together.

In the course of our daily conversations, he told me that my Number Three sister, Qiao, the one with the beautiful voice, had committed suicide four years earlier, when her daughter had informed the authorities of her mother's anti-Communist opinions. In turn, I told him that Zhen Ji, his Number Three son, my brother, had joined the Nationalist Air Force and had been killed in a plane crash in 1952.

"I always felt something bad must have happened to him, because I knew he would have somehow found a way to contact us," he said sadly. I remember thinking my father was going to cry, but he didn't.

My father's voice erupted with emotion. "I have no tears anymore," he rasped. "They are all dried up. Your mother, Yun Hui, I think it was a blessing that she passed away before me. She was suffering greatly. Her bound feet, which always caused her so much pain, and which she never complained about, identified her as part of the aristocracy and she was shunned. Even many of our family were afraid to associate with us. Also, as we became older, it was difficult for us. I had no strength left. I could not carry her and she could not walk. One day, although we had both been hungry for a long time, I realized that your mother had lost a lot of weight. I knew she was sick, but there was nowhere to go for help."

After a lengthy pause, he pointed to the picture of Mao he was forced to hang on the wall and said with such a strong voice that I was taken aback, "I never thought I could have it in my heart to hate anyone, but I hate him for what he and the Communists have done to the country and for destroying our family."

✿ ✿ ✿

Two weeks into my trip, I left my father's bedside and traveled to our old family home in Wuxi, only to find out that the home had been razed to build a factory, and that the cemetery where my ancestors had been buried had been dug up to create farmland. I became so sad when I realized I wouldn't be able to tell my father I had "swept the graves," a Chinese tradition called *sao mu*, because their graves no longer existed, that I quickly took off to Shanghai to see my favorite cousin, "Bamboo Brother" and his family. We had a wonderfully warm reunion, which raised my spirits, and I then completed my requisite tour of Mao's birthplace in Hunan before finally returning to Beijing.

✿ ✿ ✿

As my thirty-day visa was about to expire, my father asked me to get an extension. "Can't you stay just a little longer, Number Seven daughter?" I talked to the Overseas Visitors Office and was denied. As consolation, I suggested to my father that we have a small family party. The idea pleased him to the point that he even mustered the strength to participate a little in the planning. "Speak to Quan-Quen And have her help you with the food," he instructed me. Quan-Quen had been living in the same courtyard complex as my father since her husband, my Number Two brother, had been sent to a heavy labor camp for speaking out against Mao. In the intervening years since she had come to live with us as my brother's wife, Quan-Quen had changed considerably; she was no longer the spoiled and haughty girl I remembered. In fact, she and her son were quite kind to my father, and it touched me deeply. Without complaint, she took care of him on a daily basis, bringing him food and hot water for his tea, and my nephew would come to bathe him.

Together Quan-Quen and I planned the party. Thanks to my cigarette bribes, my escort had become quite relaxed and continued to look the other way whenever I did something that seemed against the rules.

Again, I bought food at the Friendly Store: chicken, shrimp, pork, some fresh vegetables like cabbage and spinach, walnuts to make a sweet dessert soup (one of my father's favorites), plus beer, wine, more cognac, and Johnnie Walker Black Label, which my brothers-in-law liked. We contacted as many relatives as we could, and a few days before I was scheduled to return to the States, we all crowded into my sister-in-law's room where together she and I had prepared the food. My Numbers Two and Eight sisters, plus their husbands and children, attended, and my eldest brother, Quan-Quen's husband, was able to get special permission to join us (only after we were able to find someone else I could pay off with a bribe of black-market cigarettes). Their son carried my father in and gently sat him on a chair, a seat of honor. We drank, we ate, we toasted, and for a few brief hours, time stopped, and we were able to believe life was normal.

✿　✿　✿

During my short trip away from Beijing to Wuxi and Shanghai, I had left a couple of my suitcases with my belongings in my father's room. I wanted to protect them from being searched during absences from the hotel, an occurrence that had become all too frequent, as well as ridiculously apparent. Two days before my departure, my nephews went to retrieve them. Within a half hour they returned to the hotel, breathless, and said, "Yei-yei is very sick, and you need to come with us so we can get him to the hospital!"

I ran with them to my father. He was barely breathing when we got there. He indeed seemed on the brink of death, so my nephews picked up his cot, maneuvered it down the narrow alley, and with me alongside and trying to keep up, rushed him several blocks to the hospital. As the doors to the so-called "emergency" room flew open, we were stopped in our tracks by the guard who presided over a corridor crowded with cots just like ours, all cradling people who were in much the same condition as my father.

"Hold on," barked the guard. "How old is this man?"

"He's ninety-seven," my nephew replied, "and he needs immediate help."

"If he's not dead already, he should be. Take him out of here."

My nephew turned to me and whispered, "Auntie Number Seven, show him your American passport."

I stepped between my nephew and the guard, pulled out my magical American document and said, "But he's still breathing. Can't you see that? I beg you, please have a doctor look at him." My voice was firm and in control, but my hands were shaking.

"Okay, go on to that room over there," said the guard.

"Over there" was a small cubicle with a nurse or a doctor, I don't remember which, who took my father's pulse, shined a light in his eyes, and said without any hesitation, "This man is dead."

And with that, we were dismissed and ordered to take my father's body to the morgue, my nephews still carrying him on his dingy cot.

✿　✿　✿

Burial was against government rules at the time because of the huge population and lack of land, so being told at the morgue that we needed to take my father to the crematorium within twenty-four hours was another shock I had to absorb. My nephews and I quickly contacted all the relatives to arrange the details.

According to tradition, in order for my father to walk respectfully into the afterlife, he needed to be dressed in a new *zhang-pao* (man's long robe) and, more importantly, wear a hat and shoes. Together, the family brainstormed how to acquire the resources for sewing him some new clothes. Strict rationing greatly limited what was available. The only fabric we could come up with was black cotton, which we all agreed would not be appropriate for my father—black was only worn by coolies or manual laborers. After much frantic searching we assembled an acceptable outfit consisting of a ready-made blue jacket which, though not the proper length, was at least unworn and a better color, some new white cotton pants, and clean white socks. Unfortunately, the only shoes we could find were plastic, and irony of ironies, the only head covering was a Chairman Mao hat with the red star. "Better than nothing," I thought to myself in false consolation. I sent my nephews on their bicycles to find some flowers, but there were none to be had anywhere. Instead, I bought some red paper and twisted it into rose shapes, then tied them together to form a wreath

At last, we put my father's decently clothed body into a rented wood casket (wood being so scarce that everything was recycled), placed the casket in a borrowed truck, and climbed aboard, my nephews trailing on their bicycles, for the sad, raggedy procession to the crematorium.

✿　✿　✿

Several years after my father's death and the end of the Cultural Revolution, I returned to Beijing to restore the family plots. Through general neglect and the overt maliciousness of Mao's Red Guard they had been reduced to rubble. Although my father had purchased our family plots in the once elegant and prestigious cemetery on the east side of Beijing outright, the Chinese government demanded thirty years' worth of "back rent," plus an outrageous monthly fee for upkeep. Since I was the only member of my family left who could afford it, I complied.

There's a Chinese custom of burial called *yi guan fen mu*, which means that if you don't have a body to bury, you're allowed to bury the deceased's person's clothes. When I arrived in Beijing, the first thing I did was find a tailor to sew clothes for my father with silk fabric I brought with me from the United States. I also brought my brother Zhen Ji's uniform, which I had been able to get from the Nationalist Forces when we lived in Shanghai, and which I had kept for years. This time I didn't have to rent a coffin, I had bought two, one for my father and one for my Number Three brother. All my living sisters gathered for the ceremony: Number One, Ning; Number Two, Yi; Number Five, Qin; Number Six, Sun; and Number Eight, Jing. Though my Number One brother, Xiu Ji, had died, his widow, Quan-Quen, who had helped me prepare our farewell dinner, was with my nephews, who had been so kind. Carefully, we laid my father's new royal blue robe, short black vest, white pants, cotton shoes, and lastly, a beautiful embroidered hat, in one of the coffins, and then my brother's Nationalist Air Force uniform complete, of course, with his shoes and cap, in the other.

With his surviving children looking on, my father, Sun Long Guang, and his son, Sun Zhen Ji were finally laid to rest next to my mother, Sun Shueh Yun Hui.

DESSERTS

Over the years, one of the questions I've most frequently been asked, not only by my students when I taught cooking at The Mandarin, but also by my Western friends, is, "Why aren't there more—and frankly better— Chinese desserts?"

My first thought in answer to that question is that I think it's a fair generalization to say that, as a whole, the Chinese people don't have a sweet tooth, and consequently don't really understand or share the Western appetite for sugar. Consider the fortune cookie, which I'd never seen until I came to the United States. To me it represents the way the Chinese immigrant restaurateurs tried to appeal to Western tastes for sweets, without coming up with anything delicious or authentic because of a cultural and culinary disconnect. The best we could offer, if our cookie wasn't particularly tasty, was to at least make it entertaining.

Another answer is that the Western concept of dessert—a sugary concoction served at the conclusion of a meal—traditionally does not exist in China. Most Chinese favor sweet treats that are eaten as little snacks alongside a cup of tea, and those served at banquets usually appear as interludes between courses, not at the end of the meal.

Two other reasons for the cultural disconnect when it comes to dessert have to do with ingredients and technique. First, in China we like to use beans, peas, rice, seeds, and nuts in our desserts, ingredients a Westerner would not normally think of as part of the sweet pantry. Certainly you don't see much cream or butter, and never chocolate or vanilla. Then there is the matter of technique. Historically, and out of necessity, the Chinese were forced to develop efficient methods to cook food that used the least amount of firewood, such as stir-frying, steaming, and stove-top frying in oil in a wok. Ovens, which needed to be fueled over long periods of time, were simply not available, which is why many of our sweet dishes are steamed or fried. Pastries are bought at bakeries and rarely, if ever, made at home.

At our family dinner table in Beijing, as well as in most other Chinese homes, "dessert" was always a bowl of fresh or dried fruit. My father particularly loved to finish a meal with the dates, persimmons, and walnuts that came from the trees he tended in our courtyard. Every so often, my mother would make him a sweet walnut soup that he was especially fond of. Fresh fruit, however, is still, even in modern China, the favored ending to a meal, whether at home or even in a restaurant, although many of the higher-end restaurants now in large cities like Shanghai, Hong Kong, and Beijing are serving more Western-style desserts. But as a general rule, more elaborate and traditional desserts are saved for banquets and special occasions.

The desserts in this chapter are meant to be served after a meal because I learned early on that that was what my guests at The Mandarin preferred. It's what I've become accustomed to myself after all these years (I've also developed quite a fondness for chocolate, but that's another story).

Sweet Walnut Soup

he tao lao

AT OUR LAST PARTY TOGETHER IN BEIJING, my sister-in-law and I made this sweet soup for my father because it reminded him of the beloved walnut trees that he grew in our courtyard. Make sure you really love the people you make this soup for, because, in a typical Chinese quest for culinary perfection, the recipe requires you to skin both the walnuts and dates. Sweet soups made of nuts, beans, or lotus seeds are common in China, often served as respites between courses during long banquet meals. Authentic or not, served warm or chilled, it makes a great ending to a Chinese meal.

✿ ✿ ✿

I have to admit that the thought of peeling walnut and date skins seemed arduous at best, and maybe even a little perverse. When I asked Cecilia if these tasks were really necessary, she explained that since the walnut skins make the soup bitter and the date skins are tough, yes, there was no way around it. Thank goodness our labors were rewarded. The soup was delicious. —L.W.

Makes about 8 (½-cup) servings, or 16 (2-ounce) demitasse servings

2 cups walnut halves

½ cup dried Chinese red dates

4 teaspoons sugar

1 teaspoon kosher salt

¼ cup heavy cream

A few soaked and skinned Chinese dates, chopped with toasted walnuts, for ganish (optional)

Cognac, for finishing (optional)

TO PREPARE THE WALNUTS, put them in a small saucepan with water to cover by 2 inches. Bring to a boil over high heat, decrease the heat to maintain a simmer, and cook 45 minutes, or until they're very tender. Strain the walnuts and reserve the cooking liquid (you should have at least 1 cup). While the nuts are still warm, peel off the skins. If the walnuts become difficult to peel, bring a kettleful of water to a boil, place the unpeeled walnuts in a strainer, and then slowly pour over the boiling water. You can do this more than once.

TO PREPARE THE DATES, put them in a bowl, cover with boiling water, and let soak 30 minutes. Strain the dates and reserve the soaking liquid (you should have at least 1 cup); carefully peel off the date skins. If they become difficult to peel as they cool, place them in a strainer and slowly pour over a kettleful of boiling water, which should heat them just enough to loosen the skins. It also helps to dip your fingers in water to rinse off the sugar that makes them sticky.

TO MAKE THE SOUP, put the skinned walnuts, dates, 1 cup reserved date liquid, 1 cup walnut liquid, sugar, and salt in a blender. Puree on high speed until very smooth, scraping down the blender bowl once or twice. Add the cream, then process a few more seconds to blend. Season more with sugar and salt, if necessary.

Serve the soup in 8 small bowls or 16 demitasse cups. You can garnish with some soaked Chinese dates chopped with toasted walnuts, or a little splash of cognac.

Eight-Precious Rice Pudding
ba bao fan

ALTHOUGH YOU SELDOM SEE SWEET DISHES served at the end of a meal in China, Eight-Precious Rice Pudding is the exception. In fact, it's actually become a quite common conclusion at banquets both in China and in the U.S. I think the popularity of this steamed rice cake (not really a pudding), originally a Shanghai specialty, is due both to its festive appearance and its symbolism—eight is a lucky number. Each of the eight "precious" ingredients (which can vary from chef to chef and region to region, but are usually a combination of dried fruits, nuts, and seeds arranged artfully on top) holds some kind of auspicious Chinese meaning, typically that you'll have lots of sons or make lots of money. Though the preparation may seem lengthy, the dessert is really not at all difficult and can be made in advance. Also, the ingredients can be varied according to what's available; all kinds of dried fruit work, as well as a variety of nuts.

✿　✿　✿

Cecilia uses the Japanese red bean paste (called ogura-an), made by Morinaga, which doesn't need additional sweetening. Stir in a little sugar and oil to taste for other brands. The dish can be prepared up to forming the pancakes, then covered and refrigerated for up to 1 week before steaming, or frozen for up to 1 month. If frozen, let the pudding thaw in the refrigerator for 1 day before cooking.

Shelled fresh gingko nuts can be found in small vacuum packages (usually about 3 1/2 ounces) in the produce section of many Asian markets. They're pale yellow and look like 1-inch-long footballs. Lotus seeds are sold dried in packages and resemble small brown olives.

Forming the pudding in a glass bowl allows you to see the design on the underside. It's not necessary to use glass, but it is fun; metal bowls work, too. We used a bowl that is about 8 inches wide on the top and holds about 1 1/2 quarts of liquid. —L.W.

Serves 10 to 12

2 cups sweet glutinous rice, rinsed and drained

3 1/4 cups water

1/4 cup shelled fresh gingko nuts

1/4 cup dried Chinese red dates

1/4 cup raisins

1/4 cup dried pineapple, cut into 1/2-inch pieces

1/4 cup dried apricots, cut into 1/2-inch pieces

1/4 cup lotus seeds

1 cup sweet red bean paste, sweetened to taste

1/2 cup rock sugar or granulated sugar

In a saucepan, combine rice and 2 3/4 cups of the water and bring to a gentle boil over high heat. Cover, reduce heat to low, and simmer until all the water is absorbed and the rice is tender, but still has a little resistance in the center (bite a few grains to test), about 15 minutes. Transfer to a plate and set aside to cool.

While the rice is cooking, put the gingko nuts in a bowl and cover with boiling water. Let sit 3 minutes, drain, and set aside.

In a small bowl, soak the dates in hot water for 30 minutes, until softened. Set aside.

In a small saucepan, cover the lotus seeds with water and bring to a boil over high heat. Reduce heat to medium-low to maintain a steady simmer, and cook 10 minutes, or until tender, and drain. Transfer to a bowl and remove any green threads from the center of the lotus seed with a toothpick and discard. Set aside.

TO FORM THE PUDDING, spray or lightly oil an 8-inch heatproof glass or metal bowl. Place the raisins in the bottom of the bowl and arrange the pineapple, apricots, dates, and gingko nuts in a circular pattern around the raisins in a decorative pattern.

Taking a handful of the cooled rice, form it into a flat pancake in your palm, and gently place the rice on top of the fruit in the bowl, being careful to not disrupt the pattern of dried fruit. Continue forming rice pancakes and stacking them in the bowl until you've used up half of the rice and created a fairly flat surface over the fruit (press down gently on the rice as you go, to create even layers).

Carefully spread the red bean paste over the surface of the rice layers and then top with lotus seeds.

Again forming pancakes with the remaining rice, finish filling the bowl and gently press down to even the top layer.

Fill the bottom of a steamer with water and bring to a boil over high heat. Place the glass bowl in a steamer tier, set over the boiling water, and steam, covered, until a skewer inserted in the center of the pudding comes out clean, about 45 minutes. Allow to cool slightly, just until the bowl can be handled with ease. Place a serving platter on top of the bowl, invert and carefully unmold the pudding.

Shortly before serving the pudding, about 10 to 15 minutes ahead, make a sugar syrup by combining the remaining $1/2$ cup of water and the rock sugar in a small saucepan, and bring the liquid to a boil over high heat. Decrease the heat to low and simmer 5 minutes, stirring occasionally until the sugar is dissolved. Remove from the heat and set aside.

To serve, pour some of the sugar syrup over top of the pudding. Slice into wedges and serve warm with additional syrup, if desired.

Coconut Tapioca Pudding
ye zi bo ding

I HAVE CONSULTED ON THE MENU OF THE popular pan-Asian Betelnut Peijiu Wu in San Francisco since the restaurant opened in 1995. When Alex Ong took over in 2001, he welcomed my mentoring him on the Chinese aspects of the menu. This dessert of his, which draws inspiration from China, Thailand, and France, is an ideal dinner party dessert that can be made ahead and served cold or room temperature.

✿   ✿   ✿

The recipe calls for small pearl tapioca, so do not substitute the instant, parboiled kind, which will change the texture and cooking time. The recipe calls for small pearl tapioca, so do not substitute the instant, parboiled kind, which will change the texture and cooking time considerably.

Dried Chinese red beans are sold in cellophane packages or in bulk in Asian markets. You can substitute Japanese azuki beans. Cecilia prefers the beans to have a firm bite—definitely a Chinese thing—but Alex cooks them longer to suit his Western customers' tastes. If you like crunch, cook the beans for only 60 minutes Alex and Cecilia both like Chaokao brand coconut milk for its consistency and rich flavor.

The pudding can be served cold or at room temperature. The optional mango garnish, though not typically Chinese, makes the dessert more contemporary. —L.W.

Serves 6

Red Beans

¹/₂ cup dried Chinese red beans or azuki beans

4 cups water

¹/₂ cup sugar

Custard Sauce

5 large egg yolks

2 tablespoons sugar

1¹/₂ cups whole milk

1¹/₂ teaspoons vanilla extract

Tapioca Pudding

³/₄ cup sugar

2 cups whole milk

1 (13¹/₂-ounce) can coconut milk

1¹/₂ cups water

¹/₂ cup small pearl tapioca

¹/₂ teaspoon vanilla extract

Big pinch of kosher salt

2 mangoes, peeled, seed removed, and cut into ¹/₂-inch cubes (optional)

continued

TO COOK THE BEANS, put them in a medium saucepan with the 4 cups of water. Bring to a boil over high heat, decrease the heat to medium-low, and simmer, uncovered, for 1 hour, adding more water, if necessary, so the beans remain submerged throughout cooking. If you bite into a bean it should be tender all the way through; if it isn't, cook longer. When the beans are done to your liking, add the 1/2 cup sugar and cook 10 minutes longer.

Set the beans aside to cool in their cooking liquid. You should have about 1 1/2 cups. The beans can be refrigerated in an airtight container in their cooking liquid for up to 4 days or drained and frozen for up to 2 months.

TO MAKE THE CUSTARD SAUCE, whisk the egg yolks with the 2 tablespoons of sugar in a bowl until blended and smooth.

In a saucepan, heat the 1 1/2 cups whole milk over medium-low heat until it just begins to bubble around the edges, about 7 minutes. Whisk the milk gradually into the egg mixture, then pour the mixture back into the saucepan. Cook over low heat, stirring constantly with a wooden spoon, until the mixture coats the back of the spoon and doesn't run back together when you draw your finger through it, about 10 minutes. Stir in the vanilla.

Have a large bowl filled with ice and water near the work area. Strain the sauce into a bowl and nestle the bowl in the larger ice-filled bowl, stirring occasionally until the custard sauce cools to room temperature. The custard can be transferred to a covered container and refrigerated for up to 2 days.

TO MAKE THE TAPIOCA, put the sugar, the 2 cups whole milk, coconut milk, and the 1 1/2 cups of water in a saucepan and bring the liquid to a boil over high heat. Add the tapioca, let return to a boil, stir well, then decrease the heat to medium or medium-low. Simmer, stirring frequently with a wooden spoon to prevent sticking, 30 to 35 minutes, or until the tapioca pearls are tender all the way through, but still have a little resistance when you bite them.

Transfer the pudding to a bowl, stir in the 1/2 teaspoon vanilla and the salt, and set aside, stirring occasionally, until it has cooled to room temperature.

TO ASSEMBLE THE DESSERT, drop a generous tablespoon of the reserved cooked azuki beans with a little of their liquid in the bottom of 6 (1-cup) cups or glasses. Top each with 1/2 cup or so of reserved tapioca pudding. You can serve the pudding, at this point, drizzled with the custard sauce and topped with a few mango cubes, or chill it without the custard sauce and mango, covered with plastic wrap pressed lightly on the surface, for up to 1 day. Just before serving, spoon the custard sauce onto the chilled pudding, and finish with some mango.

Peking Dust

beijin nai you li zi fen

PEKING DUST WAS SUPPOSEDLY created in the 1920s by a European chef at a hotel in Peking (now Beijing), which probably accounts for the use of chestnuts and cream. It's a simple but delicious combination of peeled fresh chestnuts and nuts ground into a paste and then served chilled and molded into a dome. You'll also often find it accompanied by sweetened whipped cream. My good friend Su Yung Li's version is my favorite, and she kindly shared her recipe with me.

✿ ✿ ✿

Cecilia, ever the pragmatist, realized that peeling the thin skin from a pile of chestnuts is a thankless chore, and found roasted and peeled chestnuts in vacuum bags at the Asian market where she shops. They're half the price of the imported French chestnuts.

Truly, the best way to puree the warm chestnuts with the almond paste and butter is with a food mill, which gives the mixture a lighter and fluffier texture. More people have food processors than food mills, so the instructions are written for the former, but if you have a food mill, by all means use it. The trick in either case is to make sure that the chestnuts are warm so they will easily combine with the butter and almond paste. Also, make sure your almond paste is pliable in the tube. —L.W.

Serves 8 to 12

Generous ¹/₂ cup dried Chinese red dates

1 pound peeled chestnuts

2¹/₂ cups whole milk

4 tablespoons unsalted butter, at room temperature

3 ounces almond paste

3 teaspoons vanilla extract

1 cup heavy cream

2 tablespoons sugar

Spray a 3-cup bowl with nonstick cooking spray. In another bowl, soak the dates in hot water for 30 minutes, until softened. Drain the dates and reserve the soaking liquid. Set aside.

TO COOK THE CHESTNUTS, put them along with the milk in a large saucepan and bring to a boil. Decrease to a low simmer and cook, uncovered, until the chestnuts are very soft, about 1 hour and 15 minutes. Drain the chestnuts, reserving the milk.

TO MAKE THE PUREE, using a food processor fitted with a metal blade, combine the soaked dates, warm chestnuts, butter, almond paste, 2 teaspoons of the vanilla extract, and 2 tablespoons each of the reserved milk and date soaking liquid, pulsing until thoroughly combined. Add more liquid, a tablespoon at a time, if the mixture is too thick to process. It should be very thick and just barely move easily around the blade. Discard the remaining liquids.

Pour the mixture into the prepared bowl, cover with plastic wrap, and refrigerate until firm, at least 2 hours or up to 1 week.

To serve, whip the cream with the sugar and the remaining 1 teaspoon vanilla until it holds soft peaks.

QUICK RECIPES FOR BUSY COOKS

I THOUGHT WHEN I RETIRED that I would be a woman of leisure. I pictured a life playing mah-jongg, entertaining, and traveling. Although I do all those things, I've also continued to work, consulting with several restaurants on their menus, as well as fundraising for a couple of nonprofit organizations that are near and dear to my heart. So with work, dining out, and entertaining I've found that my days are busier than I ever could have imagined.

When I had the restaurant to keep me busy, I ate there or often brought food home. Now, however, I don't have that luxury. I've had to develop a repertoire of nourishing and tasty dishes that can be put together with minimum of fuss. But while most Chinese dishes actually require very little time at the stove, the preparation—all the mincing, slicing, and chopping—can be pretty tedious.

Although many of the recipes in this book are fairly simple to prepare, and reflect my preference for clean, pure, and fresh flavors, in this chapter I've collected a few favorites that I turn to again and again when I'm short on time.

Over the years I've learned a few tricks. Modern appliances such as microwaves and rice cookers are great tools for the busy cook. A small food processor can mince garlic and ginger in a flash, so once or twice a week I'll process a small quantity to keep in the fridge. I choose vegetables that don't require a lot of cutting, such as bok choy or broccolini, and bagged and washed spinach. And even though I like to keep a pot of chicken broth simmering on the stove so I can make a quick soup, I've found that a good-quality canned chicken broth is a great time-saver. And one last tip: I always keep a supply of wontons and noodles in the freezer.

Water Spinach with Chiles

kong xin cai chao la jiao

IN RECENT YEARS, water spinach has become widely available in Asian markets in the United States. I'm a big fan of spinach, but this plant, which has long hollow stems and small green leaves, tastes only mildly like its namesake. It's much more delicate in flavor. In Asian markets you may also see it called ong choy, swamp cabbage, or kangkung. It's the contrast of smooth leaves and crunchy stems that I love. When a craving for this vegetable hits, I've been known to drive across the Golden Gate Bridge just to buy it from New May Wah on Clement Street in San Francisco.

✿　✿　✿

There are two kinds of water spinach available. One is dark green in color from the stems to the leaves, and the other has pale green stems with dark leaves. The former is found almost year-round. As an interesting side note, water spinach is related to the Asian variety of sweet potato. —L.W.

Serves 6 to 8 as part of a Chinese meal and 4 to 6 as a Western-style entrée

1 bunch water spinach

3 tablespoons peanut or vegetable oil

3 whole garlic cloves, peeled and smashed

6 whole dried red chile peppers, tops trimmed and seeded

Pinch of kosher salt

1 tablespoon soy sauce

Splash of Chinkiang black vinegar or good-quality balsamic vinegar, for finishing

Using a sharp knife, trim the tough ends of the water spinach and discard. Coarsely cut the remaining leaves and stalks crosswise into 4-inch pieces. Set aside.

Heat a large wok over high heat until a bead of water dances on the surface and then evaporates. Add the oil and swirl to coat the pan. Toss in the garlic, chiles, and a pinch of salt; stir to coat in the oil, and cook for 1 minute, until both have started to turn brown. (It might be advisable to have your oven vent hood turned on high, as the volatile oils released by the heated chiles can permeate the air and become quite strong.) Add the water spinach and, using tongs or chopsticks, toss to coat in the oil, picking up the garlic and chiles with the leaves as you turn the greens. Cook until the leaves have wilted, 2 to 3 minutes. Pour in the soy sauce and toss to combine all the ingredients well. Remove the pan from the heat and drizzle over a splash of vinegar.

Turn out onto a platter and serve immediately.

Cecilia's Garlic Noodles

da suan lao mian

EVERY TIME I MAKE THESE NOODLES, someone always asks me for the recipe, which is so simple it's almost embarrassing. I created it one day on a whim in the kitchen of The Mandarin, Beverly Hills when a few of my favorite customers asked for a new noodle dish. We never put it on the menu, but somehow word spread and it became one of our most requested special-order dishes.

There is definitely a garlic flavor, but because the garlic is cooked and slightly caramelized, it's sweet and not sharp. If you really love garlic, go ahead and add more. To dress up the noodles, which just somehow seemed so plain to me, I would sometimes add enoki mushrooms.

✿   ✿   ✿

Just as in cooking Italian pasta, it's imperative that the noodles are not rinsed after they're cooked. The starch that remains in the water combines with the garlic and liquid to make a "sauce" that clings to the noodles.

The garlic needs only quick cooking; be careful that it doesn't scorch and turn bitter. If it does, throw it out and start over again.

There are so few ingredients here, feel free to add more soy or oyster sauce as you would like in the spirit of improvisation. But be careful. The beauty of this dish is in its simplicity. —L.W.

Serves 6 to 8 as part of a Chinese meal and 4 to 6 as a Western-style entrée

Kosher salt

1 pound fresh ⅛-inch-wide Chinese noodles

3 tablespoons vegetable oil

6 garlic cloves, minced

1 to 2 tablespoon soy sauce

2 to 4 teaspoons oyster sauce

Have a colander ready by the sink for draining. Bring a large saucepan of water and a pinch of the salt to a rapid boil over high heat. Fluff the noodles to separate the strands. Add the noodles and cook until they are just tender, but still retain a little "bite," about 2 minutes. Immediately dump the noodles into the colander, drain well, but do not rinse them. Don't worry if they clump; they'll separate in the wok.

Heat a large wok over high heat until a bead of water dances on the surface and then evaporates. Add the oil and a pinch of the salt and swirl to coat the pan. Add the garlic and cook, stirring constantly, until soft and golden, but not brown, about 30 seconds. Add the noodles, soy and oyster sauces, and another pinch of salt. Toss until all of the ingredients are mixed well and heated through, but not browned, about 1 minute more. If the noodles seem to be sticking together, add a splash of water. Taste the noodles for seasoning and add more oyster sauce or soy sauce if you think they need it.

Turn the noodles out onto a platter and serve hot.

Shrimp with Edamame

mao dou chao xia ren

FROM THE TIME I LIVED IN TOKYO, I've loved edamame, fresh soybeans, but for years they were only available in Japanese markets. Now you can find them at every corner grocery store, it seems. This quickly pulled-together dish is wonderful after a day when you just want to make something with ingredients that can be picked up on your way home from work.

☼ ☼ ☼

You can often find shelled fresh edamame in the produce sections of supermarkets. If not, you may have to shell them yourself, which is not difficult of course, just a bit more time-consuming.

Make sure you remove the pan from the heat as soon as you're done cooking the shrimp with the edamame so the shrimp does not continue to cook and the edamame beans don't lose their bright green color. —L.W.

Serves 6 to 8 as part of a Chinese meal and 4 to 6 as a Western-style entrée

1 pound medium shrimp, shelled, deveined, and tails removed

2¼ teaspoons kosher salt

2 teaspoons cornstarch

1 large egg white, lightly beaten

3 teaspoons Shaoxing wine

2 tablespoons premium soy sauce

2 tablespoons chicken broth

1 teaspoon sugar

2 tablespoons peanut oil

1 cup shelled edamame

¼ teaspoon freshly ground white pepper

In a bowl, gently mix the shrimp with 2 teaspoons of the salt. Cover the shrimp with cold water and slosh around a few times. Drain well and transfer the shrimp to a clean bowl. Mix the shrimp with the cornstarch, egg white, and 2 teaspoons of the wine. Set aside for 5 minutes.

TO MAKE THE SAUCE, whisk together the soy sauce, chicken broth, and sugar in a small bowl until well combined. Set aside.

Heat a large wok over high heat until a bead of water dances on the surface and then evaporates. Add the peanut oil and the remaining ¼ teaspoon of salt and swirl to coat the pan. Toss in the shrimp and cook for 1 minute until they are just pink. Pour in the sauce, bring the liquid to a boil, and toss to coat the shrimp well. Add the edamame, remaining 1 teaspoon of wine, and white pepper and stir-fry for 15 seconds, just to evaporate the alcohol and warm the beans through (be careful, because the beans will lose their color if cooked too long). Immediately remove the pan from the heat.

Turn the shrimp mixture out onto a platter and serve hot.

Spinach with Bean Curd

bo cai ban dou fu

SPINACH, I THINK, IS MY FAVORITE VEGETABLE, maybe after asparagus, but I always hated having to clean it. Now you can buy prewashed spinach, and while it's certainly more expensive, to my mind it's worth every penny. I use spinach frequently now, and here it's combined with pressed and seasoned bean curd, making this a very nutritious dish indeed.

✿ ✿ ✿

Cecilia buys what is called "pressed tofu," which comes both plain as well as seasoned (simmered in soy and spices). Cecilia also likes to doctor her seasoned, pressed tofu by simmering it again with more soy and wine. Just to keep things simple, find a brand that you like that comes already seasoned and use it as is. Already seasoned baked or pressed tofu is readily available in most supermarkets. Flavorings and seasonings vary among brands. —L.W.

Serves 4

2 tablespoons soy sauce

2 tablespoons Shaoxing wine

1^1/$_2$ teaspoons Asian sesame oil

2 tablespoons peanut oil

2 ounces seasoned, pressed tofu, cut into
   ^{1}/$_8$-inch-square julienne strips

1 teaspoon peeled, minced fresh ginger

12 ounces fresh spinach

TO MAKE THE SAUCE, whisk together the soy, wine, and sesame oil in a small bowl until well combined. Set aside.

Heat a large wok over high heat until a bead of water dances on the surface and then evaporates. Add the peanut oil and swirl to coat the pan. Add the tofu and quickly sear it by stirring constantly 15 to 20 seconds. Toss in the ginger and continue to stir until it is soft and golden, but not brown, about 20 seconds. Add the spinach and, using tongs or chopsticks, toss to coat it in the oil, then cook until the leaves have just wilted, about 30 seconds. Pour in the sauce, bring the liquid to a boil, and stir to combine well. Remove from the heat.

Using a slotted spoon or tongs, carefully transfer the spinach and tofu to a platter. Drizzle over a bit of the remaining cooking liquid and serve hot, or at room temperature as a salad.

Baby Bok Choy with Garlic and Ginger

sheng ziang chao cai xin

THIS IS MY "GO-TO" RECIPE that I use when I want a quick stir-fried green vegetable. If I find a package of baby bok choy at the market for a good price, they'll wind up in my lunch when I get home. A tablespoon of oyster sauce (if you like it) added at the end is nice.

✿ ✿ ✿

In addition to the bok choy, you can substitute spinach, Swiss chard (any color), kale, or any other greens you like. You'll just have to adjust the steaming/braising time depending on the "toughness" of the greens and how bitter they are, adding more water while they cook, if necessary. —L.W.

Serves 4 to 6

1 tablespoon peanut oil

1/2 teaspoon kosher salt

1 teaspoon minced garlic

1 teaspoon peeled, minced fresh ginger

1 pound baby bok choy, halved lengthwise

1/2 cup water

1 tablespoon soy sauce

1/2 teaspoon sugar

1 tablespoon oyster sauce (optional)

1 teaspoon Asian sesame oil, for drizzling

Heat a large wok over high heat until a bead of water dances on the surface and then evaporates. Add the peanut oil and salt and swirl to coat the pan. Add the garlic and ginger and stir constantly for about 20 seconds, until soft and golden, but not brown. Add the bok choy and, using tongs or chopsticks, toss to coat the bok choy in the oil, also picking up the garlic and ginger as you turn the greens. Pour in the water and soy sauce.

Cover the pan and continue to cook on high heat for about 2 minutes, until the water is almost evaporated, the leaves are wilted, and the stems are crisp-tender when pressed with a knife. Remove the pan from the heat, add the sugar, and if you're using it, add the oyster sauce. Toss well to combine.

Transfer the bok choy to a serving platter, pour any leftover cooking liquid over the top, and drizzle with the sesame oil.

Stir-Fried Pork with Leeks
da suan chao la rou

PORK AND LEEKS ARE A POPULAR combination in Hunan Province. Usually the pork is pork belly that has been steamed and cut into thin slices for stir-frying, as in Sichuan Twice-Cooked Pork (page 124), which is absolutely delicious but also requires some forethought to prepare (unless you're using leftover steamed pork belly, of course). One day, after coming home from a shopping excursion in Chinatown with a piece of cured pork, I decided to stir-fry it with some leeks that were also in my market basket. Wow, it was so good! And easy, too.

☼　☼　☼

This is the kind of dish that lends itself to improvisation. You can use leftover red-cooked (page 120) or twice-cooked pork (page 124), or even a good-quality smoked slab bacon, diced 1/4 inch thick. Simply adjust your cooking time accordingly. Remove the leeks when they're golden, add the meat and cook until it's begun to crisp, then return the leeks to the pan to finish. If you're a spice lover, throw in a few whole dried chile peppers in the beginning to cook with the leeks.

Serves 6 to 8 as part of a Chinese meal and
4 to 6 as a Western-style entrée

1 large leek, trimmed and well rinsed, halved
　　lengthwise, and cut diagonally into 1-inch pieces

1 piece (about 3 1/2 ounces) cured pork

2 tablespoons peanut or vegetable oil

Heat a large wok over high heat until a bead of water dances on the surface and then evaporates. Add the oil and swirl to coat the pan. Add the leek and cook, stirring constantly, until it has started to soften, about 1 minute. Toss in the pork and continue to cook over high heat until the leek has turned golden in color and the pork has started to crisp, about 2 minutes more.

Turn out onto a platter and serve immediately.

SOURCES

There are so many reliable sources for food and equipment purveyors (and not just Asian) that this list only scratches the surface. These are some of our favorites. We've alphabetized the list but also given a line description of what they sell.

Adriana's Caravan
800.316.0820
www.adrianascaravan.com
Extensive selection of spices, oils, vinegars, fresh and dried mushrooms

Benton's Smoky Mountain Country Hams
423.442.5003
www.bentonshams.com
Hickory-smoked country hams, sold whole and in small portions

Earthy Delights
800.367.4709
www.earthy.com
Fresh and frozen peeled chestnuts, fresh wild mushrooms, and artisanal oils and vinegars

Flying Pigs Farm
518.854.3844
www.flyingpigsfarm.com
Heritage breed fresh pork belly

Grimaud Farms
800.466.9955
www.grimaud.com
Muscovy duck

Kalustyan's
800.352.3451
www.kalustyans.com
Extensive selection of spices, seasonings, condiments, and teas

Kikkoman
www.kikkoman.com
Soy sauces

Lee Kum Lee
www.lkk.com
Asian sauces and seasonings

Maple Leaf Farms
800.348.2812, ext. 26
www.mapleleaffarms.com
Duck

Niman Ranch
866.808.0340
www.nimanranch.com
Naturally raised beef, pork, lamb

99 Ranch Market
www.99ranch.com
Asian supermarket chain with locations in California, Washington, Nevada, Georgia, and Hawaii

Oriental Pantry
978.264.4576
www.orientalpantry.com
Hard-to-find Asian foods, exotic spices, and savory sauces

Penzeys Spices
800.741.7787
www.penzeys.com
Extensive selection of spices and herbs

Preferred Meats
800.397.6328
www.preferredmeats.com
Beef, Berkshire pork, lamb

The Spice House
312.274.0378
www.thespicehouse.com
Extensive selection of spices, herbs, and seasonings

Ten Ren Tea Company
888.650.1047
www.tenren.com
Unique selection of Chinese teas

The Wok Shop
888.780.7171
www.wokshop.com
Asian cooking tools such as woks, steamers, cleavers, and dishware

Uwajimaya
www.uwajimaya.com
Large Asian grocery retailer in the Pacific Northwest with a wide selection of produce and dry goods

Williams-Sonoma
877.812.6235
www.williams-sonoma.com
Online and mail-order catalogs for equipment and ingredients

Yank Sing
415.957.9990
www.yanksing.com
Chili sauces and oils

INDEX